The Corporate State

This book critically examines key features of the contemporary organizational landscape by focusing on major beneficiaries of recent historical political-cultural transformations involving the embrace of market fundamentalism and a market society: corporations, those who direct them, and those who use them for their own benefit.

Part I examines the big US-based tech firms (i.e., Facebook, Google, Apple, and Amazon), highlighting numerous tensions and contradictions between their highly cultivated, flattering, yet unwarranted public images and the reality of how they operate as extremely competitive, at times deceptive, profit-seeking entities. A focus on these firms also highlights just how dramatically the economic realm has been transformed over the past few decades due to accelerating advances in information technology and corporate-managed globalization. Part II explores how the state has been pushed back via privatization and corporate predation in such areas as health care, military/security, criminal justice, philanthropy, and education and concludes by looking forward with a vision of a knowledge-caring society that must rebalance corporate-managed market fundamentalism.

Through the use of clear cases that bring the theory to life for students, the book is ideal as a supplementary text for advanced undergraduate and graduate students in a range of coursework in the fields of organizational theory and behavior, leadership in organizations, and management responsibility and business ethics. It will also be of great interest to students of sociology, specifically in the areas of complex organizations, economic sociology, theory, political sociology, and law and society.

Robert M. Orrange is Professor of Sociology at Eastern Michigan University. He is the author of *Work, Family, and Leisure: Uncertainty in a Risk Society* and *Social Structure: Organizations and Institutions*.

The Corporate State
Technopoly, Privatization and
Corporate Predation

Robert M. Orrange

Routledge
Taylor & Francis Group

LONDON AND NEW YORK

First published 2020
by Routledge
2 Park Square, Milton Park, Abingdon, Oxon OX14 4RN

and by Routledge
52 Vanderbilt Avenue, New York, NY 10017

Routledge is an imprint of the Taylor & Francis Group, an informa business

British Library Cataloguing-in-Publication Data
A catalogue record for this book is available from the British Library

Library of Congress Cataloging-in-Publication Data
Names: Orrange, Robert M., author.
Title: The corporate state : technopoly, privatization and corporate
    predation / Robert M. Orrange.
Description: Abingdon, Oxon ; New York, NY : Routledge, 2020. |
    Includes bibliographical references and index.
Identifiers: LCCN 2019046986 (print) | LCCN 2019046987 (ebook) |
    ISBN 9780367366858 (hardback) | ISBN 9780429348105 (ebook)
Subjects: LCSH: Corporate power—United States. | Big business—United
    States. | Business and politics—United States. | Social responsibility
    of business—United States. | High-technology industries—United
    States—Case studies.
Classification: LCC HD2785 .O77 2020 (print) | LCC HD2785 (ebook) |
    DDC 338.7/40973—dc23
LC record available at https://lccn.loc.gov/2019046986
LC ebook record available at https://lccn.loc.gov/2019046987

ISBN: 978-0-367-36685-8 (hbk)
ISBN: 978-0-429-34810-5 (ebk)

Typeset in Bembo
by Apex CoVantage, LLC

Printed in the United Kingdom
by Henry Ling Limited

For Gideon Sjoberg (1922–2018)

Contents

Introduction

"We're facing 25 years of prosperity, freedom, and a better environment for the whole world. You got a problem with that?" (Schwartz and Leyden 1997). Such was the tagline of a *Wired* cover story written at the height of the dot-com boom on the precipice of the 21st century. Over the past few decades, our beloved tech firms have been at the forefront of technological and societal change. And those that have emerged as the most prominent among them, namely, Facebook, Google, Apple, and Amazon, among others, now pervade our very lives. And, in turn, we have generally welcomed them in with open arms, for they, or the products and services they offer, in essence represent vehicles through which we actualize our highest ideals: they enable individual freedom, endless possibilities to connect and share with others, and the means for self-expression and self-fulfillment.

Recently, however, this optimistic view of big tech has come under increasing scrutiny. It seems that over the years, we hardly even took notice of how the largest of these firms have come to amass so much power and influence over our lives and our society. Or, perhaps, we took it for granted as just the way things are, which has been pretty good, at least on the surface. But as we look below the surface (or interface), many of us have become increasingly skeptical and uneasy about the relationship these firms have forged with us and wonder whether they really represent and advance our ideals and values to the extent they seem to claim that they do. Perhaps you have become aware of, or heard about, problems with Russian hacking and the 2016 presidential election; the spread of fake news on the internet; major breaches and violations of consumer privacy; growing problems with online addiction, particularly among younger generations; and even the perplexing notion that these firms have become monopolistic bullies seeking to suffocate the competition at every turn.

Perhaps you have begun to wonder what is really going on? And, how it all came about in the first place? This book places these questions in a larger context and views the current scene as a reflection of broader transformation in state and market relations dating back in large part to the Reagan-Thatcher era of the 1980s. Here, we can observe the revolutionary shifts in how we envision the relationship between the democratic state and the capitalist "free" market over the past several decades.

This transformation also reflects some more fundamental changes in state and market relations surrounding how spheres of governing have been transformed, looking at who has become more entrenched in the governing process, namely, corporations, the elites who direct them, and corporate interests, generally speaking. Here, we explore this larger history highlighting this transformation in how we are governed, pointing out the way in which "markets" increasingly came to be viewed as the best means and mechanisms for governing what had been viewed as our collective, shared, endeavors and responsibilities—the functions of the state.

Part of this transformation involved a resurgence, decades in the making, of classical economic thought applied to our popular imagination. It is widely accepted that a, if not the, major figure in this movement was the late economist Milton Friedman, described by one of then President Ronald Reagan's economic advisors as "the most influential economist since Adam Smith" (quoted in Cassidy 2009: 72). Adam Smith's *The Wealth of Nations*, published in 1776, remains a foundational, even sacred, text on how free markets operate. Smith employed the metaphor of an invisible hand that guides, directs, and regulates the activities of myriad individuals, who merely seek no larger ends than their own personal gain, into a benign economic system that, over time, benefits and directs ever greater wealth and prosperity to the whole of society. Friedman was a central figure in this renaissance of market fundamentalist ideas, which have been embraced with religious zeal among many of its adherents as if they reflected fundamental laws of nature manifest through divine provenance. He, along with Austrian economist Friedrich Hayek, helped create the famed "Chicago School" of economics upon joining the University of Chicago in the late 1940s. While an influential academic economist, Friedman's greatest contributions to the resurgence of classical economic thought came in the form of his more popular works.

His most influential popular writings date back to 1962 when *Capitalism and Freedom* was published and culminated in his wildly popular *Free to Choose*, which was published in 1980 accompanied by a ten-part television documentary, translated into well over a dozen languages and sold roughly one-and-a-half million copies worldwide. He asserted that democratic-capitalist societies faced stark choices regarding how they wished to coordinate productive economic activity: one involved succumbing to the coercion exercised by the totalitarian state, while the other involved the voluntary cooperation of individuals in a free and open marketplace. Because these market fundamentalists, led by Friedman, Hayek, and others, were unwavering critics of the state, they opposed its involvement in virtually all of the functions it had come to perform aside from certain sensitive military, security, and criminal justice activities, but even those were not free from scrutiny, as well shall see.

Friedman railed against all forms of government regulation—and the agencies charged with overseeing them—in areas such as food and drugs, consumer product safety, environmental protection, protections for financial investors, and efforts to maintain fair and orderly financial markets. The only effective form of regulation was the self-regulation and discipline imposed by the market. He was also highly skeptical, if not downright hostile, to government activities and questioned the government's involvement in public projects and services such as highway construction, education, social security, public housing, and setting minimum wage rates, to name a few. Freidman was also unwavering in his support for individual economic freedom, not only as an end in itself but also as fundamental to securing political freedom. He linked these freedoms to longstanding cultural beliefs in the rugged individualism that shaped the American character and argued that big government would destroy not only innovation and prosperity but also the freedoms set forth in the Declaration of Independence (Cassidy 2009).

These fervent critics of the state finally found their unabashed champion in the figure of Ronald Reagan, the Hollywood actor-turned-politician, who became a two-term president during the 1980s and whose legacy endures long after his public service ended. Friedman, who had been close to Reagan since the latter's days as governor of California in the 1960s, was appointed to the president's Economic Policy Advisory Board after serving as economic advisor to Reagan's 1980 presidential campaign (Cassidy 2009). This backdrop provides an important context through which we also examine the key areas of traditional state activity that have eventually been outsourced or, in many cases, taken over by corporations, or corporate interests, in the post-Reagan era, and which invariably become focused on the governing process that feeds them the resources (taxpayer dollars) they so crave. Here, among the many possibilities, we home in on a selection of those having nothing less than profound and troubling long-term consequences for our democratic society: health care; security functions of the state, including military, criminal justice, and immigration; education and the larger reform agenda in which it has been immersed; and, finally, the triumphal notion that governing—and, really, government itself—most effectively advances democracy through the actions of NGOs (nongovernmental organizations) and civil society actors and organizations.

The market fundamentalist presumption that markets are the best mechanisms to discipline and order virtually all aspects of social life points to one simple conclusion: what's valued = what sells. Everything is monetized and assigned a price. The emergent 21st-century tech sector came to represent a new frontier through which our freedoms could be more fully expressed. However, in the marketplace of ideas, what is true is not always what is valued. Oftentimes, untruths and fake news sell politically, while some corporations devote vast resources to advertising and public relations campaigns and promote products, services, and even an image of the world that distorts our sense of the individual and public good. Some firms and industries even cover over or obscure hidden and unflattering truths about what they have on offer that, if widely understood, could prove damaging to their revenue streams.

Once it was revealed that the dark side of the information economy reared its ugly head during the 2016 presidential election, it was as if Milton Friedman's dream of a free and open marketplace for ideas, news, and information ended up in a little shop of horrors. The more we peer through the once-opaque interface linking our smartphones to big tech and its multitude of partners hidden in the shadows, the more disturbed we become at what we see. Longtime tech writer Kara Swisher (2018) put it bluntly: "Facebook, as well as Twitter and Google's YouTube, have become the digital arms dealers of the modern age . . . by weaponizing pretty much everything that could be weaponized," including "social media," "the First Amendment," "civic discourse," and "most of all, politics."

Theoretical backdrop

A note on governing and government

Political scientist Susan George (2015) writes with alarm about the growing hordes of corporations, industry groups, and their CEOs, lobbyists, and technical-expert representatives—profit oriented, yet unaccountable to the wider public—who have increasingly come to exert direct and indirect influence over governments. At times these entities work directly though government, while at others they may influence, cajole, and even usurp the responsibilities of elected officials through their lobbying or through industry-linked committees and organizations that offer advice and counsel. Their efforts have even led to the formation of quasi-governmental bodies that, in conjunction with wider efforts, have led to the rise of a type of "illegitimate authority" that exercises power and influence over the body politic (George 2015: 2). These entities increasingly exert an outsized influence over law, regulation, and policy in areas ranging from public health, taxation, financial regulation, trade, to security policy (George 2015; Wedel 2015, 2009).

To clarify, government is typically understood to be carried out by clearly identifiable democratically elected officials (George 2015). Key features (and problems) associated with the rise of modern democratic systems of government were identified roughly a century ago by German social scientist Max Weber. He envisioned a larger trend whereby systems of rule historically based on custom and tradition would increasingly be replaced by rational-legal systems of political authority, defined most centrally by adherence to impersonal rule of law (Weber [1921] 1968). This fostered the expansion of democratic systems, which became a core feature of the modern world. Democracy has meant increasing rights for citizens to have some influence in the formation of policy and the selection of their leaders. Weber believed that given the large scale and scope of the modern nation state, the representative forms of democracy would be the most viable, wherein elected officials are invariably granted significant decision-making authority (Kivisto 2004).

Weber has also identified deep and intricate connections between the nature of modern capitalism and democracy, for industrial capitalism during the rise of the machine production came to be characterized by the growth and expansion of bureaucracy and larger systems of technical control. Rational scientific management increasingly defined large-scale enterprise, which for Weber was increasingly organized along bureaucratic lines in the modern world.

This trend toward large-scale organization and bureaucracy did not simply define capitalism since the age of machine production, but also democracy and democratic governance, as technical experts and rational administration come to assert increasing degrees of authority over the practical functioning of the state. As the state grows in complexity and develops expanded capacity for action, technical experts come to take on increasingly central roles in the functioning of its various branches. Weber applied the metaphor of an iron cage to his understanding of how modernity was unfolding, and this bleak image, replete with connotations of entrapment and bondage, emerges out of both capitalist and democratic-state-based institutions (Kivisto 2004; Weber [1904/1905] 1958, [1921] 1968).

Capitalist democracy today is best understood through the legacy of Max Weber than that of Adam Smith and his contemporary heirs. The predominance of the bureaucratic type of administrative organization, in both spheres of business and government, means a world of large-scale organizations characterized by hierarchical systems of authority (or a chain of command), a complex division of labor, a high degree of technical specialization, and complex sets of rules and regulations that guide the operations of the organization and its members, broadly speaking (Weber [1921] 1968). By contrast, Smith's contemporaries cling a more atomistic view of capitalism wherein independent and autonomous individuals carry out a multitude of individualized transactions all disciplined and given order by the principles of the market. Weber's emphasis on the central role of bureaucracy in modern democratic-capitalist systems slings an enormous wrench into the market fundamentalist worldview.

Returning to the contemporary scene, corporate and industry interests have been great beneficiaries of the shift in our political lexicon over recent decades, which has moved away from government toward the ideal of governance, for the process of governance is assumed to involve a range of interested stakeholders in a process of collective decision making, among which actual governments or elected representatives of the people may be found. Governments may have a greater or lesser involvement in a host of governance issues that affect citizens, who, in turn have not simply material, but also moral, political, and civic rights to participate in the affairs of their cities, towns, regions, and countries (George 2015). But, if government is deemphasized in the governance process, what does that mean for citizens whom it is obligated to represent (DuGay 2000)? While it seems likely that the concept of governance resonates with our contemporary culture of individualism and the idea of personal, even stakeholder, empowerment, in actuality, one ironic consequence of this shift in our political lexicon has been a deemphasis on the role of government in the act of governing. Yet organized business, corporate, and industry interests have far greater resources and capacities to shape and influence the process of governing than do average citizens—the former's cheery, branded, public relations campaigns aside. These powerful interests have enjoyed a windfall of legitimacy and political influence from the triumph of Smith's heirs, with their depictions of a free and open marketplace of goods, services, ideas, and influence, and their entreaty that all that is governable be outsourced to the market.

How liberals learned to love the market

While the decade of the 1980s was defined politically by Republican President Ronald Reagan, in the 1990s the mantle was handed back over to the Democrats and their two-term president, Bill Clinton. However, this time, Clinton and his "New Democrats" were practically falling over themselves to demonstrate their support for the ascendant market fundamentalist creed. And so, the decade of the 1990s, the first post–Cold War decade after the fall of the Soviet Union, became one not just characterized by market triumphalism at home in America, but was also very much promoted abroad. Our new cultural heroes had become the entrepreneurs, especially those who disrupted longstanding industries reigned over by stodgy and sluggish old-line corporations, with their slovenly and dependent (union) employees. These were the new breed of revolutionaries, opening up new markets and disrupting old ones, fighting for the only kind of justice worth having: the blind justice provided by market discipline, the ultimate arbiter of value. In the "new economy" of the 1990s, it was the consumer citizen who was said to have become sovereign (Frank 2000).

This was also the era in which corporate branding had generated a profound impact upon the wider culture, with the dominant brands becoming ever-present, penetrating into virtually all aspects of cultural life. Among them, it was Nike that emerged as a defining template, setting a standard that others would follow. Its CEO, Phil Knight, was unabashed in proclaiming that Nike and other companies that had traditionally designed and manufactured products were coming to redefine their mission as fundamentally about marketing. Their "Just Do It" slogan became truly epochal, conveying something ephemeral, even spiritual, akin to an attitude or a set of ideals that defined a lifestyle. And it was also Nike to first enlist Michael Jordan, who quickly became the world's ultimate and defining "superbrand" (Klein 2001). Corporations even at times adopted the mantle of revolution in their advertising to market products against what was decried as drabber conformist offerings of competitors. Brands also got wise to the fact that segments of youth had become disaffected by all of the incessant marketing and advertising that had colonized their lifeworlds, and so they grew savvy at pitching products with a dose of self-incriminating cynicism, or even irony, when it served the bottom line (Frank 1997).

Not only did the market make deep cultural inroads during the 1980s and 1990s, but it also came to easily coexist with, if not fully support, our desires for spiritual and personal fulfillment. This was almost perfectly captured by the public's love affair with Oprah and the extraordinarily popular *Oprah Winfrey Show*. It debuted in 1986 and drew numerous imitators throughout the 1980s and 1990s. Part of Oprah's mission was for the show to have a strong spiritual dimension to it. She wanted viewers to realize their sacred existence as spiritual beings, the sons and daughters of creation. Her teachings generally reflected Christian views, and really those associated with traditional religion, as she emphasized love and concern for those who were suffering, life as struggle, and the need to confess our wrongs and strive for redemption. She was also deeply committed to helping viewers achieve happiness and personal fulfillment. The "Oprah effect," as it came to be known, was extremely powerful, perhaps unrivaled among that of any celebrity. She could catapult the sales of a lesser-known product by sharing her enthusiasm for it with her audience. She was also known to give away products to her audience, which always generated lots of excitement, and she regularly shared her enthusiasm for newly discovered products with her audience. In Oprah's world, consumerism mixed seamlessly with the quest for self-fulfillment, a spiritual mission in life, and the desire to do well and good at the same time (Wu 2016). America liked the message!

Next, we have our (once?) beloved tech sector. Here we have the merging of a larger social purpose to the modern corporation—one with a conscience, or even a soul. Apple's landmark commercial introducing the Macintosh, which aired during the 1984 Super Bowl, could be said to have kicked off this era of tech hubris. It depicted images alluding to George Orwell's dystopian *Nineteen Eighty-Four*. Whether it was about IBM and the struggle for dominance over the development of the personal computer, or a more general message of empowerment and originality directed against larger forces of bureaucratic conformity, the Mac was coming to save the world!

Our beloved tech firms also developed mottos pointing to some larger meaning or purpose that defines the essence of these corporations. For instance, we have Google's unofficial motto "Don't be evil," which lasted for roughly 15 years (but is no longer). Facebook's evolving mission statement at one point in 2009 had become "Facebook gives people the power to share and make the world more open and connected," and Apple's most enduring advertising slogan has been "Think different."

Some link the industry persona of Silicon Valley back to a morphing of ideals associated with the 60s, hippies, counterculture, and a new type of vision for the kind of company the tech world has striven to develop. As sociologist Fred Turner points out, these companies seem to promote idealized images of themselves and their industry that, upon closer inspection, don't quite mesh with the reality. Many embrace an enlightened liberal attitude regarding social, cultural, and environmental issues, and they are known for creating collaborative, creative, and communal workspaces for their highly educated, elite, mostly white and increasingly Asian, male programmers and engineers (Fox 2014; Turner 2006). During the decade of the 1990s, the Valley's techno-libertarian leaders were staunchly opposed to government regulation and oversight and were certainly not interested in affirmative action in employment. However, in recent years, tech leaders point to how their mission statements have evolved to promote core values and beliefs affirming the importance of diversity and inclusion in the workplace—just don't look at the numbers, and please disregard the lawsuits (Mundy 2017).

In fact, it took until 2014 for Google to lead the way (followed by other tech companies) in even publishing data on the number of women and minorities it employed, while simultaneously committing to substantial investments in improving those numbers. Unfortunately, three years later, the *Atlantic* ran its infamous cover story "Why Is Silicon Valley So Awful to Women?", as little had changed throughout the industry (Mundy 2017). Then, in November 2018, sparked by revelations that Google had given the creator of its Android software a $90 million exit package in response to what it deemed were credible accusations of sexual harassment, 20,000 employees worldwide staged a walkout, demanding that they receive better treatment from the company (Wakabayashi and Benner 2018; Wakabayashi, Griffith, Tsang, and Conger 2018). One positive development that has emerged in its wake has been Google's shift in policy where it no longer requires employees to sign nondisparagement agreements— a wider industry practice that has contributed to a longstanding culture of secrecy around cases of workplace sexual harassment. Other major tech firms have begun to follow suit (Benner 2017; Wakabayashi 2019). In the spring of 2019 the House Subcommittee on Consumer Protection and Commerce began hearings to explore what can be done about the persistent issue of a lack of diversity in tech (Sumagaysay 2019).

As we shall explore, our leading entrepreneurial heroes, rebels, if you will, today run organizations that have morphed into profit maximizing, tax avoiding, territory-dominating corporate behemoths. This book helps us to look behind the curtain of Silicon Valley's techno-utopian image, behind the Gorilla Glass screens of our smartphones, to examine these entities more realistically as large-scale complex organizations, oftentimes having contradictory aims and purposes.

A Pragmatist-Weberian approach to mind, self, and capitalist society

The underlying theoretical perspective informing this work is what I call Pragmatist-Weberianism, which draws on the theoretical advances made over several decades by sociologist Gideon Sjoberg and his colleagues (Orrange 2017; Sjoberg 1999; Sjoberg, Gill, and Tan 2003; Vaughan and Sjoberg 1984). Here we see the social nature of mind and self, first developed by early pragmatists John Dewey and George H. Mead (who is known as the founder of symbolic interactionism in sociology). Central to our human nature, the social mind is characterized by wide-ranging capacities, including the ability to create images, think abstractly, draw upon a social memory, and use various logics and modes of reasoning. Moreover, a central feature of the social mind is its capacity for critical reflection, both individual and collective; however, the social mind emerges only through interactions with others and is shaped in important ways through those ongoing interactions.

Sjoberg's major contribution was to take this pragmatist understanding of human agency and place it in the context of modified Weberian insights on the modern social democratic world characterized by complex systems of rational-legal authority, intermeshed with ever-expanding capitalist bureaucratic systems worldwide. Bureaucratic organizations are characterized by an overarching emphasis on efficiency, a hierarchy of authority, and a complex division of labor, rules, and regulations, among other things. These characteristics have central bearing on the process of reflectivity. For instance, the actor's position within a hierarchy of authority and division of labor affects the types of knowledge and information that is at his or her disposal. Vast differences in knowledge exist between managers at the very top and the middle and lower echelons of the organizational hierarchy. In addition, the system of authority within an organization can serve to limit reflectivity among those below and their knowledge about the activities of higher ups. In this work also of importance are the knowledge, goals, plans, shared understandings, and *fundamental interests* that exist among those elites at the top of the organization, perhaps shared to a greater or lesser extent with trusted and essential technical-professionals within, but which at times can be sanitized, idealized, and fundamentally transformed through marketing and public relations efforts (and other more formal types of reporting) for consumption by a range of outsiders, be they investors, government officials, politicians, and consumers.

In a broader sense, the relationships forged between state and market are lived and experienced, if not necessarily understood or acknowledged, by citizens and consumers in myriad ways. However, the corporation invariably has a Janus face. Those differential interests that often exist between individuals in positions of authority and members of the wider organization, as well as a range of interested others on the outside with whom it interacts, when viewed from a broad critical perspective, can reveal potential ruptures in our relationships with them. These will become more apparent as we explore the relationships we as citizen consumers have with big tech. Following Sjoberg and colleagues, in so doing we make use of Jurgen Habermas' (1984, 1987) notion of society as both *system*—characterized by Weber's formal rational administrative organizational dimensions and profit-oriented corporations—that coexist with the *lifeworld*—which involves both the public sphere of social life and associated democratic ideals, and private worlds of family-friendship and community, replete with evolving communicative norms, practices, and understandings that sustain them along with our humanity.

While market fundamentalists and other supporters of the Reagan revolution are quick to point out the potential dehumanizing features of expanding government bureaucracy, they and our corporate leaders rarely if ever consider the potentially negative implications of expanded corporate power and influence that have accompanied this shift. At the end of his prolific life, the economist and public intellectual John Kenneth Galbraith chidingly observed in *The Economics of Innocent Fraud* (2004) how corporate executives stubbornly refuse to acknowledge they, in fact, oversee, the operations of large-scale bureaucracies. No, instead, market fundamentalist ideas reserve bureaucracy as an unflattering descriptor of all things government. However, it takes large-scale organization, coordination, resources, and technical personnel to operate vast multinational business operations today.

According to a pair of recent and prominent Nobel Prize–winning economists, George Akerlof and Robert Shiller, corporations in our land of free markets and sovereign consumers have actually been busily at work making "phools" of all of us: something they do, in large part, because competitive market pressures induce this behavior. In their work, *Phishing for Phools* (2015), they document how a range of corporations (banks, pharmaceutical companies, cigarette manufacturers, investment firms, etc.) get "phools," or consumers, to do things that are in the phisherman's interest but not the phools'. These economists urge us to wake up to the possibility that Janus-faced corporations may utilize their oftentimes vast and superior resources in pursuit of their narrowly profit-oriented agendas to phish us. Extending their argument to big tech—the focus of the first section of this book—we examine how they have phished deep into the public and private spheres of our lifeworlds.

Management scholar James Hoopes (2006) observes that with advanced information technologies, a new world not so much of the invisible hand of the market but that of management is affecting workers and citizens in profound and oftentimes (when it comes to the largest and most powerful corporations) very undemocratic ways. We would also add consumers to the list of those whose lives have been both potentially improved and deftly manipulated by the modern managers who sit atop our beloved tech firms. He continues, "In a democratic society, all forms of power, and especially corporate power, should be suspected rather than trusted. Paradoxically, only managers who know and acknowledge that they have no claim on our trust deserve our moral respect" (Hoopes 2006: 95).

Putting the 21st century in context

The knowledge society

In his widely influential *Capitalism and Freedom*, Milton Friedman (1962) asserted that "[t]he great advances of civilization . . . have never come from centralized government" (quoted in Madrick 2014). Such notions in the post-Reagan era have come to be largely and unquestioningly accepted by our business leaders and economists, and, perhaps, much of the wider public. For far too long, our leading tech firms have fed off the mythology surrounding their founders as independent-minded geniuses, visionaries, whose companies' emergence and spectacular successes were nurtured in a pristine competitive market ecosystem untainted by government interference and support (Madrick 2014; Shaw 2018). This ideology has served our tech leaders, if not the rest of us, very well over recent history. And, yet, following economic historian Joel Mokyr (2002), we would all do well to adopt a much broader perspective on the development of science and, more broadly, knowledge (from the abstract/

theoretical to the practical/applied), its distribution, use, and accessibility, as a fundamental dimension of our (or any) advanced social order.

While the reigning ideology may persist that government has played virtually no role in the success of our tech entrepreneurs and, therefore, has no legitimate right to intrude upon the prerogatives of our innovative tech firms, forgotten is the broader societal-government support that helped to lay the groundwork for the sector's emergence dating back to the 1950s and 1960s—an era in which big science really came into its own in the US. The electronics industry's earliest startup firms drew upon expertise that was nurtured in America's great universities, not in the garages of some high-school-dropout-turned tinkerers. Furthermore, the political-economic context of the Cold War and the government-military-space complex was entrepreneurial in nurturing and driving technological advances, most notably through the Defense Advanced Projects Research Agency (DARPA; Mazzucato 2011). This complex also provided lucrative markets offering exorbitant prices for early innovations, such as transistors, that, only later, were converted into the mass production systems for the consumer market. As economist Mariana Mazzucato (2011) convincingly argues, government investment in tech tends to be in the earlier stages of development, something that private sector venture capital shies away from. In fact, federal funding accounted for over 50 percent of all research and development in the US from 1950 through the late 1970s (Madrick 2014). Mazzucato (2011) also points out how government research has been visionary, opening fields of technological development to novel ideas in areas such as information technology, biotechnology, nuclear energy, and nanotechnology, not to mention the inception of the internet itself (also see Madrick 2014).

The case of Apple is instructive. The company actually spends less than the other big tech firms on research and development. However, its genius has been to integrate new technologies—such as touch screens and facial recognition—into appealing new commercial products, while those initial technological breakthroughs were originally funded by government military and intelligence agencies (Mazzucato 2011). Apple, by the way, is the most profitable of all the big tech firms, as it charges exorbitantly high prices for its highly desirable and stylized products. Furthermore, the company is notorious for avoiding paying its fair share of taxes to the US government and is able to do so through the use of now-infamous and intricate off-shoring schemes to funneling those profits though foreign subsidiaries located in tax havens around the globe.

In spite of all the rhetoric, a close relationship between our high-tech firms and the agencies of the national security state remains today. In many respects we have what Fred Block (2008) refers to as the hidden developmental state: a situation where the state still nurtures early phase developments in science and technology but the fact that it is doing so remains obscure and not granted sufficient priority, given the reigning market ideology. With Silicon Valley we really have a hybrid public-private economy (Weiss 2014). The government still invests in research and startups that drive innovation, which tech firms incorporate into new consumer products. Meanwhile the national security state treats these commercial applications as testing grounds for future military applications of the technology, but do so in ways that are largely unrealized by the public. Executives from some of our leading tech companies are deeply involved in this process and have been members of national defense and intelligence advisory boards, including Google's (really Alphabet) Eric Schmidt and Jeff Bezos of Amazon. In fact, Google has received serious criticism and pushback from its engineers and programmers about the company's close relationship with the national military/security apparatus, and it seems the company will have to walk away from some future contracts in response to those objections (Shane and Wakabayashi 2018; Wakabayashi and Shane 2018).

Tech firms have enjoyed the robust profits that flow from the commercial applications they have developed out of government-sponsored taxpayer-funded research. Furthermore, many are in possession of vast amounts of sensitive data, while the industry has developed extensive data analytics capacities with which to exploit them. Companies such as Cambridge Analytica, and its parent company SCL, which have been implicated in the 2016 election meddling scandal for the misappropriation of vast amounts of Facebook users' data, have actually been recipients of government contracts for cyber-military projects (Shaw 2018).

Marketing expert–turned tech critic, Scott Galloway (2018), recounts how during a hearing in the aftermath of the Russian interference into the 2016 US presidential election, the chairman of the Senate Intelligence Committee "pleaded with the General Counsels of some of our biggest tech firms, 'Don't let nation-states disrupt our future. You're the front line of defense for it,'" which for Galloway "represented a seminal moment in our history, when our elected officials handed over our national defense to firms whose business model is to nag you about the shoes you almost bought, and remind you of your friends' birthdays."

For its part, Google, which had, as of 2010, shut down its search business in China, citing government censorship requirements and its efforts to hack the Gmail accounts of human rights activists, has been seeking ways to develop inroads back into the country's vast and lucrative markets. And so, in 2017, Google announced it would establish a Chinese-based center devoted to artificial intelligence (AI). It also announced that it would appoint the then head of Stanford University's Artificial Intelligence Lab and AI arm of Google's Cloud business to lead the new center. A post on the company's website by the new head stated, "The science of A.I. has no borders and neither do its benefits" (Tejada 2017). China has recently embarked on an ambitious 2025 plan aimed at becoming a world technological leader while seeking to wean itself off of foreign-made software and equipment. Apple, as well as other tech firms aiming to grow their Asian markets, has also made commitments to establish research and development centers in China (Mozur, Wakabayashi, and Wingfield 2017). It is as if the Chinese government has assumed a role once played by the US government during the post–World War II and Cold War era, but thanks to the Reagan revolution we now suffer from collective amnesia about that aspect of US history (Gruber and Johnson 2019; Manjoo 2018a; Tollefson 2018). Ironically, we may have entered a critical inflection point with the advent of fifth-generation, or 5G, networks, as the Trump administration, in a rare move garnering significant bipartisan support, issued orders in May 2019 to ban American telecommunications firms from purchasing foreign-made equipment that could pose a threat to national security, taking aim at China and its leading telecommunications firm Huawei (Kang and Sanger 2019).

Global rules and ruling

Our big tech firms have a truly global reach, affecting consumers, citizens, and governments worldwide. For instance, Apple's business with China represents roughly 20 percent of the company's global sales, and its most important market after the US, as the iPhone has become a status symbol among its growing middle class (Mozur, Wakabayashi, and Wingfield 2017). The company's production operations also sit atop one of the most impressive and sophisticated global supply chains that is also centered in China.

By some estimates, Google accounts for over three-quarters of all internet searches worldwide (Duhigg 2018). That's one company basically handling the world's search for information. And Google's Android operating system software backs roughly 80 percent of the world's smartphones (Nicas 2018a).

For its part, Facebook is on a humanitarian mission to bring the internet to the entire world, and, maybe, pick up some paying customers along the way (Grossman 2014). But in recent years, Chinese firms have begun challenging the global supremacy of US tech firms and will likely increasingly do so in the future. China's Tencent now boasts a social network with one billion users, which is actually less than half of the number of global users on Facebook. Alibaba currently has over 500 million active users for its online shopping apps. Both companies have built their bases around China's massive internet market, which is estimated at over 700 million users (Mozur 2017a). Meanwhile, in its efforts to thwart Amazon's growing retail supremacy, Walmart recently invested $16 billion to gain a majority stake in Flipkart, India's leading e-commerce company. This was just one deal among a record $2.5 trillion in mergers during the first half of 2018, much of which was driven by the looming threat of tech dominance in a range of industries including media and health care (Grocer 2018a).

An important question that has only grown in urgency is how to regulate all of this global commerce and, specifically, that associated with big tech, a major focus in this book. While in the ensuing years following the Reagan revolution the tech sector was widely viewed to have ushered in a new era of free, open, and self-regulating markets, only recently have concerns grown about the need for some oversight, particularly in the wake of the 2016 presidential election (Kang 2017; "Once Considered" 2017). Instead, as the *Wall Street Journal* points out, it is the European Union (EU) that has been the de facto regulator of big tech, leading the way for the rest of the world to follow, while the US has simply taken a back seat (Schechner and Drozdiak 2018).

More specifically, it has been Margrethe Vestager, the once Danish political activist and centrist party leader who was appointed competition commissioner of the European Commission and solidified the EU's reputation as the world's leading enforcer of antitrust law. European regulators are more sensitive about whether dominant firms stifle competition, while the US has tended to focus more narrowly on whether they negatively impact end consumers. Europeans are also much more actively supportive of users' rights to data privacy, something that represents a major threat to the advertising-based business models employed by Facebook and Google (Schechner and Drozdiak 2018).

The EU has placed big American tech firms under antitrust scrutiny in recent years. For instance, in 2018, the EU issued a record $5.1 billion fine to Google for abusing its dominance over European smartphone makers by requiring them to install Google products when they utilize its Android software, after it imposed a previous record fine of $2.7 billion in 2017 on Google for unfairly favoring its own comparison shopping service in search results (Condliffe 2018; Nicas 2018a).

Until recently, US antitrust enforcers have been less inclined to take on big tech, while the leaders of these firms have (until recently) been more dismissive of the EU's efforts to regulate their firms' behavior. For instance, in 2016 newspaper interview, Apple's CEO Tim Cook referred to EU allegations that the company paid ultralow taxes in Ireland as "total political crap." We will discuss Apple's tax avoidance schemes in a later chapter devoted to the company. And, in a 2015 interview, then President Obama appeared dismissive of the EU's investigations into US tech firms, viewing them as economically driven to help their own less innovative firms compete by erecting barriers against US companies.

There are certainly critics who claim the US has failed to effectively police our big tech firms. For instance, while many view Facebook's acquisition of Instagram as one of the best acquisitions of all time, others criticize it as a massive regulatory failure on the part of the US in allowing the company to vastly expand its social networking monopoly (Wagner 2018). Meanwhile, other countries have been following Europe's lead for several years now, including Brazil, India, Russia, and South Korea, which all, for instance, have maintained deeper suspicions about Google's dominant search business (Schechner and Drozdiak 2018). In recent years, it seems that state attorney generals began leading the way in scrutinizing big tech, while activists in California, the home of big tech and Silicon Valley, have had some very significant legislative success in advancing consumer privacy at the state level that has enjoyed bipartisan support (Lohr 2019a; Confessore 2018).

But that all seems to be changing, as Congress has been holding regular hearings focused on the tech giants' anticompetitive practices, with harsh criticism now emanating from both sides of the political aisle. Furthermore, federal regulators began antitrust investigations during the summer of 2019, with the Justice Department taking responsibility for Apple and Google, and the Federal

Trade Commission (FTC) set to examine Facebook and Amazon (Kang, Streitfeld, and Karni 2019; Lohr, Isaac, and Popper 2019). In fact, this shifting political climate was recently punctuated by a historic $5 billion fine levied by the FTC against Facebook for violating a 2011 settlement over user privacy (Isaac and Singer 2019; Kang 2019).

Plan for the book

In *Part I: Technopoly* we examine the free-wheeling tech sector and how big tech firms seemingly have been free to do whatever they want during the past two decades, as we sat idly by assuming that forces of market discipline and consumer sovereignty would lead to the best of all possible worlds. Here, we devote opening chapters to our most omnipresent Janus-faced tech firms: Facebook, Google, Apple, and Amazon. We focus on how these firms impact our economy, society, and democracy in ways we may not ever consider or realize given our primary relationship with them has been as user-consumers.

Part II: Pushing Back the State: Privatization and Corporate Predation provides a deeper historical look at the Reagan revolution and, more important, what it displaced, namely, the post–World War II New Deal era. We question some of the eventual outcomes of the Reagan revolution and triumph of market fundamentalist ideas by looking at profoundly consequential developments associated with the growing power and influence of corporations and their predations through the areas of health care reform, as well as key arenas of privatization associated with the security functions of the state including the military, security, and criminal justice sectors. Here we highlight the rise of the military-industrial complex, which soon morphed into a form of military Keynesianism, only later to be accompanied by a new and disturbing form of criminal justice Keynesianism.

Next, we take up the movement that accompanied the Reagan revolution to celebrate, renew, and advance democracy through the growth of nonprofits (or NGOs) and a strengthening of civil society. Here, we identify a parallel growth in what has been called philanthrocapitalism, wherein big philanthropy, much of which has been funded and directed by our fabulously wealthy tech and finance entrepreneurs, has come to supplant traditional functions of government through new democratic notions of governing. In this context, we highlight the efforts of philanthropic corporate elites to push for education reform, including the privatization agenda and for-profit public schools, all much championed in earlier decades by none other than Milton Friedman. Unfortunately, these experiments to privatize America's schools have been most commonly pushed forward in poorer, urban, school districts serving predominantly minority children, who, honestly, would likely be best served by having the kinds of educational experiences available at the schools to which Bill and Melinda Gates send their own children.

We conclude by briefly highlighting the need for the Reagan revolution that championed a market-dominated economy and society to give way to a more balanced, sustainable, and equitable vision of a caring society—one still supported by markets, but which is able to confront major societal risks we face moving forward. These include growing challenges associated with the US becoming a truly aging society in the context of growing retirement and broader health crises, the persistence of poverty, employment uncertainty (much of which is driven by AI advances associated with tech), and environmental and ecological challenges. Adapting to present and future societal risks will require a rebalancing of market fundamentalism toward a more institutionally robust knowledge and caring society.

Part I

Technopoly

1 Facebook

Let the hacking begin!

One of Facebook's earliest, most emblematic, and defining mottos was "Move fast and break things" (Reagan 2009)—and many things did eventually break. It pointed to a kind of "outlaw" hacker culture that emblemized the company's roots. In fact, Facebook's corporate headquarters reside at "1 Hacker Way" in Menlo Park, California. By 2009, as the company had reached a high point in its Janus-faced idealism, its mission statement proclaimed, "Facebook gives people the power to share and make the world more open and connected" (Reagan 2009). This marked an era of tech triumphalism, which peaked during the early days of the Arab Spring, when Facebook and Twitter were the platforms through which democracy advocates toppled authoritarian regimes. But the triumphs were rarely long lasting, as authoritarian rulers reclaimed seats of power in capitals across the Middle East, while in advanced Western democracies, it was becoming clear that social media could also be a force for nasty cyber-mob-induced activism, like the misogynistic "Gamergate" campaign that engulfed the gaming community in the fall of 2014 ("Once Considered" 2017). By May 2017, the company announced its latest motto was to "Move fast, and please please please don't break anything," which seems to hold more relevance than Zuckerberg and his top executives have fully come to realize ("Facebook's New Motto" 2017).

The company motto in its early days, proclaiming "The Facebook is an online directory that connects people through social networks at colleges," reflected the (by today's achievements) more modest origins of the firm, and the internet of its time (Reagan 2009). It all began—as the now-infamous story goes—when Mark Zuckerberg decided to take on the task for himself of digitizing the historically print-based student directory at Harvard, called a facebook. In 2004, Zuckerberg caught word that Harvard University's computer services had begun working on developing an electronic facebook and thought he could develop a better version and launch it ahead of the university's. In one of his early escapades (recounted on his blog at the time), while confessing to be "a little intoxicated," he gained unauthorized access to Harvard's student picture database online and proclaimed the now famous tagline "Let the hacking begin" (quoted in Wu 2016: 290).

The early Facebook that emerged was different than other popular social networking sites at the time, such as AOL, which during the 1990s had successfully begun drawing in mainstream users by offering a wider range of social experiences based around chat rooms and forums. From today's vantage point, it is hard to imagine this earlier internet, which for many represented a somewhat-intimidating and unknown universe only to be explored by the bravest of souls: techies, geeks, and nerds. But AOL and others fell victim, on the one hand, to trolls who invaded their forums and chat rooms, of course using aliases, and toxifying the social environment with their outrageous incendiary comments and, on the other, to commercial and other spammers who bombarded users with unwanted solicitation (Wu 2016).

Possessing sharp intuition about the nature of social desirability (what's cool) and a keen social sense regarding the dynamics of both connecting and competing as powerful motivations driving user engagement (he studied computer science and psychology at Harvard), Zuckerberg envisioned a system beyond dating and "hooking up," which had been another central focus of the early internet, given an environment that fostered anonymous usernames and profiles. Here, he recreated an already-existing social community of classmates, new acquaintances, and wider social networks within and across college campuses that eventually evolved over several years into a system primarily focused on keeping up with old friends and family (more online than off) and proved to be a solid foundation for maintaining a loyal user base. That said, he remained somewhat cagey about the possibility that a major source of early user engagement lay in the potential for hooking up. In fact, Facemash was a creation of that earlier hacking episode, becoming a Harvard-only version of the rating site "Hot or Not." This endeavor led to charges against him by the school's administration board, which shut down the site, while Zuckerberg got off with only a warning—instead of a federal indictment (Wu 2016).

The company's success was not based on any revolutionary technological breakthrough or algorithmic innovation, but instead was built upon solid execution and stable if not highly innovative coding. The site was characterized by simplicity and limited functionality, while the company maintained strict control over the user page frame and format. Facebook's overall concept mirrored that of an earlier social networking entrant called Friendster, which itself was copied by numerous other new social networking entrants, but in the end collapsed under the digital weight of its own success and could not keep up with user demand (Wu 2016).

Zuckerberg had a keen eye about what appealed to his users and was also extremely wary about allowing advertising to degrade the user experience early on, and this proved to be an attractive feature of the site. In contrast, MySpace, a major competitor, was less concerned about verifying user identities and more interested in rapidly increasing their numbers and loading up the site with advertising to rapidly grow revenue. But make no mistake about it—advertising was the holy grail behind cultivating users at Facebook. As early as 2004, Zuckerberg began pitching advertisers on the addictive qualities of the site and the potential for nanotargeting consumers at a level practically unimaginable in the pre-internet era. In the end, Facebook rose to the top, handily beating its competition by focusing on growing new users first and foremost in order to amplify its network effect whereby the value of the overall system grew with each new user (Wu 2016).

A digital advertising behemoth colonizing your lifeworld

There are over 7.5 billion people living in the world today, and Facebook has a meaningful relationship with only about 2 billion of them (Galloway 2017a). Only?! Not only is that an astounding figure, but as recently as 2016, the company reported that users spent an average of 50 minutes a day across its Facebook, Instagram, and Messenger platforms (which leaves out time they may be spending on WhatsApp). And this figure was up from about 40 minutes in 2014. Not surprisingly, the 18- to 34-year-old demographic spends the most time on Facebook, notwithstanding the now-popular notion that young adults have abandoned the site. According to the Bureau of Labor Statistics, the only other daily leisure activity that takes up more time is watching television programs and movies, which members of this young adult demographic are increasingly doing on mobile devices (Stewart 2016).

Perhaps you've just come to realize that when you are on Instagram (or Messenger or WhatsApp for that matter), you are sharing all that information with Facebook; and sharing is something Facebook's platforms are very good at (not with outsiders, of course). All those users, spending all that time sharing across multiple platforms, whether they realize it or not, facilitates the accumulation of a vast amount of intelligence for the network. As mentioned earlier, the more users who join the Facebook community, and the more they share, the more the company's network effect, its scale and intelligence, and therefore, its value, increases. To whom? Why, to advertisers, of course.

To grasp the immensity of Facebook's scale and its ability to target an audience (intelligence), consider an example of what other digital migrants and I grew up thinking was the greatest advertising event in any given year: the Super Bowl. In 2018, its audience reached just over 100 million viewers (Crupi 2018). And to reach that broad mix of viewers, advertisers paid big money, approximately $5 million per 30 second commercial (Hanbury 2018). During the 2018 Super Bowl, we saw commercials for Pepsi, Coke, Diet Coke, Budweiser, Bud Light, avocados from Mexico, Doritos, Mountain Dew, Amazon Alexa, E*Trade, Febreze, Groupon, Hyundai, Kia, Lexus, Turbo Tax, Kraft Foods, and M&Ms (Hanbury 2018). Impressive! And the reality is that several name brands return each year and spend all that money because they enjoy a hefty boost in sales revenue each year after the event. Now, consider Facebook's potential audience (user base) 365 days a year. On top of that, think of the potential it offers advertisers to target segments of that user base to deliver highly tailored content to any narrowly defined demographic within that base, versus spraying a vast and far less differentiated assemblage of fans and other onlookers with the equivalent of a garden house in the hopes of quenching their thirst for a jumbled mix of consumer products (see Galloway 2017a).

With that in mind, it may seem a little more than obvious that Facebook and its peer Google consume the lion's share of digital advertising—over 50 percent of all such global mobile advertising spending. For 2016, the two accounted for just over 100 percent of digital advertising growth in the US, made possible because their competitors actually lost revenue (Galloway 2017a; also see Kafka 2016).

Tech marketing expert Scott Galloway (2017a) also points out that Facebook may just be destined to become the largest media company in the world, and it has the enormous advantage over other traditional media entertainment companies of getting its content for free, from you the user—or *prosumer*, following sociologist George Ritzer (2015; Ritzer and Miles 2019). The others, be they Netflix, CBS, or Disney (ABC), must spend billions of dollars to create original content. So the next time you post a picture with friends while out at a party, be sure to let them know that while you may not be studying, at least you're working—working for Facebook (for free, of course). These top-tech firms are so dominant that it seems there is a one-way flow of top talent from the most prestigious advertising firms over to Facebook and Google, but little if any traffic heading back their way (Galloway 2017a).

Facebook provides the cyber-social playground and feeds microtargeted information about us to advertisers, who, in turn, insert themselves into our ongoing social conversations. And while we may carefully manage our comments, pictures, and posts to create a more idealized image of ourselves and our exciting lives for all those "friends" in our network, Facebook knows us on a much deeper level than most of them do. Company executives explain that it draws upon this knowledge with the "goal to make ads on Facebook just as useful and relevant as posts people see from friends and family" (Metz 2017). All of this is accomplished with the "legal fiction of consent" (Editorial Board 2019).

Most users are aware that Facebook keeps track of pages they like and ads they click. It also registers the brand of phone and the type of internet connection and records location settings from user devices. Once users log in, Facebook records virtually every other website they visit while browsing the web. However, even when users are logged off, it can still amass much of their browsing data, should they visit any pages with a "like" or a "share" button (they're ubiquitous!), or should they click on an advertisement linked to its Atlas network. They also provide publishers with a code called Facebook Pixel that they (along with Facebook) can use to build records on any Facebook using visitors. Next, Facebook supplements and enhances its own user web-tracking information by collaborating with other data brokers, including major credit reporting firms such as Experian, that build consumer data bases over many years from government and public records and other private sources, creating in all likelihood the most comprehensive consumer profiles ever assembled. All these efforts add up to (roughly) 98 personal data points that the company uses to make sure ads are as useful and relevant as posts from family and friends

(Dewey 2016). These include user age, gender, parents, residential location, level of education, employment information, income level, relationship status, shopping behavior, major life events, political engagement and leanings, musical tastes, TV viewing interests, type of car, credit cards, tastes in clothing, types of groceries purchased, and if one is a heavy user of beer, wine, or other spirits, as well as major life events such as birthdays (Jones 2016). Need I go further?

Facebook's ad system evolved to plug right into the user newsfeed, the primary interface for the network. The ads are ideally tailored to mesh seamlessly with other organic content (what we expect to see from family, friends, and favored media outlets, etc.). But these ads are pages specifically built by businesses, advertisers, or other organizations and are carefully targeted based upon the rich user information database amassed by Facebook over the years—the fundamental reason for its existence. Facebook does favor ads that are deemed more relevant to user preferences for content, and paid advertisements are labeled "sponsored" or "promoted." However, the line between ads and content can eventually become very blurred, because once a user "likes" an ad, further posts by its sponsor may end up in the user's feed automatically, without being tagged as such. Because these posts are seen as more credible, Facebook is more likely to share them in the feeds of users "friends" (Metz 2017).

Conveniently, Mark Zuckerberg (Facebook's founder) proclaimed in 2010—as the company was undergoing one of its major systemic changes to the privacy settings of its users—that the prevalence of social networking had come to a point where people no longer have the expectation of privacy (Johnson 2010). Perhaps, he was correct in simply stating what was an obvious shift in wider norms around privacy evolving throughout society. This ongoing tug of war between the company and its users, and really the public at large, reflects a keen sense on the part of its founder about how to test and push the boundaries of privacy, and then back off when things get too hot, only to try again at a later point in time. From a free market point of view, this is just part and parcel of the evolution of cultural norms and values honed in the marketplace of ideas. However, what seems to be at work is the company's instrumental interest (collecting data for the purposes of growing advertising revenue) in shaping/colonizing the lifeworld norms around privacy and sharing.

About that $5 billion fine and your privacy

The Federal Trade Commission (FTC) assessed a record $5 billion fine against Facebook in 2019 for mishandling user data and deceiving users about its use. Times have changed! This was partially in response to the Cambridge Analytica scandal (more on that shortly), as well as a major investigative report by the *New York Times* in 2018, based on company documents along with interviews with 50 former employees and corporate partners, which revealed that Facebook had been violating a 2011 consent agreement with the FTC by providing unwarranted access to users' personal data to over 150 companies, with some deals dating back to 2010 and others still active as late as 2017. While the deals involved mostly tech companies, they also included other firms such as online retailers and various media sites. And Facebook struck some of these deals with very big tech firms including Microsoft's Bing search engine, Yahoo!, Netflix, Spotify, as well as Amazon. While the company can claim it never sells user data, instead it has created data sharing partnerships with other companies that serve to advance its own interest in growing revenue. And while the partnerships it has formed over the years were generally made public, the company was successful in keeping details of the sharing agreements confidential (Dance, LaForgia, and Confessore 2018).

For instance, the report disclosed that

> as of 2017, Sony, Microsoft, Amazon, and others could obtain users' email addresses through their friends. Facebook also allowed Spotify, Netflix and the Royal Bank of Canada to read, write, and delete users' private messages, and to see all participants on a thread.
>
> (Dance, LaForgia, and Confessore 2018)

Spokespeople for these companies seemed to indicate that they were unaware of the extent of the access they had been granted. The company's data sharing agreements with device makers, included Apple, which was able to "hide from Facebook users all indicators that its devices were asking for data. Apple devices also had access to the contact numbers and calendar entries of people who had changed their account settings to disable all sharing" (Dance, LaForgia, and Confessore 2018).

The original privacy breach that led to the 2011 consent agreement with the FTC occurred in 2009. At the time, Facebook changed the privacy settings for its 400 million users, inadvertently making some of their personal information accessible to the internet. It had originally promoted this new feature associated with the change as "instant personalization," claiming it was a way for its partners to customize what people saw on their sites. However, this move drew strong complaints from users and privacy advocates, and the FTC cited those changes as a deceptive practice (Dance, LaForgia, and Confessore 2018).

Facebook often straddles the line between serving its users and deceiving them, only to pull back, if temporarily, when users and privacy advocates resist or cry foul. In 2018, The Guardian reported on confidential Facebook internal documents released by the UK parliament that emerged from a California lawsuit, which provide some insights into how Zuckerberg and top executives thought about growing revenue streams for the site. Here we see glimmers of how the company has viewed its relationship with users and competitors, and how it managed privacy issues (Levin 2018a; Wong 2018).

Documents reveal how in one instance, back in 2013, shortly after Twitter launched its Vine video app, Facebook responded by limiting access to user data. A Facebook vice president "wrote that Vine allowed users to find friends via Facebook, saying, 'Unless anyone raises objections, we will shut down their friends API [application programming interface] access today.' He added: 'We've prepared reactive PR.' Zuckerberg responded: 'Yup, go for it.' Twitter eventually shut down Vine" (quoted in Levin 2018a).

In fact, one document seemed to indicate that Zuckerberg was intimately involved in making decisions regarding how data access would be managed for key competitors. It stated, "We maintain a small list of strategic competitors that Mark personally reviewed. Apps produced by the companies on this list are subjected to a number of restrictions outlined below. Any usage beyond that specified is not permitted without Mark level sign-off" (quoted in Levin 2018a).

Interestingly enough, was the fact that while they seemed to limit data access for certain perceived competitors, the company provided "special" access to other tech firms, including Airbnb, Lyft, and Netflix, it "whitelisted" (Levin 2018a). Along these lines, a Netflix communication confirming the agreement with Facebook stated, "We will be whitelisted for getting *all* friends, not just connected friends" (quoted in Levin 2018a).

The documents also reveal how back in 2015, as Facebook began rolling out features that enabled it to log text messages and phone calls through smartphone apps, it was actively deliberating over the possibility that it could trigger a privacy scandal, which eventually did occur. One internal email message stated candidly, "This is a pretty high-risk thing to do from a PR perspective but it appears that the growth team will charge ahead and do it. . . . We think the risk of a PR fallout here is high" (quoted in Levin 2018a).

Finally, the documents provide some insight into the evolution of Zuckerberg's thinking about how storage and access to user data, or personal information, could potentially be conceptualized in a manner analogous to money and banking (note how Facebook has also been developing its own cryptocurrency). In one email he mused about how the company could potentially charge developers an annual fee to access user data each year. In a related message Zuckerberg contemplated,

> For example, banks charge you interest for as long as you have their money out. Rather than letting devs pay a one time fee to fetch data, we could effectively do this by mandating that devs must keep data fresh and update their data each month. . . . Another idea is charging different developers different rates for things. The whole banking industry is based on charging people different rates.
>
> (quoted in Wong 2018)

Of course, the company objected to the release of the documents and argued to the effect that any speculation made based upon them would be doing so significantly out of context (Levin 2018a; Wong 2018). Shortly after the fine was announced, the *Wall Street Journal* reported that Facebook had posted strong revenue, earnings, and user growth (Horwitz and Seetharaman 2019).

Absorbing the competition

Cue the *Jaws* theme music. Now let's try and imagine Facebook as it scans the depths of its vast cyber habitat looking for innovators encroaching on its territory. Flush with capital, Facebook, like the rest of the Four, can easily afford to devour and absorb its competition. Its greatest acquisition, Instagram, was purchased for $1 billion in 2012, and grew from 30 million users to 400 million by 2015 (Wu 2016). Some balked at the outrageous price paid at the time for a company with only 19 employees. In retrospect, the purchase is looking like the bargain of the century, as Instagram, which has a fraction of the users claimed by Facebook, generates more overall user engagement, something advertisers love (Galloway 2017a). Next, it purchased messaging app Whats-App in 2014 for a heftier price at $22 billion, but that seems to be paying off handsomely as well (Dayen 2017a). The company was recently fined $122 million by the European Commission for misleading regulators into thinking it would be unable to automatically match user Facebook accounts with their WhatsApp accounts (Singer 2018). Of course, they eventually did begin sharing that user data, while the fine was a small price to pay to do so. Keep in mind how these acquisitions add to Facebook's overall network effect.

Sometimes new and innovative firms do not wish to be acquired by the digital giant. In that case, Facebook, with its market power and vast user base, simply rolls out lookalike prototypes of the object of its desire, nudging its users to abandon it in favor an adequate substitute integrated into the company's user platform. The most recent high profile instance of this is the development of its stories feature to copy Snap, in an effort to drive the new upstart to the margins. Since its $33 billion IPO in 2017, Snap has been struggling to maintain a healthy stock price and to ease investor concerns that it won't end up a casualty of its much larger nemesis (Galloway 2017a).

In spite of its struggles to establish a robust market niche, Snap has been more successful than many other new and innovative apps that have fallen victim to an early warning system that is, surprisingly, bundled into the popular Onavo app. This virtual private network provides secure anonymous browsing for users on Android devices. However, Facebook's ownership of the app is buried in the privacy policy, which can be read upon installation. Too late! While Onavo (which was purchased by Facebook from an Israeli data analytics startup in 2013) facilitates secure browsing for its smartphone users, Facebook can utilize the anonymized data it collects from them when they are off the Facebook grid, so to speak, to identify early on new apps that are growing in popularity. It enabled their early detection and purchase of WhatsApp, which had become popular outside of the US. This also gives the company a leg up on creating alternative versions of newly emerging apps, which are specifically designed to be used within the Facebook universe. One indicator as to the significance of the threat to new innovation posed by Facebook's use of the Onavo app has been the wary receptions that new startups invariably receive from tech investors, namely, venture capitalists, who are anxious to assess the likelihood that Facebook will create its own copycat versions of their apps. There has been a growing trend of venture capitalists shying away from tech innovators who are seen to be competing with Facebook (or Google or Amazon, for that matter), and this has created a strong disincentive on investing in new tech startups that come to close to the giants (Dwoskin 2017).

Facebook has acquired over 90 companies since 2007, and of those, roughly 40 percent were subsequently shut down (Wu and Thompson 2019). Chris Hughes, co-founder of Facebook along with Mark Zuckerberg, has recently become a vocal critic of the company's market dominance, and is working with leading antitrust scholars in advising the FTC and Justice Department about how they might pursue an antitrust case against the firm. They view the company's acquisitions as part of a defensive strategy to protect its dominant market position. In fact, there is a high degree of skepticism about Zuckerberg's recently proclaimed "pivot to privacy," certainly on face value, but also because it involves plans to integrate the company's three messaging platforms—WhatsApp, Instagram, and Messenger—which would make it even that more difficult to one day break them up (Lohr 2019b; Wong 2019)!

Destroying traditional media and eroding democracy

In the early 2000s, traditional media companies that sought to engage readers online did so through dedicated websites or via search engines, with Google having become by far the dominant one today. By 2009, these companies were experiencing increasing traffic from desktop users through shared links on Facebook, and many entered various types of sharing agreements with the company in search of readers and revenue. For instance, the *New York Times* entered an agreement where users could read *Times* content directly on Facebook. While such agreements opened up possibilities for growing readership and, hence, new sources of advertising revenue for traditional media outlets, as usership increased and smartphones grew in technological capacity and popularity, it became clear that Facebook was the place where readers got their news, in addition to making connections with friends and family. And so, news media companies have had to adapt to the fact that Facebook is where many of their readers live: that they control the distribution pipeline, and traditional media must compete with an array of other content passing through the Facebook newsfeed. In stark terms, this means Facebook controls the access, and the advertising, while media companies have become subordinate players, starved of, and desperate for, those advertising revenues which are their lifeblood (Galloway 2017a; Herrman 2016).

Sixty-seven percent of Americans get news from social media, and Facebook is by far the number one site through which this happens (45 percent of Americans get news from Facebook; Shearer and Gottfried 2017; Matsa and Shearer 2018). As Scott Galloway (2017a) argues, "Facebook has become, de facto, the largest news media firm in the world" (122). However, the company has long insisted on simply being viewed as a (neutral) platform. Serious news outlets, by contrast, no matter how much skepticism they may be under by politicians and segments of the wider public, understand that they have a significant role to play in a democratic society and are responsible to the public for reporting the news in a fair and accurate manner. Taking such editorial responsibility seriously would significantly cut into all that advertising revenue Facebook and other social media outlets have been hording for themselves, while leaving traditional news media on a starvation diet. Furthermore, they would likely open themselves up even further to the growing criticism (and it is growing into an orchestrated movement) on the political right claiming they are part of a liberal censoring media establishment (Grynbaum and Herrman 2018).

Facebook's business model depends upon likes, clicks, and sharing to keep that advertising revenue gushing in. And nothing seems to drive engagement and sharing more virally than content that is outrageous, confrontational, angry, and, at times, even funny. That's what gets attention and increases sharing, which is what has driven visibility on the Facebook newsfeed. In fact, there is an entire hyperpartisan self-referencing media world that operates solely within the Facebook network, but is connected to media outlets outside of it. And, of course, there are dimensions to it on the political right and the left, but the former is generally richer and more robust than the latter. These ecosystems feed on and exacerbate political polarization (Herrman 2016; Galloway 2017a; "Once Considered" 2017).

Because concern for the truth, objectivity, fact-checking, have historically been the purview of traditional news media, but are not essential criteria driving the business model of clicking and sharing on Facebook, the free market for ideas has become more of a swamp where predators go phishing for phools. While we should not over idealize the way in which traditional news media have fulfilled their role as democracy's fourth estate, the larger concern is a social media–driven news ecosphere that, sadly, preferences fake news when it drives clicks, engagement, and, hence, generates advertising revenue (Galloway 2017a; "Once Considered" 2017).

Facebook's preferred method for asserting some editorial judgment to screen out offensive or downright deceptive content has been to use AI-driven algorithms. The company has, at times, claimed that doing so removes the partiality and bias of human judgment. But these algorithms are designed by humans and do not have to capacity to make subtle distinctions and judgment calls better carried out by experienced, knowledgeable, yet fallible, human editors. It seems that Zuckerberg and his top executives have been almost constitutionally averse to the use of skilled human editors over algorithms and have not readily been able or willing to acknowledge the limits of AI screening. Furthermore, they are ever cognizant that algorithms represent the yellow brick road to profitability in Facebook's line of business, as humans are so, um, costly (Galloway 2017a).

Their myopia about the potential represented by algorithmic editors as well as the company's aversion to employing costly human one's, have been revealed through media accounts in the wake of the furor over fake news and Russian meddling in the 2016 presidential election. Zuckerberg and his top officials were exceedingly slow to acknowledge the extent of the problem that meddling in the electoral process poses for our democracy. The company's reluctance to do so was revealed by the fallout accompanying the exit of Facebook's chief information security officer, Alex Stamos, whose impending departure was announced in March 2018 amid ongoing internal tensions among top executives surrounding the extent to which Facebook should share information with the public about how the platform was misused during the 2016 election season. It seems some top executives believe the company would have been better off saying little about the election interference. Tensions around this emerged between the legal and policy advisory teams and Stamos' security team. For instance, after carrying out investigations during the summer of 2016, by that November Stamos and some of his engineers had uncovered that Russians had been aggressively pushing DNC leaks and propaganda on Facebook. Meanwhile, that same month Zuckerberg had publicly dismissed the notion that fake news influenced the election as a "pretty crazy idea" (Perlroth, Frenkel, and Shane 2018). Stamos pushed to disclose as much as possible about interference into the election, which the company pushed back against, preferring to avoid mentioning Russia explicitly in their public disclosures. That is, until the company was forced to reverse course in the fall of 2017 after a *Time* article revealed the Russia story (Perlroth, Frenkel, and Shane 2018).

A public relations expert who had been hired to head executive reputation efforts at the company, but who eventually left disillusioned, observed that Facebook was preoccupied with polling and monitoring the public reputations of Zuckerberg and Chief Operating Officer Sheryl Sandberg, and let concerns about the company's image override disclosing the whole truth (Perlroth, Frenkel, and Shane 2018). In fact, later in-depth reporting revealed that while Zuckerberg embarked on a public apology tour and Sandberg spearheaded lobbying efforts to deflect growing criticism of the company, Facebook also employed the services of a political consulting firm specializing in opposition research. And so, while the company displayed a "mea culpa" conciliatory public face, it employed researchers to undermine the credibility of its critics, including the Senate intelligence committee, which had commenced hearings on Russian activities on Facebook. The consulting firm, Definers Public Affairs, employed a strategy that involved the conservative leaning NTK network, a website that appeared to be a generic news aggregator. Yet many of NTK's stories were written by Definers' staff, several of which were aimed at criticizing Facebook's big tech rivals as well as undermining the intelligence committee's work, while raising questions about the motives of some its members (Frenkel, Confessore, Kang, Rosenberg, and Nicas 2018; Nicas and Rosenberg 2018).

The Stamos departure is also comprehensible considering the, at times, embarrassing messaging on the part of some Facebook executives, now long after the 2016 election. For instance, in February 2018, the company's vice president for advertising, Rob Goldman, tweeted that he had "seen all of the Russian ads and I can say very definitively that swaying the election was 'NOT' the main goal" (Roose 2018a). This, in response to Department of Justice Special Counsel Robert Mueller's indictments focused on the Russian Internet Research Agency, having just concluded that swinging the election in favor of Donald Trump was, in fact, a primary goal of the Russian Facebook campaign. Trump gleefully retweeted Goldman's comments in support of his own insistence that there was no collusion with Russia.

A month after the Stamos affair, another Facebook vice president, Andrew Bosworth—who himself had tweeted in 2017 that the effects of Russian interference and fake news in 2016 were "marginal, even in a close election"—got caught up in a firestorm of controversy surrounding a leaked internal company memo (not intended for outside consumption) defending Facebook's growth at any cost business model (Frenkel and Bowles 2018). In it, he asserts,

> Maybe someone dies in a terrorist attack coordinated on our tools. And still we connect people. The ugly truth is that we believe in connecting people so deeply, that anything that allows us to connect more people more often is "de facto" good.
>
> (Frenkel and Bowles 2018)

This June 2016 memo, titled "The Ugly," continues,

> We connect people. Period. That's why all the work we do in growth is justified. All the questionable contact importing practices. All the subtle language that helps people stay searchable by friends. All the work we do to bring more communication in. The work we will likely have to do in China some day. All of it.
>
> (Mac, Warzel, and Kantrowitz 2018)

The memo, while provocative and in keeping with Bosworth's longstanding reputation at the company, stirred up internal controversy at the time, but was also likely intended to rally the troops and keep them committed to the firm's core mission. In actuality, its message may not have run too far afoul of Zuckerberg's own vision, as co-founder Chris Hughes emphasizes how from their "earliest days, Mark used the word 'domination' to describe our ambitions, with no hint of irony or humility" (Hughes 2019).

Furthermore, an extended February 2018 account in *Wired* about Facebook's response to election meddling over the previous two years points to top management's predilection for AI-driven solutions to all problems, and their strong aversion to human editors. The article profiles a former contract employee and recent graduate of Columbia Journalism School, who had been leaking internal communications at Facebook that were focused on thorny political questions the firm faced during the hotly contested 2016 presidential election. He was part of a group of roughly 25 contract employees with backgrounds in journalism who were working in Facebook's New York office on a newsfeed called Trending Topics that focused on popular news subjects. The feed was generated by an algorithm but moderated by these journalists, who were subtly but keenly made aware of their temporary status within the company and who knew their jobs were doomed from the beginning. In fact, they were training those algorithms, in part, to eventually replace them, and they knew it. The story reinforced how the company views employees as more costly, meddlesome, inconvenient, and not readily scalable, in comparison to algorithms, which don't require time off, bathroom breaks, health insurance, or paychecks (Thompson and Vogelstein 2018). It actually seems rather obvious. Doesn't it?

We can see how Facebook's longstanding public position that it is a tech platform has enabled it to grow revenue and profits far more robustly, even recklessly, than had it operated as a publisher or media company. However, a lawsuit filed in 2015 by a startup app aggrieved that Facebook had restricted access to "friends" data, led the company to argue in its defense that its decisions reflected a "'publisher function' and constituted 'protected' activity," which "includes both the decision of what to publish and the decision of what not to publish" (Levin 2018b). Who said you can't have it both ways?

Russian hacking and Cambridge Analytica

And so, during the 2016 election the Russians took full advantage of Facebook's algorithmic emphasis on sharing, and the tools that enabled it to profile and target citizens, track those efforts, and maximize the impact of its advertising and sharing campaigns. As evidenced by a February 2018 US Justice Department indictment, focusing primarily on the Internet Research Agency, a notorious Russian troll factory, the majority of election interference was focused on Facebook and Instagram, which were mentioned 41 times in its 37-page report. Facebook eventually revealed that 150 million of its American users had seen Russian propaganda (Frenkel and Benner 2018; Isaac and Wakabayashi 2017).

As far back as 2014, Russians working for a firm called the Internet Research Agency (IRA) were employed to add comments and share posts on a range of social media platforms. The goal was to grow the number of American followers in online groups focused on a range of issues including religion, immigration, and race as part of a larger campaign to sow discord among the electorate. The Russians would also steal the identities of real Americans or create fake accounts with fake personas in order to increase sharing on social media. Some online groups had grown to hundreds of thousands of followers by 2016. In addition, some of the fake accounts were used to organize political rallies in the US. The organization also spent hundreds of thousands of dollars to pay for ads on Facebook and other social media platforms, namely, Twitter, while it also created YouTube channels to sow discontent among the electorate, often paying for these efforts using stolen PayPal accounts. The staff at IRA eventually grew from under 100 employees to over a thousand by 2015 (Frenkel and

Benner 2018; MacFarquhar 2018). Much of this is explored in greater depth in Special Counsel Robert Mueller's *Report on the Investigating into Russian Interference in the 2016 Presidential Election* (Mueller III 2019).

Paralleling the Russian scandal behind the 2016 election have been alarming revelations about the extent to which a political data consulting firm, Cambridge Analytica, improperly gained access to private data of potentially over 80 million Facebook users (Kang and Frenkel 2018). The company provided tools to target, psychologically profile, and influence voters' behavior. It was formed, in effect, as an American shell company out of the elections division of SCL Group, a British intelligence and defense contractor, receiving a major $15 million investment by billionaire Republican donor Robert Mercer. The company got its name from Steve Bannon, an early investor and board member who would eventually become chief executive of Trump's 2016 election campaign (Rosenberg, Confessore, and Cadwalladr 2018).

It was the head of the elections division at SCL, Alexander Nix, who would eventually become CEO at Cambridge Analytica, and who courted Mercer and Bannon, both of whom were intrigued by the potential that psychographic profiling held for winning electoral campaigns and shaping the wider political culture. Meanwhile, Christopher Wylie, the now famous whistleblower who helped found Cambridge Analytica, and his team of researchers were given the charge of building psychographic profiles of voters on a national scale, which represented an extremely expensive and time-consuming project. However, Wylie identified a potential shortcut, as researchers at Cambridge University's Psychometrics Center had devised a technique to map personality traits onto what people liked on Facebook. And while the Cambridge Center declined to work with Wylie's team at SCL, they eventually secured the services of a psychology professor at the university, Dr. Kogan, who built his own app, called "thisisyourdigitallife," and began harvesting data in June 2014 (Collins and Dance 2018; Rosenberg, Confessore, and Cadwalladr 2018). All that was divulged to Facebook and its users of the app (in the fine print, of course) was that that information was being collected for academic purposes. While only 270,000 users participated in the study and consented to having their data harvested, the professor was able to provide over 50 million raw profiles to the firm, of which roughly 30 million contained enough detailed information that could be combined with other records to build psychographic profiles (Granville 2018; Rosenberg, Confessore, and Cadwalladr 2018).

While Professor Kogan declined to provide further details on what transpired, citing nondisclosure agreements with Facebook and Cambridge Analytica—so convenient for the corporations and such an inconvenience for democracy— eventual whistleblower Christopher Wylie, along with further journalistic interviews with former employees, revealed that Cambridge Analytica likely continued to possess most or all of the private Facebook data. Furthermore, it was revealed that the company, in its efforts to harvest the Facebook data on millions of American users, received help from at least one, and likely several, employees of a Silicon Valley private contactor named Palantir Technologies that provides services to American spy agencies and the Pentagon (Confessore and Rosenberg 2018a). Palantir, which never entered a formal contractual relationship with Cambridge Analytica, was co-founded by wealthy libertarian investor Peter Thiel, who also serves on the board of . . . wait for it . . . Facebook.

So, was Facebook hacked? Well, technically, no. Personal information was not stolen from Facebook servers; instead, it was given away. The company regularly allows researchers access to user data for academic purposes, a practice to which users give their consent upon creating an account. But the company does prohibit such data to be transferred in the manner done so by Professor Kogan—namely, to data brokers, advertisers, or in his case, a political consulting firm. In fact, back in 2007, Zuckerberg publicly announced that he was opening up the social network platform to outside developers and invited them to build apps on top of it (in a manner analogous to an operating system). Third-party apps collect vast amounts of personal and detailed information about users, who can theoretically opt out of such practices, but few likely do so. This practice has been very good for Facebook, as it provides users with evermore opportunities to spend time on the site, which drives advertising and other revenue for the company itself. Furthermore, there are many positive ways in which all of this open information has been used, such as helping NGOs better respond to natural disasters, or even the common practice of importing digital address books across devices or apps. And, while much of this openness still remains, by 2015 Facebook had removed the ability of third-party developers to collect detailed information on the friends of users who installed an app, and it continues to modify these policies amid growing privacy concerns. Unfortunately, Cambridge Analytica gathered its data in 2014 (Frenkel 2018; Roose 2018b).

If you have ever taken a personality quiz such as "thisisyourdigitallife," you may be familiar with your Ocean score, or how you rate according to the five major psychological traits of Openness, Conscientiousness, Extraversion, Agreeableness, and Neuroticism. In its case, Cambridge Analytica gained access to profiles and real names of those Facebook users who downloaded its app. It then used responses from a few hundred thousand users to make inferences about millions of others with similar behaviors and demographics. Today, it is commonplace for political consulting firms and marketers to link our online personas with our offline selves through a process known as "onboarding." Apparently, Cambridge Analytica may have a few thousand data points on each of us. With Facebook's help, and through other government open records sources, microtargeting of specific individuals on the part of marketers and political campaigns is quite feasible. In fact, with Cambridge Analytica's assistance, the Trump campaign utilized microtargeting and a kind of "psychographic advertising" to create "dark posts," or ads directed to select voters with tightly crafted messages aimed at influencing their behavior. For instance, dark posts were used to influence certain groups of black voters to abstain from voting for Hillary Clinton (Funk 2016). And just to place Cambridge Analytica's work in a wider context, its parent company SCL has a long track record of experience in its over 25 years of existence, which includes working for political and military clients in countries such as Afghanistan, Kenya, Mexico, and Somalia. Specifically, in 2017 SCL received almost $500,000 from the US State Department for information on how recruits are motivated to commit terrorism through Islamic State extremist propaganda (Hjelmgaard 2018). In May 2018, Cambridge Analytica announced it would file for bankruptcy. Top executives at the company, along with some from its parent, SCL, along with the Mercer family, have moved to create a new firm, Emerdata, based in Britain, likely as part of a clever rebranding strategy. They have also teamed up with a Hong Kong financier who is a business partner of Erik Prince (more on him later; Confessore and Rosenberg 2018b).

Facebook and its peers have enjoyed a long run facing limited scrutiny from politicians, regulators, and the public at large. The 2016 election, Russian hacking, and data breaches have thrust them into the political and regulatory spotlight. They have been successful at avoiding such scrutiny for quite some time by cultivating progressive brand images through their public relations campaigns, while they also have been extremely successful in their lobbying efforts. For instance, since 2006, most online political activity has faced far less regulatory scrutiny than have traditional television, radio, and print media. The Federal Elections Commission (FEC) has justified exemptions for political activity on the internet because it is (was) "unique and evolving" and therefore distinct from other media in a manner that "warrants a restrained regulatory approach" (Vogel and Kang 2017). This conformed with the view dating back to the 1990s that the internet represented a free and open marketplace of ideas ("Once Considered" 2017). When the FEC moved to strengthen online disclaimer requirements in 2011 and 2016, the companies either ignored requests for input or suggested that new rules could "stand in the way of innovation" (Vogel and Kang 2017). Facebook also seemed to take advantage of partisan divides at the Commission, realizing that while they may not be exempt from disclaimer requirements on political ads, enforcement would not be forthcoming. One former commissioner, in reflecting on the political fallout of the 2016 election, commented, "[I]t was kind of like the chickens coming home to roost" (Vogel and Kang 2017). We will see. It was reported in January 2018 that the Four spent a combined roughly $50 million in lobbying and other activities intended to influence the government in 2017—a new record (Romm 2018)! It would not be surprising to see them ramp up these efforts in the years ahead—and they may need to!

Facebook's foreign policy

Facebook continues to seek global expansion abroad in its quest to gain new users and grow revenue. It has been engaged in a broader global mission (Zuckerberg has even addressed the United Nations) aimed at bringing the internet to the entire world, which skeptics or cynics (you decide) claim is simply part of a plan to lure in new users with the aim of eventually making them paying customers (Grossman 2014; Hempel 2016). The developing world, namely, parts of Asia and Africa, represents the next frontier though which Facebook aspires to add another billion users over the coming years. And, yet, increasingly, governments around the world have become more assertive in efforts to control online speech, commerce, and politics. According to research by the *New York Times*, from 2012 to 2017 at least 50 countries have passed laws to gain greater control over how people use the web (Mozur, Scott, and Isaac 2017). And so, as Facebook—and, increasingly WhatsApp, which holds even greater potential for spreading false information due to features that enable users to remain anonymous (Goel 2018)—seeks to expand its global market reach, we increasingly see it engaging in acts of diplomacy that me might typically assume are the purview of government.

For instance, in one case, a computer engineer, who had posted a poem online that was critical of the communist regime in Vietnam, was hauled into a local police station and commanded to hand over his Facebook password. This occurred weeks after Facebook's head of global policy management had met with a top Vietnamese official and pledged to remove information that violated the nation's laws. Facebook claims that it has a consistent process by which governments report illegal content. However, the Vietnamese government asserted that Facebook had agreed to create a new communications channel with the government and would prioritize its requests to remove posts about party leadership that officials deemed inaccurate. The company has strong business interests in placating governments such as Vietnam, as the regime had earlier called on businesses not to advertise on Facebook and other foreign sites. If local businesses had followed the government's requests this would have meant a sharp decline in revenue for the social networking company (Mozur, Scott, and Isaac 2017).

Along similar lines, Facebook is trying to become the internet in Africa, as it competes with rivals such as Google and China's Tencent. Roughly 170 million people, over two-thirds of all internet users throughout the continent, use Facebook, while over 50 percent of the population remains without internet connectivity. The company has made great inroads in Kenya, forging partnerships with local carriers to offer free, but stripped-down, versions of its services that can work on less powerful mobile devices. It is also working with about 30 regional governments on a range of digital projects. But some worry that the company is amassing too much power across the continent, which could have the effect of squeezing out potential online rivals or competitors. In a few instances countries have taken direct action against Facebook. Chad once blocked access to the social network during elections, and Uganda tried unsuccessfully to take legal action in Irish courts, Facebook's home outside of the US, in efforts to gain access to the identity of a political blogger critical of the governing regime (Mozur, Scott, and Isaac 2017).

Facebook and other big tech companies have experienced pushback from regulators around the world in recent years, with Europe leading the way in such efforts, while others are following suit. European regulators aspire to give users greater control over how their data is shared and used, and there seems to be greater concern among Europeans, specifically, that their data are being controlled by big American companies. For instance, after purchasing Whats-App in 2014, members of Facebook's global policy team began strategizing about how to win the approval of regulators for their plans to integrate data sharing on the app into the wider Facebook family. And while this sharing exists for its US customers, the company faced a major backlash among the public and privacy officials in Europe, beginning with Germany and spreading to other countries throughout the continent. Increasingly, countries around the world are looking to the Europeans, and the EU in particular, to set the standards for best practices regarding data sharing and regulating big tech, in general (Mozur, Scott, and Isaac 2017).

The United Nations (UN) has also taken Facebook to task. It did so through an August 2018 report on Myanmar's treatment of the country's Muslim Rohingya minority. In it, the UN called for the head of Myanmar's armed forces, along with several high-level military officials, to be prosecuted for genocide. This was outlined by *BuzzFeed News*, which conducted its own analysis documenting extensive hate speech on Facebook's platform during a period from March 2017 to February 2018 (Rajagopalan, Vo, and Soe 2018). The analysis highlights how lawmakers in Myanmar regularly posted hateful anti-Muslim content, even explicitly calling for violence in some cases. The UN's report singled out Facebook as "a useful instrument for those seeking to spread hate," and noted how the company's response to the crisis had been "slow and ineffective" (quoted in Rajagopalan, Vo, and Soe 2018). Facebook has responded to concerns raised by NGOs and other activist organizations by promising to take a more proactive approach to the problem. While it is well known that Zuckerberg generally favors automated AI-driven solutions to Facebook's content management processes, local civil society groups have expressed concerns that the company has not employed enough content reviewers who can speak Burmese, Myanmar's major language. Furthermore, leading human rights scholars interviewed by *BuzzFeed* seemed to imply that Facebook lacked an appreciation for how dehumanizing rhetoric spread through mass media can be a catalyst for violence and ethnic cleansing against vulnerable minority groups, as was the case with how radio was exploited during the 1994 Rwandan genocide (Rajagopalan, Vo, and Soe 2018).

Now, the biggest, and frankly most elusive, prize for Facebook has been China, which actually began blocking Facebook in 2009. Zuckerberg has been known to fawn over Chinese leaders, mostly to no avail. But he remains persistent, even at one point asking the Chinese president, Xi Jinping, over a 2015 White House dinner if he might suggest names for his expectant first born child—a request generally reserved for respected elder relatives. Furthermore, in 2016 Facebook began prototyping a tool that could be used to suppress posts in specific regions of the country, which would facilitate the social networks compliance with Chinese censorship policies. But it was never deployed (Mozur, Scott, and Isaac 2017).

Ironically, while China keeps Facebook out, the company has been more than willing to help it spread propaganda abroad. In fact, the Chinese government is one of Facebook's most valued customers, and the company has been more than willing to help its state run affiliates, such as China Central Television (CCTV), the major state-owned broadcasting network, and Xinhua, its official news agency, learn how to most effectively use the platform to spread government propaganda in the US and throughout the wider world. It may likely spend in the realm of a million dollars a year on Facebook ads. Much of this effort appears in the form of soft news propaganda heralding the success and benevolence of the Chinese government. Some of these efforts even focus directly on audiences in the US, while China has also has endeavored to court African nations and the wider world by offering an alternative to Western media. The bottom line: China is keenly aware of the potential that Facebook holds as a tool for molding political attitudes and shaping public opinion. That is why its leaders are so keen to use it to influence attitudes abroad, while denying access to their own citizens back home (Mozur 2017b; Mozur, Scott, and Isaac 2017).

In recent times, the Chinese government has begun to assert more direct control over and involvement in its own big tech companies. This is happening as President Xi Jinping begins his second term and moves to further consolidate his rule over the country. The government aims to harness the knowledge and capital of its leading tech firms to advance national goals laid out in its "Made in China 2025" plan, which include initiatives focused on electric cars, robotics, semiconductors, and leading the world in AI. For instance, Alibaba (e-commerce) has been designated as the national champion for developing smart city infrastructure. Tencent (messaging) will lead the way in medical imaging. Baidu (internet search engine) will develop smart driving cars. In turn, China's big tech firms are striving to keep government leaders happy, as the Communist Party moves to make its presence within the companies evermore visible. For instance, at a major high-rise office building owned by Tencent, a chart is prominently displayed that shows how many employees are party members, and images of the company's penguin mascot appear with a hammer and sickle on its chest (Zhong and Mozur 2018).

Facebook and the attention economy—feeding on addiction

Facebook and other firms in the attention economy feed on generating likes and sharing to grow advertising revenue, and, as a consequence, Facebook continuously seeks to exploit users' tolerance for invasion of their privacy, regularly testing and probing those limits (Galloway 2017a). Yet, in our individualistic market-based society, it is common to simply assume that consumer choice is what drives the way in which businesses like Facebook operate, and therefore, users could simply discipline these companies into acting on behalf of their interests. Recently, some within the tech world itself, have begun pushing back against that notion. One former software developer and entrepreneur, Tristan Harris—whose company was acquired by Google in 2011, where he eventually became a design ethicist—has contributed to a growing social movement in Silicon Valley that seeks to encourage ethical design into software development. While at Google, Harris quietly circulated what became a manifesto of sorts in which he wrote, "never before in history have the decisions of a handful of designers (mostly men, white, living in SF, aged 25–35) working at three companies had so much impact on how millions of people around the world spend their attention" (quoted in Bosker 2016).

Harris has spent his adult life in tech and was first introduced to the dark arts of manipulation, what has been referred to as hacking human psychology, while pursuing a master's degree at Stanford University, where he joined its Persuasive Technology Lab. It was run by experimental psychologist B.J. Fogg, who developed quite a following among aspiring tech entrepreneurs attracted to his principles of "behavior design." By the way, shouldn't there be some kind of professional code of ethics against this stuff? While there, Harris learned about how successful websites and apps tap into deep seated human needs, and really, anxieties. For instance, LinkedIn developed a hub-and-spoke icon to represent each user's network. The design proved extremely successful because it tapped into people's craving for social approval, making them anxious to continuously grow their own personal networks (Bosker 2016). Marketing scholar and social psychologist Adam Alter (2017) argues along similar lines that encouraging behavioral addiction has become the design imperative for digital devices, social media, and online gaming.

But just how effective has all of this persuasive technology really been? What has been its overall impact on society? While research exists pointing to limited effects on wellbeing (Przybylski and Weinstein 2017), perhaps the most comprehensive research pointing to nothing less than massive impact has been carried out by psychologist Jean Twenge and her colleagues (Twenge 2017; Twenge, Martin, and Campbell 2018). Twenge's academic work over more than two decades has explored generational differences and change. Over recent years, she has identified some alarming trends among adolescents. Large-scale survey research indicates that beginning around 2012 significant shifts in teen behaviors and emotional states have occurred. Sharp rises in reported feelings of loneliness, depression, and risk factors associated with suicide, have become linked to higher levels of time spent online. And while Twenge explored a range of explanations to account for this spike (for instance, the impact of economic distress on families in the aftermath of the 2007–8 financial crisis) the one that stands out and which cannot readily be discounted is the introduction of the iPhone in 2007. It was at this point where members of the post-millennial generation—those born between 1995 and 2012, or iGen, as she refers to them—became the first to experience the full impact of mobile technology (Twenge 2017).

Twenge pinpoints the twin sources of anxiety now more keenly experienced by members of iGen, and girls in particular, as first, significant increases in reports of feeling lonely or left out. The other is associated with posting on social media and the anxiety surrounding anticipating and getting likes (also see Gajanan 2015). In fact, getting likes is not simply an obsession of the young and innocent, but it has turned into a full-blown industry. The "Follower Factory," as it is referred to in the *New York Times*, highlights how widespread the practice of paying for a following has become, especially among celebrities and politicians (Confessore, Dance, Harris, and Hansen 2018). It also represents a highly lucrative business for the firms that offer these services. Why try and convince people to like your posts when it is so much more convenient to purchase them? The whole endeavor seems to give new meaning to the notion of fake friends.

The pervasive use of mobile technology, and its widespread integration into people's lives is now so complete that some now speak of it as wearable, like some essential piece of clothing one puts on every day and would not consider leaving the house without. Legal scholar and tech critic Tim Wu (2016) and others suggest that that smartphone has become a kind of artificial limb that many of us simply cannot function without. In fact, Twenge (2017) highlights how these devices are so ubiquitous that most teens go to sleep with their smartphones. She argues that the devices are implicated in research indicating that members of iGen are more likely to be sleep deprived, which is also linked to depression. Surveys now indicate that a majority of adults also cannot go to bed without their smartphones (Dreifus 2017).

Perhaps amid the public outcry over fake news, Russian election interference, and general misuse and abuse of users' personal information, followed by Zuckerberg's very public mea culpas, which included appearances before the US Congress and the European parliament during the spring of 2018, we might see the wounded tech titan tread more carefully into the lives of its users. Not so fast. Back in December 2017, the company had already launched a new and controversial app called Messenger Kids, designed especially for the under 13 market, which few big tech companies have dared to pursue. The app, intended for use by children as young as six years, is a service that can only be set up by a parent who uses his or her Facebook account to do so. The company points out that no advertising is permitted on the app, and parental controls make it safer to use than other traditional social media sites intended for use by people over 13 (Isaac and Singer 2017).

Shortly after Messenger Kids was introduced, dozens of pediatric and mental health experts sent an open letter to Facebook (organized by the nonprofit Campaign for a Commercial Free Childhood) urging them to discontinue the service. In it, they claimed the service preys on a vulnerable group (children under 13) who are developmentally unprepared to take part in online social networking activity (Kang 2018). In promoting the new service, Facebook claimed that it worked closely with leading experts in developing Messenger Kids, which took roughly 18 months. The online tech news site *Wired* reported that the company failed to disclose that many of those same experts had received funding from the organization (typically to cover logistical costs associated with other collaborative initiatives). Furthermore, the company did not seek input from prominent critics in developing the app; ones such as Common Sense Media were not consulted until the process was nearly over, and the nonprofit Campaign for a Commercial Free Childhood only learned about the app days before it launched. Meanwhile, prominent scholars on children and technology such as Jean Twenge and sociologist Sherry Turkle only learned about the app after its launch (Ortutay 2018; Tiku 2018). Critics argue that many features of the social network are available in the new app, including emojis, selfies, video chat, and group texting—a perfect recipe for hooking the next generation of users (Kang 2018).

Recently, some experts have pointed out that in actuality Apple is the company best situated to make a conscious effort to design products that facilitate users' capacities to moderate their time spent on social media and the internet, primarily because its business model does not depend upon addiction (Manjoo 2018b). In fact, two of Wall Street's largest investors have called upon the company to do just that. In a surprising, almost unprecedented, action, Jana Partners, an activist hedge fund, along with Calstrs, a major pension fund manager, wrote an open letter to Apple in January 2018, urging the company to take into account its products' health effects, especially on children, and to make it easier for parents to limit their children's use of iPhones and iPads (Gelles 2018). A striking statement indeed, as these two investors together own about $2 billion of Apple's stock. And now, some tech executives are also coming forward and acknowledging that their products are actually designed to be addictive. Of course, the biggest challenge remains that so much of the attention economy, and the culture of usage that has been forged in its wake, depends upon encouraging addiction. Have we collectively witnessed a colossal instance of market failure in the form of externalized political, social, and health-related costs? Can tech be tamed of its urge to phish for phools?

2 Monopoly

Google it!

While almost a quarter of US adults do not identify with any organized religion (Pew Research Center 2015), marketing scholar Scott Galloway (2017a) points out that many of us, increasingly all of us, regularly turn to a higher power, a deity of sorts, to answer all of life's questions—from the pedestrian to the sublime. And who or what is this entity to which we entrust so many of our private thoughts, secrets, and desires? Why Google, of course. With its simple and elegant home page, free of any clutter or advertising, Google has become one of our most trusted and dependable confidants.

The company set out to earn our trust from the very beginning. Its longtime unofficial motto has been "Don't be evil." This lasted from the beginning of the 21st century until the company was reorganized under its now parent company, Alphabet, in 2015, wherein the motto was modified to "Do the right thing." However, the original motto remained as the opening line of Google's corporate code of conduct until the spring of 2018, when "Don't be evil" was relegated to the final line of the document (Conger 2018). Over the course of its history, Google's privacy policy has undergone 30 revisions and, in the process, expanded from 600 to over 4,000 words. The evolving manner in which it handles your personal information has been essential to its long-term profitability. In this chapter, we will explore why living up to its original highminded ideals may not be as easy as it seems. After all, Google is an immensely profitable enterprise whose value (market capitalization) stood at roughly $825 billion as of August 2019 (Warzel and Ngu 2019; Yahoo! Finance 2019).

It is probably fair to say that most of us love Google. It is something we are heavily reliant upon at school, work, and throughout our daily lives. Google has been my constant companion during this book project, although I must confess that writing this particular chapter makes me feel a bit uneasy about our relationship. But, generally speaking, we rarely take notice of the central place it holds in our lives, taking it for granted almost in a manner analogous to having running water or electricity. Increasingly, critics claim we should treat Google as a public utility, given that it is almost invisible in its ubiquity (Galloway 2017a). In fact, by some estimates, it accounts for 87 percent of all online searches worldwide (Duhigg 2018). But the concern is less about the direct effect it has over users—although you may become alarmed to learn just how much private information we have surrendered to the company in return for all of those free searches—than the manner in which Google exercises enormous power over its competitors and even its industry partners. In the pages that follow, we will first explore Google's business model, or how it makes all that money while offering a seemingly free service. Then, we explore the case for why Google just may, in fact, be a monopoly, and how its anticompetitive business practices are directly linked to its core business model. In the meantime, remember, "Don't be evil!"

The business model: it's all about advertising

Google has built up an enormous reservoir of trust among its user base. It has done so by providing organic search results that are accurate and relevant to our queries, while paid content is clearly labeled as such. And so, we continue to search ever more. Consider all the many queries you have made on Google; even for things you have wanted to see or learn about which you might be embarrassed, even ashamed, to share with anyone else. All this trust, and all of that sharing, enables Google to weave together a rich tapestry of information about how we behave, and what we might wish for or desire. This grants the company unheralded power to generate advertising. They use that power as gatekeeper to any commercial entity that wants to learn about us in order to serve up products and services that might just fulfill those needs and desires, sometimes even soliciting us in anticipation of what we may wish for prior to our own realization that we wanted to make a purchase in the first place (Galloway 2017a).

The power of Google search has transformed the way in which traditional marketing has been conducted. Until recently, the dominant approach involved sorting people into more generic demographic groups and lifestyle categories. Now, because it is possible to identify each of us and our unique tastes, preferences and interests—although certainly still part of demographic-lifestyle groupings—this has enabled tailor made advertising and messaging at the most granular individual level. Google, along with Facebook, has completely transformed an entire industry that they are not directly a part of. They merely serve that industry. And who or what do they serve them? They serve them you, which is made possible by everything they know about you, which is more than anyone else has ever known.

They are so good at serving advertisers that Google, and of course Facebook, must be looked at as driving factors contributing to the decline of traditional new media, the fourth estate, by, once again, starving them of revenue. In a manner similar to Facebook, Google has subordinated and commodified traditional news media. Sadly, they do a much better job of extracting value from news articles than, say, the *New York Times* and other major news outlets do themselves. Galloway (2017a) tells the story of how back in 2008, the *Times* might just have been able to redirect the fateful relationship between traditional news media and newer online social and search media upstarts in a manner more favorable to the former (and perhaps, to our democracy), but they missed out on the opportunity. Back then, Google was less dominant (hard to imagine) and needed content to feed the search impulse among its user base. If the *Times* had moved to turn off Google, not allowing it, or any other internet media company to crawl its content for free, and instead forced them to pay for or license (even exclusively) its content, the balance of power could have turned out much differently. However, the view among the leadership at the *Times* was that their relationship with Google was more equitable, and that the *Times* was getting valuable traffic from the search engine in exchange for its content. The problem was that Google was able to aggregate so much more user information on users it directed to *Times'* content than the news outlet ever could, and so it generated vastly greater advertising revenue from the deal. In fact, certain critics of big tech today have called for some type of tax on companies like Google and Facebook, whose advertising revenues have skyrocketed over the last decade or more, while newspaper advertising revenue has undergone a dramatic decline. The internet giants seem to get all the benefits from hosting news links from traditional media outlets but provide none of the journalistic value (Dayen 2017a).

Feeding a wider consumer data ecosphere

New York Times tech writer Brian Chen (2018) recently shared with readers what he found after downloading a copy of his Facebook data. Noting that his profile is sparse and that he rarely clicks or shares while on the site, he had assumed the company would not have collected much data on him. Wrong! Much to his surprise, he leaned that roughly 500 advertisers, many of which he had never even heard of before, had his contact information. Facebook had his entire phone book as a result of updates he made to it after setting up Messenger (its messaging app). Curiously, the company kept a permanent record of the roughly 100 people he had deleted from his friends list over the past 14 years. They had also kept a history over the past two years of each time he opened Facebook, the browser and devise used to open it, and in some cases his physical location. Chen conceded that this could very well serve a legitimate security purpose in order to flag suspicious activity, but it remains alarming nonetheless. And while the company claims that they provide tools to allow people to take out information they have put into Facebook, it is not so easy to do so with basic information (i.e., birthday). The company seems to have been run on a general policy of not deleting anything they collect on users.

Facebook, in Chen's words, was just the tip of the iceberg. His Facebook data tallied about two-thirds of a gigabyte (650 megabytes). In comparison, he ran a similar experiment on Google, where for his personal email account alone, Google's archive measured eight gigabytes. Do you use Gmail? Also, if you are not using an iPhone, then your smartphone likely uses Google's Android operating system, and you download all your apps from the Google Play store. Chen found that Google had kept a history of many news articles he had read over the years. They were kept in a log because the news sites had loaded ads served by Google—this, irrespective of whether he had clicked on any such ads, and in the majority of cases, of course, he had not. In another folder, Google had a record of apps he had opened on his Android phone since 2015 (Chen 2018).

It is now becoming clear that advertisers and other marketing firms can obtain information on us in a variety of ways. In so doing, they represent a larger ecosphere of which Google and Facebook are a part. As noted, roughly 500 brands, many of which he had never even heard of, had Chen's contact information. Upon inquiry, Facebook told him that these brands might have obtained his contact information elsewhere and loaded it into a Facebook tool called Custom Audiences, which facilitates efforts on the part of businesses to target Facebook user profiles and serve them ads. Facebook also offers ten different tracking technologies, which utilize cookies or invisible pixels that collect information on your browsing activities that brands can utilize and load into Custom Audiences to serve you ads on Facebook. Also, it may be the case that you share information with one entity, such as a credit card or airline loyalty program, and they in turn share with other entities that, in turn, serve you ads on Facebook (Chen 2018). Of course, given all of the bad publicity the company has received surrounding its lax oversight of user data, Facebook has been engaged in ongoing efforts to tighten up its relationship with data brokers and other third-party entities in the hopes of allaying users' privacy concerns, while striving to maintain its revenue streams (Hern 2018).

Google has recently been under scrutiny from Ireland's privacy watchdog for the European Union, the Data Protection Commission, which has been investigating whether the company has been feeding personal data from users to advertisers in contravention of its own privacy policies. The investigation is examining whether "sensitive data, such as race, health, and political leanings," are being used to target ads on its advertising exchange, Authorized Buyers, formerly known as DoubleClick (Murgia 2019).

For many years now, firms have simply purchased consumer information from large data providers, and then used that information to serve targeted ads on social media, browsers, or other websites. These providers play a major role in the wider consumer data ecosystem. One of the very largest among them is a firm called Acxiom, located outside of Little Rock, Arkansas. An in-depth story (expose) on the firm, dating back to 2012, opens with, "It knows who you are. It knows where you live. It knows what you do." And continues, "It peers deeper into American life than the F.B.I. or the I.R.S." The author describes Acxiom as the "quiet giant" of the multibillion-dollar database marketing industry (Singer 2012). While few of us have ever heard of this company, it was believed at the time to have amassed the largest commercial consumer database: about 1,500 data points each on roughly 500 million active consumers worldwide, including a majority of US adults (Singer 2012).

While Acxiom has marketed itself as "a global thought leader in addressing consumer privacy issues and earning the public trust" (quoted in Singer 2012), in practice the company seems much more devoted to serving the interests of its paying corporate clients, counted among which are almost half of all Fortune 100 companies, than protecting consumer privacy. For many years now, the company has moved beyond now common online tracking techniques, such as the use of "cookies," in pursuit of a more comprehensive digital marketing strategy aimed at integrating online, mobile, and offline behaviors, in the hope of developing more complete consumer behavioral portraits. Acxiom has had a head start in the process, today having a database of offline consumer information that is now nearing 50 years in the making. Its PersonicX classification system, assigns consumers to one of 70 detailed socioeconomic clusters (Singer 2012).

In order to pursue its mission of becoming an advanced consumer data refinery (versus simply a data mining company), it has aggressively recruited tech talent from companies such as Google, Amazon, and Microsoft. It even hired away a vice president of advertising at Microsoft to become its CEO. Not surprisingly, privacy advocacy groups, such as the nonprofit Center for Digital Democracy, have raised concerns that the industry is forging a new era of consumer profiling, while the in-depth story raises the question of whether the industry's activities should be likened to "stalking" consumers (Singer 2012).

Privacy advocates worry about the way in which industry data brokers use ranking systems to classify groups of consumers as high value prospects and others as low value ones—otherwise known as "waste" in the industry (Singer 2012). This points to ways whole segments of the population can simply be excluded or discarded in the world of online commerce. Or consider Acxiom's Consumer Data Products Catalog, where corporate clients can make purchase selections from hundreds of details ("elements") about individuals or households to supplement their own marketing databases. The company has a "Race model," providing information on major racial categories, which on the one hand may provide ways of engaging diverse communities for marketing purposes, but also runs the risk of being used as a form of "ethnic profiling" or stereotyping (Singer 2012).

Much of the large-scale data mining carried out by the industry has been perfectly legal. It seems that federal authorities, namely, the Federal Trade Commission (FTC), while having raised concerns about this secretive industry over the years, has not really taken effective actions, or convinced Congress to do so, in order to keep up with this rapidly changing privacy landscape. Unfortunately, the database marketing industry has operated in the shadows and has not been required by law to provide consumers with copies of their own reports or files, which would enable them to seek corrections, unlike that which has been required of consumer credit reporting agencies (Singer 2012). Speaking of which, this latter industry, which forms another segment of the wider consumer data ecosphere, has recently proven itself colossally incapable of protecting vital personal and financial consumer information.

The 2017 Equifax breach was probably the event that really started getting wider alarm bells ringing over consumer data and privacy. The company, which among the three major consumer credit reporting agencies that include Experian and TransUnion, reported a major breach in September 2017 that affected roughly 150 million American consumers. Hackers gained access to company files through a weak point in its website software, and were able to steal Social Security numbers, driver's license numbers, names, birthdates, and addresses. Security analysts and privacy experts posited that this kind of breach was among the worst that could happen to consumers. The previous year, hackers had stolen W-2 tax and salary data from an Equifax website, and more recently W-2 tax data from an Equifax subsidiary. Security experts were highly critical of the company for not improving security after those earlier breaches (Bernard, Hsu, Perlroth, and Lieber 2017).

Equifax handles data on more than 800 million consumers worldwide. But make no mistake about it, we consumers are not its customers, or at least the ones that really matter. The company, which has been in business for over a century and been profitable over recent decades, embarked on a mission over the last ten years or so to deliver even stronger growth for Wall Street investors. The strategy involved a massive expansion of the personal data they collect on consumers, and then finding ways to market a multitude of new products and services with that data.

Equifax used big data and created algorithms to "scrub" social media in order to obtain new data on consumers and link to existing company files. They also had analysts developing new types of algorithms, which enabled them to market new services aimed at predicting consumer behavior and pitched these to lenders and other business. They expanded global operations to 24 countries mainly through acquisitions. Finally, through a major purchase of a company called Talx in 2007, they began offering human resources products. They grew Talx's payroll information business by expanding the company's base of 142 million employment records to roughly 300 million today. In just over a decade, the company was able to double its revenue, and in the process transformed its corporate culture becoming much more aggressively profit oriented, all the while emphasizing safety and data security as a selling point. In various promotional materials it proclaimed, "Data breaches are on the rise. Be prepared. . . . You'll feel safer with Equifax" (quoted in Cowley and Bernard 2017).

Once again, everyday consumers are not Equifax's customers—although they do offer some consumer products, and sell products and services to, say, LifeLock, which then sells identity protection to end consumers. But Equifax (and the other consumer reporting agencies) are really in the business of servicing financial institutions and employers. Much like the case with Facebook and Google, we consumers are the product that gets "sold." Over the course of one's adult life, Equifax amasses an ever-expanding file on each of us that may include places of address, driver's licenses, social security numbers, telephone, cable, and other utility bills, rental histories, medical debts, any type of criminal record, and so on. Apparently, its record on any one of us could be hundreds or thousands of pages long (Cowley and Bernard 2017).

It is not surprising that many of us (consumers) were outraged over the breach, as we have had little or no say in how these companies operate.

Meanwhile, their business clients had limited recourse in dealing with, or disciplining, Equifax. A senior vice president at the Mortgage Bankers Association captured the predicament of their member financial institutions, noting, "We don't really have a chance to opt out of the credit report system" (quoted in Cowley and Bernard 2017). They are stuck with a cartel of three major consumer reporting agencies, and so are we. Not much of a free market there to discipline bad actors. Speaking of which, it was also revealed that three senior executives at Equifax sold shares of company stock worth $1.8 million in the days just after the breach (Bernard, Hsu, Perlroth, and Lieber 2017).

Monopolizing its territory

Google's parent, Alphabet, having about 80,000 employees, promotes itself as a diversified company, but in actuality derives 90 percent of its revenue from advertisements (Duhigg 2018). Back as early as 1998 Google's founders acknowledged that by relying on advertising the company would find it difficult to produce the highest quality products for consumers (Wu 2016). This compromise is most apparent in the competition that Google's Android faces with the iPhone, as Apple's business model is not fundamentally built upon generating advertising revenue—instead they charge exorbitant prices for their products. Furthermore, this dependency led Google executives to embrace a strategy aimed at protecting their search dominance, and, in particular, product search, the most lucrative of all its services. Internal company memos dating back well over a decade highlight Google executives' concerns about protecting search profitability, and the need to ward off potential rivals who might encroach upon this territory (Duhigg 2018).

A major preoccupation among top executives at Google has been to master what is known as vertical search. Apparently, this type of search is far more complex and sophisticated, and therefore difficult to master, than simple searches linking a few key words together and then identifying websites with these combinations. Instead, vertical searches involve what is referred to as parameterization. It entails developing complex algorithms that must integrate larger sets of variables, or parameters, that may be of interest to users conducting web searches. Because these capabilities are so highly valued, there is a lot of tech talent out there dedicated to mastering and monetizing the art of vertical search. Internal memos from around 2005 highlight how top executives were keen to protect vertical search. "What is the threat if we don't execute on verticals? Loss of traffic from Google.com because folks search elsewhere for some queries," wrote one executive, while another asserted, "Long term, I think we need to commit to a more aggressive path" (quoted in Duhigg 2018). These discussions were also reflective of a mandate that came down from co-founder Larry Page to more aggressively push Google's offerings.

One of the ways to get more traffic was to list Google's price comparison results at the top of any given search, even if the company's search algorithm did not naturally prioritize them. Another way was to change the rules governing Google's search algorithm, and in 2006 the company initiated a major update, followed by another a few years later. Google claimed one reason for the adjustments were to discipline entities that sought to unfairly game the system in order to gain favorable, but undeserved, listings. Critics argued, however, that Google itself engaged in similar practices as those it was disciplining and demoting in its search results, which meant it was nearly impossible for rival vertical-search engines to compete with the search giant (DuHigg 2018).

Some firms that have tried to compete directly with Google, believing they have developed superior services, have ended up on the losing end of the struggle. One such rival, a young upstart called Foundem.com, which you have likely never heard of, developed a price comparison search engine. After years of testing among its founders' friends and acquaintances, the company formally launched right around the time that Google had made a conscious decision to protect its search territory. During the first two days of its initial launch, Foundem experienced a burst of traffic from queries made on Google and other search engines. But within 48 hours, the company found it had been relegated from the front page of Google's search results down a dozen or more pages, while it continued to receive high rankings from other search engines. Foundem's owners, who were fairly well known in the tech world, and had contacts with people inside Google, could never get the company to respond to its emails and phone calls inquiring as to why they had been demoted in its search results. Back in England, their home base, the company had won awards for their search products, but remained basically invisible on Google. Eventually, they took up antitrust complaints against the company in Europe and in the US (Duhigg 2018).

Next, consider the case of Yelp, which provides user generated reviews of local businesses, and a company with which you are most likely familiar. It originally had a run of good fortune with Google, appearing at the top of countless Google searches during its early years. In fact, Yelp was so successful that Google tried to purchase it in 2009, but its owners refused. Shortly thereafter, Google began simply including Yelp's content in its own search results, which led to a dramatic decline in traffic directly to Yelp's website. The company, along with TripAdvisor and Citysearch, have made complaints to the Federal Trade Commission (FTC) over the years about what they claimed to be unfair treatment by Google. In Yelp's case, Google responded to the FTC by noting that Yelp could simply remove its content entirely from Google search. I guess if you were unhappy with the water service you were receiving from the local municipality, or perhaps the electricity being provided by your regional energy provider, you could simply discontinue service in protest, and look for other alternatives (Duhigg 2018).

The mobile industry stack

Companies like Google, Facebook, and Apple operate in multiple yet related markets. These form "interlocking ecosystems" wherein companies cooperate and compete with one another (Iyer and Rangan 2016). A good example of such an ecosystem that highlights Google's industry dominance is the mobile industry stack. Here within the mobile device ecosystem we find layers of functionality, starting with the mobile devices themselves. At the base of the system are found device makers such as Apple, Samsung, and China's Huawei. As we move up the stack each layer of functionality is dependent upon the one below it, and so those firms that dominate one layer can use their power to control how the layer above it functions. Next are the mobile operating systems, which include Apple's iOS and Google's Android. On top of that is the distribution layer, where we find the App Store and Google Play. Finally, there are the apps themselves that we purchase or download for free from the store located in the distribution layer.

While Apple relies upon a vertically integrated stack, meaning it uses its own products for each layer, Google works cooperatively and competitively with partners but still dominates nonetheless. Its open source operating system, Android, can be adopted by any device maker and, theoretically, modified to suit their needs. However, Google requires mobile device makers to sign anti-fragmentation agreements should they wish to pre-install its proprietary apps such as Google Play and Google Search. This means the device makers must forgo the option to modify the Android OS, and in practice serves to practically lock out other search engine providers and distribution level store fronts. European regulators have raised serious antitrust concerns about Google's dominance of the mobile industry stack because roughly 90 percent of device makers in Europe use Android. For its part, Google argues that its services have made it much more efficient and cost effective for device makers to bring products to market (Iyer and Rangan 2016).

The case of Skyhook wireless highlights some of the ways in which Google exerts its dominance over the mobile industry stack. This particular startup invented a new navigation system and won contracts with mobile device makers Samsung and Motorola. In an internal email that came to light in a later lawsuit, a Google manager speculated that Skyhook's system was, in fact, more accurate than Google's. Shortly thereafter, a Google official pressured the two device makers to terminate their relationships with Skyhook, which both of them eventually did. Google admitted to no wrongdoing in the lawsuit and was forced to pay out on a patent infringement claim, but Skyhook's owners eventually ended up having to sell their company at a discount (Duhigg 2018).

Google, like Facebook, has expanded its presence throughout the interlocking ecosystems in which it operates in significant part through acquisitions. So much so that in 2011, Eric Schmidt, Google's longtime executive chairman, boasted that they were buying a company a week. Some of their most significant acquisitions include purchases of online ad servicing company Double-Click, as well as YouTube and Android (Dayen 2017a).

For its own dubiously cooperative involvement in the mobile industry stack, details of Facebook's longstanding relationship with device makers came to light in 2017, much to the outrage of politicians, regulators and the wider public. Over the past decade, it has had data sharing partnerships with more than 60 device makers, including Apple and Samsung. Early agreements were forged before its apps were widely available on phones, which allowed device makers to offer some of its most popular social networking features, such as the "like" button. However, Facebook allowed the device makers access to data on users' friends without obtaining their consent. Facebook only began winding these agreements down in April 2018 (Dance, Confessore, and LaForgia 2018). What has been even more alarming are the revelations that the company had similar data sharing agreements with at least four Chinese electronics companies dating back to 2010. This included an agreement with telecommunications equipment company Huawei, which has close ties to the Chinese government and was flagged by US intelligence officials as a national security threat (LaForgia and Dance 2018).

Lessons learned from Microsoft: the original evil empire of tech

Tech critics have drawn analogies between the market dominance enjoyed by Microsoft during the 1990s and the Google of today. This, in spite of the fact that Microsoft inspired a public image that was more Darth Vader compared to Google's more honest and wholesome Luke Skywalker. At their root, each has "monopoly" inscribed into its own DNA. As Scott Galloway (2017a) points out, Google has undertaken "one of the most ambitious strategies in business history: to organize all of the world's information," or at least "become the gatekeeper to it" (154). Yet they have done so over more than a decade without really threatening potential rivals; that is, until it was too late. The innocent, likeable image, clean, searchable homepage uncluttered by advertising, buttressed by an (until recently) unofficial motto, "Don't be evil," made it all seem innocuous and innocent (Galloway 2017a).

Microsoft, on the other hand, widely came to be viewed as a bully, despised by many, and fully deserving of being cast in the role of villain. In fact, it seems they at times cultivated that image. The company was pursued relentlessly by federal and state prosecutors during the 1990s, who argued that the company was acting in a predatory manner to secure its software monopoly. And when Microsoft occasionally lost in court, its founder and CEO, Bill Gates, would seemingly thumb his nose at government prosecutors and judges, implying that the company would simply carry on with business as usual, while in other cases they were able to overturn unfavorable verdicts on appeal (Duhigg 2018). Like Google, Microsoft was also a gatekeeper, suffocating potential rivals before they could threaten the company's dominance. The most notorious of all such cases was that of Netscape, which had developed a vastly more popular web browser than Microsoft's Internet Explorer. But Microsoft was able to strangle Netscape's growth by bundling Explorer with its own industry dominant Windows operating system, and then "partnering" with PC manufacturers such as Dell to preinstall its products while excluding those of its rivals (Galloway 2018).

After the US government unsuccessfully tried to break up Microsoft, it eventually offered the company a settlement so weak and innocuous—such as agreeing to make its products more compatible with competitors' software—that nine states urged the court to reject it. Many have argued that the antitrust pursuit of Microsoft on the part of the government has been a waste of time and did not accomplish anything. This conforms with the reigning view that digital commerce is unique because competition inevitably rules the day. In that narrative, Google came along and provided superior search engines and other products and won over consumers from Microsoft, which had lost its innovative edge. As far back as 2012, Google's Larry Page embraced this notion when he asserted, "when our products don't work or we make mistakes, it's easy for users to go elsewhere because our competition is only a click away" (quoted in Duhigg 2018).

However, a different view has emerged among some contrarian legal scholars and antitrust lawyers, such as Gary Reback, who worked with clients back in the 1990s and successfully exhorted the government to sue Microsoft. Reback has shifted his sights to Google in recent years. The contrarian view holds that while the antitrust pursuit of Microsoft may have proved unsuccessful on the surface, it actually had a significant impact on how the company operated over ensuing years. Evidence from within the company, namely, in the form of reports and testimonials from former employees, indicate that the ongoing threat of antitrust prosecution and all of the negative publicity surrounding the company eventually took its toll on the defiant monopolist (Duhigg 2018).

During the late 1990s, when federal prosecutors were pursuing Microsoft, the company may have struck a dismissive and condescending tone in its public responses to those actions, while the mood within the company was filled with caution and anxiety. One former lawyer for the firm recounted how "the constant scrutiny and being in the newspaper all the time" led people to start "second guessing themselves. No one wanted to test the regulators anymore" (quoted in Duhigg 2018). Furthermore, top executives who had previously comported themselves with arrogant self-assuredness began requesting to have lawyers and compliance officers present in their meetings when software developers pitched new products, even though those individuals had been routinely ignored in the past. Furthermore, with the firm operating under the constant threat of government scrutiny, a new internal culture of compliance emerged and led to the damping down of once fierce internal debates and discussions about how to destroy the competition. And while there may have been informal talk about crushing one particular new upstart—and former employees believe that it could have readily been accomplished, as Internet Explorer was the portal through which most users would have to seek out Google—the then giant Microsoft had become gun-shy about extinguishing this latest rival (Duhigg 2018).

The European Union leads the way forward

Google and other big tech firms have faced much closer regulatory scrutiny from the European Union, especially after Danish lawmaker Margrethe

Vestager was named Commissioner for Competition in 2014 and soon became the most important antitrust official in the world. The EU spent several years bringing a case against Google, reviewing 1.7 billion search queries to see how entities fared on topics where Google has a financial interest versus those where it did not. A verdict in June 2017 found that Google had given its own comparison shopping service an illegal advantage over its competitors. The company was fined a historic $2.7 billion and was ordered to stop favoring its own comparison shopping service (Duhigg 2018).

In 2018, the European Union issued a new record $5.1 billion fine to Google for abusing its dominance over European smartphone makers by requiring them to install Google products when they utilize its Android software, thus making Google Search and the Chrome browser two of several Google default services on these devices produced by these companies. This provides Google with vast market coverage, which facilitates its capacity to serve up evermore advertising. The EU also ruled that Google must allow device makers the opportunity to create their own versions of its Android software, referred to as "forks." Previously, companies that developed modified versions of Android would have their access to Google apps blocked in response (Condliffe 2018; Nicas 2018b; Satariano and Nicas 2018).

However, even more important than the fines, may just be the shifting tides of public sentiment regarding the reality and the threat posed by technopoly. For instance, in the US, a bipartisan collection of state attorneys general moved to request that the FTC reopen its antitrust investigation of Google. And the Supreme Court allowed an antitrust case to proceed against Apple in 2019, which focused on exorbitant pricing on offer in its app store linked to excessive commissions and restrictions placed on developers who sell through it (Liptak and Nicas 2019). Of note in Google's case is a Missouri investigation, spearheaded by a Republican state attorney general, looking into whether Google has disadvantaged competitors in its searches, and we know now that the Justice Department has taken on that task. Until recently, Republicans have generally been more inclined to assert that free markets, and in particular the digital economy, operate according to their own natural mechanisms of self-correction, and therefore the government need not intervene into their operation (Duhigg 2018; Lohr, Isaac, and Popper 2019).

But it has not only been Republicans who have been reluctant to take on Google and other big tech firms over recent years—Democrats, and, namely, the Obama administration, have been similarly disinclined. In fact, in 2012, after gathering complaints about Google for several years, staff at the FTC produced a 160-page report, much of which was inadvertently leaked to the press. In it they noted that "Google has strengthened its monopolies over search and search advertising through anticompetitive means" and "had adopted a strategy of demoting, or refusing to display, links to certain vertical websites in highly commercial categories" (quoted in Duhigg 2018). Unfortunately, the FTC's politically appointed leadership declined to sue. Keep in mind, these firms have invested millions in lobbying efforts that have paid off over the years.

Furthermore, tech firms have heavily invested in academic research on digital commerce over the past decade or so, with Google having provided up to $400,000 in seed money for each of roughly 100 such projects, yet their sponsorship is not readily disclosed in much of this research (Dayen 2017a; Duhigg 2018).

Perhaps for too long, we took these companies at their word, or their "motto." Certainly, the European Union has taken a much more skeptical view of Google's potentially monopolist search and industry gatekeeping practices, along with the firm's unchecked willingness (like that of Facebook) to exploit users' personal information for profit. Maybe it is no longer good enough for them to hide behind the maxim "Don't be evil," which they have already distanced themselves from anyway. And maybe the time has come for regulators to formally hold them accountable for their actions (business practices).

3   Apple

Alas, something is rotten in Cupertino

They did it! Just as I was beginning to write this chapter in earnest, Apple Inc.'s market value climbed to just over $1 trillion: a record in the history of capitalism (although it has not remained there; Grocer 2018b). As reported in the *New York Times*,

> That landmark is the result of an extraordinary corporate success story. In a span of 21 years, a near-bankrupt computer maker evolved into the most valuable publicly traded company in the United States, pushing the tech industry away from big bulky machines and producing some of the world's most popular consumer products, like the iMac, the iPod and the iPhone. Apple's products have reshaped swaths of everyday life.
>
> (Phillips 2018)

And yet this unrivaled accomplishment also serves to highlight a growing trend of corporate consolidation throughout the US economy in recent years. Today, in a host of industries, from airlines to banking to cable television and wireless services, a smaller and more concentrated group of companies command larger shares of total profits in their particular sector. Nowhere is this more apparent than in tech. As we have already discussed, Apple and Google combined provide the software for almost all the smartphones that are produced and sold, while Facebook and Google garner well over half of all online advertising dollars in the US. More than three-quarters of all American industries have grown more concentrated since 1980, and there is fairly widespread agreement among economists that these trends are real and could very well be long lasting. Unfortunately, economists are also highlighting connections between these trends and stagnating wage growth, a declining middle class, and rising inequality in the US ("Companies Appear" 2018; "Is There a Concentration Problem" 2017; Phillips 2018; "Too Much" 2016). In the pages that follow, we will explore how Apple, one of the world's most beloved firms, fits neatly into this picture.

Harvesting from the commons of knowledge while giving nothing back

At one point in the movie *Steve Jobs*, a film about the late, great founder and CEO of Apple, a character asks, "So how come ten times in a day I read 'Steve Jobs is a genius?'" The mystique surrounding the late Steve Jobs and other tech titans is part of a larger mythology about the role played by Silicon Valley (and the wider private sector) in America's technological innovations (Foroohar 2015). But let's step back and examine that mythology in a broader context.

Since the latter part of the 20th century, it has become widely asserted to a greater or lesser extent that we now live in a "knowledge society," or perhaps a "post-industrial" society, marking an inflection point in the history of the industrial world, where services, intelligent designs, and advanced technologies point the way forward (Bell 1973). But, in following economic historian Joel Mokyr (2002, 2003, 2011), the knowledge society must be viewed in broader terms, the origins of which owe much to the institutions that fostered the growth of science, and which emerged alongside the Enlightenment; more specifically, in the form of the Republic of Letters. This virtual community emerged in Western Europe during the period of roughly 1600–1750, which just preceded the Industrial Revolution, and set the institutional conditions, incentives, and context for the creation and sharing, evolution, and refinement of new forms of what we refer to as scientific knowledge today.

Following Mokyr (2003), aspects of the pre-industrial world were rich and productive in many respects, and it enjoyed many path breaking inventions. However, it differed fundamentally from the world set in motion by the Industrial Revolution—one that generated sustained economic growth based on advancing technological development. And technological advancements increasingly came to depend upon a broadening and deepening "epistemic base," or a widely shared commons of developing scientific knowledge. In contrast, the pre-industrial era "was a world of engineering without mechanics, iron-making without metallurgy . . . mining without geology," as well as "medical practice without microbiology and immunology," and so on (Mokyr 2003: 4).

While many phases of industrialization proceeded without dependence on a deeper scientific base of knowledge, certain advances relied heavily upon this evolving commons of knowledge, and tech is clearly one of those. As Fred Block ([2011] 2016) argues, the US government played a role in supporting economic growth in the 19th century and the 20th, at a minimum by providing infrastructure such as roads, canals, and railroads, and in facilitating the diffusion of productive innovation in many sectors of the economy. However, it was World War II that witnessed a dramatic expansion in the government's technological capacities.

During World War II and its early aftermath, the government created an extensive network of laboratories staffed with highly trained scientists and engineers that served to expand its scientific and technological capacities. The Manhattan Project itself created a network of atomic laboratories that still exists today. This period also witnessed the government become the principal source of funding for foundational scientific research, which was consolidated with the creation of the National Science Foundation (NSF) in 1950. Here, it influenced the scientific community by anticipating and then funding endeavors that promised to advance new technologies that might have military applications. In general, Block ([2011] 2016) argues that government officials took on greater responsibility for pushing forward technological frontiers.

A second turning point leading to a heightened role for government in advancing technological-scientific innovation occurred during the Cold War in the 1950s and 1960s, with the Soviet launch of Sputnik in 1957, which was the first artificial satellite placed in orbit around the earth. This created a panic among US policy makers and led to the creation of a new agency, NASA (the National Aeronautics and Space Administration agency), which remains widely recognized today. It passed the National Defense Education Act, aimed at strengthening math and science education in the US. And lesser known, but extremely important, was the creation of DARPA (the Defense Advanced Research Projects Agency). A portion of DARPA's funding was devoted to speculative initiatives, supporting ideas that moved beyond the contemporary horizon of innovation and might not produce anything substantively useful for 10 or 20 years. The agency experimented with new strategies for accelerating the development of new technologies. In particular, it played a central role supporting the development of the computer industry during the 1960s and 1970s by funding the creation of new computer science departments at US universities and supporting key research on semiconductors, while it also oversaw early development of the internet (Block [2011] 2016).

During the 1960s, the DARPA program officers also were visionary in taking advantage of new developments in the early computer industry, namely, the new type of engineer–scientist run spin off firms that have come to emblemize the entrepreneurial and risk taking qualities associated with Silicon Valley today. They were able to support this new innovative environment by mobilizing the efforts of technologists in a range of settings including big firms, small startups, university researchers, and specialists in government laboratories. They were able to spur innovation oftentimes with smaller more competitive grants by funding and targeting new innovations and rewarding those who produced desired outcomes, while quickly turning off the funding sources on projects that did not bear fruit.

Block ([2011] 2016) highlights one special example of how DARPA was able to leverage the more open and fragmented nature of technological development that accompanied the emergence of Silicon Valley by financing a laboratory associated with the University of Southern California that was dedicated to fabricating computer chips from anyone who presented a potentially innovative design. By the later 1970s it became apparent that the prohibitive cost of fabrication was a roadblock to new technological improvements in computer chip design. Small firms and research laboratories could not afford the cost of production, so DARPA stepped in and took on this expense which enabled technological developments in the area to proceed at a rapid pace.

The 1980s represented a key turning point, given that the Reagan era was heralded for its embrace of market fundamentalist ideology and general denigration of all things government. But Reagan, in fact, was much more of a pragmatist in matters of government than his legacy would lead one to believe. And so, the government built on DARPA's successes and expanded initiatives that fostered decentralized technological advancement. By then, the personal computer's emergence, with Apple being the first to market in 1976, was a powerful example of the effectiveness of DARPA in spurring on the industry's explosive growth and significance.

Furthermore, by the late 1970s and early 1980s Western Europe and Japan began to catch up with, and even outpace, major industries that had been dominated by US manufacturers since the end of World War II. This threat was keenly felt in the auto industry, where many feared that Japanese firms had a growing superiority over US manufacturers. And so, the Reagan administration built on many of the steps taken during the Democratic Carter administration during the late 1970s to accelerate technological development in this more fragmented, decentralized manner. One of the most successful and important programs initiated early in the Reagan administration was the Small Business Innovation Research Program (SBIR). To this day, this program provides funding for new technological entrepreneurs, nurturing new enterprises and facilitating the transition of countless new technologies from laboratory to the marketplace. However, as Block ([2011] 2016) notes, this roughly $2 billion a year program is so obscure that it has received minimal news coverage during its long existence, and many of our congressional leaders do not recognize its value and importance.

While Democratic administrations (Clinton during the 1990s and Obama during the 2010s) have understood the importance of the state in nurturing scientific, technological, and hence economic development, they have been hampered by the legacy of market fundamentalist ideas that have triumphed since the Reagan presidency. The Trump administration is a curious aberration, given its focus on supporting technologies and industries rooted in the past, namely, coal and fossil fuels, while demonstrating no systematic interest in the scientific foundation and technological advances required to nurture the industries likely to drive economic growth in the future. Nevertheless, the power of this ideology has made it politically treacherous to acknowledge the state's central role in promoting technological development, as market fundamentalist dogma insists that that private sector should be left on its own so that it can best respond to signals from the marketplace.

After all, Milton Friedman himself asserted in *Free to Choose* (Friedman and Friedman 1980) that there is no economic justification for the government to fund scientific research. And so, for decades we have had what Fred Block (2008) refers to as the *hidden developmental state*: a situation where the state still nurtures early phase developments in science and technology, but the fact that it is doing so remains obscure and not granted sufficient priority given the reigning market ideology. One consequence is that this role of the state in this capacity is rarely recognized in political debates or given sufficient attention in the mass media. Here in the US, unlike countries in the European Union, we do not have the kind of open political discussion and debates about the government's role in supporting technological development and innovations that will help advance the country's economic competitiveness and citizens' future standards of living and overall wellbeing.

Economist Mariana Mazzucato (2011) has been one of the most prominent and authoritative voices highlighting the important role that the state has played in fostering advanced technological developments in recent years:

> Every major technological change in recent years traces most of its funding back to the state. . . . Even early stage VCs (venture capital) come in much later, after the big breakthroughs have been made. . . . We pretend that the government was at best just in the background creating the basic conditions (skills, infrastructure, basic science). But the truth is that the involvement required massive risk taking along the entire innovation chain: basic research, applied research and early stage financing of the companies themselves.
>
> (quoted in Foroohar 2015)

Mazzucato takes special aim at Apple and the technological advances that it has been able to leverage into its wonderful and stylized retail products. However, she notes that those "revolutionary technologies that make the iPhone and other products smart were funded by the government" (Mazzucato 2013). She points to the internet, GPS, touchscreen display, and even the iPhone's voice-activated personal assistant, Siri, as prominent examples of early stage government-funded research activities that made these technologies and commercial applications of them possible. She also emphasizes how "many of the "new economy" companies that like to portray themselves as the heart of US "entrepreneurship have very successfully surfed the wave of U.S. government-funded investments" (Mazzucato 2013). For instance, Google's search algorithm was funded by the National Science Foundation. Meanwhile, in stark contrast to the government largesse they have enjoyed, many have gone to great lengths to avoid paying their fair share in taxes! More on that later in the chapter.

Fighting for (and invading) user privacy at home, while complying with Chinese authorities abroad

In December 2015, a man and his wife attended a work holiday party in San Bernardino, California, and surprise attacked the guests, killing 14 coworkers and injuring almost two dozen others. The couple died hours later in a shoot-out with police. Suspecting terrorism, the FBI obtained the husband's iPhone and secured a federal court order mandating that Apple create and provide software to unlock the phone (Galloway 2017a). However, Apple stood up to the FBI request to get inside the dead terrorist's iPhone. Its CEO, Tim Cook, proclaimed the company had a moral and financial obligation to protect its users' privacy and liberty. While it was unclear as to whether the company had a winnable case, the FBI rescinded its request just before it was headed into court (Manjoo 2017a).

For its supporters, perhaps here was a case where Apple really stood by its Silicon Valley values. But as marketing scholar Scott Galloway (2017a) points out, judges issue search warrants on a regular basis, as their charge is to comply with search and seizure laws that prevent indiscriminate searches, while ordering private property, including homes and, at times, the computers in them, searched for evidence surrounding actual or preventable crimes. Have we, in Galloway's (2017a) words, "fetishized the iPhone," turned it into a "sacred object" that sits above the law (66)? Furthermore, if the company is willing to stand up for citizen/user liberty and privacy in the democratic US, what is Apple's track record in dealing with non-democratic, even authoritarian, regimes when it comes to advancing those same virtues? The case of China is instructive.

In July 2017, Apple removed several VPN apps from its Chinese app store in order to comply with a new cybersecurity law. These apps had enabled iPhone users to bypass the Chinese government's censorship apparatus and obtain access to blocked content. And while we may never know just how Apple responded in private consultations with the Chinese government, it offered no public criticism of the law at the time. Instead, a public statement on the VPN ban noted that the company "had been required to remove some VPN apps in China that do not meet the new regulations," but that the "apps remain available in all other markets where they do business" (quoted in Manjoo 2017a). In order to comply with a request from government authorities, it also removed the *New York Times* app in the Chinese app store a few months earlier.

The company also announced during July 2017 that it would partner with a Chinese state-owned company to build Apple's first data-storage center in China as part of a larger $1 billion investment in the Guizhou province of southwest China. The deal occurred in response to a strict law passed in China requiring companies to store users' data within the country. Apple's revised terms and conditions agreement, in a practical sense, means that all Chinese users' personal information stored on the iCloud, including photos, text files, contacts, and email, will be shared with the Chinese partner company named Guizhou-Cloud-Big Data (G.C.B.D.), and hence, available to Chinese authorities as well. While Apple, whose CEO Tim Cook has asserted that privacy is a fundamental human right, had claimed that G.C.B.D. would not have access to the personal data stored in its facility without Apple's permission, the new user agreement seemed to contradict such public statements (Guangcheng 2018; Mozur, Wakabayashi, and Wingfield 2017).

Back home, we must remind ourselves of a different kind of invasion of privacy is being increasingly called out. That is, the manner in which Apple's vaunted iPhone increasingly represents—at least according to a growing cadre of ethical computer programmers (Bosker 2016), child psychologists, and public health researchers (Twenge 2017), along with major institutional investors (Manjoo 2018b) that have a financial stake in the company's continued profitability—a threat to the health and wellbeing of the US's youth. Recall our discussion about tech addiction at the end of the chapter on Facebook. Many are now calling for a less addictive iPhone.

Master of the global supply chain

Apple is a greatly admired and innovative company, and with a market valuation of $1 trillion, one can only imagine all the jobs the company has created over the years. Well, yes, it has led to the creation of hundreds of thousands of jobs. Just not in the US. Many of us were first awakened to the vast production system employed by Apple through a series of investigative news stories about the company in 2012. In that context, we also learned of the now legendary story of Steve Jobs, not only as a creative genius, but also as a demanding perfectionist, and the last-minute redesign of the iPhone screen back in 2007.

Just over a month before the iPhone was set to launch, Steve Jobs abruptly ordered a last-minute modification. After having carried a prototype around in his pocket for several weeks, he noticed numerous little scratches on its plastic screen. He was convinced that the solution was an unscratchable glass screen, and ordered that it be perfected in six weeks. The company had been working on a project that explored various ways to reimagine the iPhone and had already done some preliminary work on developing a glass screen. Ultimately, a Chinese factory was awarded the contract to produce them. With generous subsidies from the Chinese government, the plant's owners had already begun constructing a new wing, and even had a warehouse filled with glass samples ready and waiting for the Apple team in the event they were awarded the contract. Engineers would be available at no cost, and on-site dormitories ensured that production line employees would be available at a moment's notice. Apple's current CEO, Tim Cook, then an operations expert, had been instrumental in convincing the company to begin focusing production on Asia, as he believed that their factories could scale up much more rapidly and their supply chains were superior to what was available in the US (Duhigg and Bradsher 2012).

Within just a few weeks of the iPhone launch, the supplier delivered the first shipments destined for final assembly to the manufacturer, which, in turn, had made a last-minute assembly line overhaul to accommodate the new glass screens. Upon their arrival in the dead of night, plant managers woke thousands of sleeping workers from their dormitories, provided them with a snack and a cup of tea, and then escorted them to the factory floor to begin 12-hour shifts at their workstations. In less than a week, the plant was producing 10,000 iPhones a day. Foxconn, the company that manufactured the phones, has become a household name among those familiar with the industry.

That particular facility employed 230,000 workers, a quarter of whom lived in company dormitories (Duhigg and Bradsher 2012).

In the intervening years, reports by investigative journalists have drawn attention to the oftentimes harsh, exploitative, and even unsafe conditions under which many of those who assemble iPhones, iPads, and other electronic devices have toiled—at least according to interviews with the workers themselves, labor and other advocacy groups, outside observers, and even company records. The problems range from employees having to work excessive overtime, in some cases seven days a week, to the employment of underage workers, crowded dormitory conditions, improper disposal of hazardous waste, and most serious of all, blatant disregard for workers' health due to unsafe factory conditions, especially where hazardous chemicals are used in the production process. Foxconn was singled out for at times harsh and overcrowded living conditions in company dorms, demanding that employees work continuous shifts, and inappropriately punitive disciplinary practices. Of course, the company issued generic public statements disputing these accounts (Duhigg and Bradsher 2012). Furthermore, the company was singled out for a rash of suicides among its young workers living in company dormitories dating back to 2010 (Barboza 2010).

Apple has not been alone among electronics companies to have such problems emerge within their supply chain relationships. These seem to have emerged in the electronics industry in a manner similar to that of the apparel industry during the late 1990s, when Nike was a leader in divesting itself of US-based manufacturing capacity and constructing a global supply chain of producers. In that case, political movements emerged—many on college campuses—in protest against global sweatshop labor, and Nike and other apparel-based brands were at times shamed into improving conditions throughout their supply chains (Klein 2001).

Investigative reports emerging back in 2012, based in part on interviews with former Apple executives and managers at some of their Asian suppliers (invariably given on conditions of anonymity), highlighted ongoing and unresolved and persistent tensions within the company between fostering crucial supplier relationships to ensure rapid production and swift delivery of new products and the desire to improve conditions within factories. In principle, Apple and other innovative tech companies would like to improve working conditions within their supply chains. The company even has a "supplier code of conduct." It has engaged in significant auditing campaigns, and produces annual supplier responsibility reports. That said, industry executives pointed out how a major overhaul to the system would slow the kind of innovation and new products demanded by customers every year (Duhigg and Barboza 2012).

Some former executives noted that suppliers would change their practices in an instant should Apple demand it. In the time period between 2007 and 2012, Apple found hundreds of violations in its audits, but fewer than 15 suppliers were terminated for noncompliance. One executive with intimate knowledge of supplier relations claimed that as long as suppliers promise to try harder, noncompliance is generally tolerated. And while back in 2010 Steve Jobs boasted at an industry conference that "Apple does one of the best jobs of any companies in our industry, and maybe in any industry, of understanding the working conditions in our supply chain," another former executive was much less sanguine. In contrast, he noted that while the company is trying hard to make things better, "most people would still be really disturbed if they saw where their iPhone comes from" (Duhigg and Barboza 2012).

One of the problems associated with such arms-length supplier relations is that Apple is viewed as such as valuable and prestigious client by its suppliers. Courting and landing a contact with Apple is cause for celebration—but then the demands begin. Apple has been known to demand intricate details from their suppliers about their operations, including the costs of parts and supplies, workforce size, and salary information on employees. After scrutinizing the supplier's financials, Apple decides what it will pay for a part, only allowing its supplier a slim profit margin. So suppliers try to find ways to cut corners, which might include less safe work environments or exploiting workers themselves in order to produce more efficiently. Then, Apple may come back the next year and ask for a price cut (Duhigg and Barboza 2012).

During its early years, while some other American tech companies had already begun to dismantle their domestic manufacturing supply operations, Apple was committed to manufacturing in the US. In fact, Steve Jobs was of the belief that hardware and software development needed to be closely integrated. Having opened plants in Colorado, Texas, and California, Jobs boasted in 1984 that the Mac personal computer was "made in America." However, by the late 1990s, with slumping sales revenues and bloated inventories, Apple embraced outsourcing under the direction of then operations manager Tim Cook. The company found a valuable partner in Foxconn, a Taiwanese manufacturer. Former Apple executives boasted of the excellent engineering staff at Foxconn, as well as its ability over the years to meet the demand that accompanied Apple's new products. Foxconn had the capacity to rapidly produce new prototypes and then ramp up production, in part by being able to hire and utilize hundreds of thousands of workers during peak periods (Barboza 2016).

But just how was this company able to produce so rapidly and cost-effectively on such an enormous scale? Well, its founder, Taiwanese billionaire Terry Gou, had developed enormous political clout among Chinese officials at various levels of government over the years, and had been extremely successful in lobbying for subsidies, cheap land, a flexible and expansive workforce, and high-quality infrastructure. Nowhere is this better captured than in Zhengzhou, known informally as "iPhone City," with its six million people located in an impoverished region of China. It is home to the world's biggest iPhone factory, with capacity to produce up to 500,000 iPhones a day. Chinese government incentives worth billions of dollars have enabled Foxconn to produce so cost-effectively and lucratively for Apple. Foxconn is also China's largest employer, with the government incentivizing and rewarding the company for creating all those jobs by massively subsidizing the costs of building large sections of its factory and employee housing facilities. It has paved roads and built power plants to help subsidize energy and transportation costs borne by the company. The government even recruits workers to fill Foxconn's factories. Furthermore, the local Zhengzhou government eliminated Foxconn's corporate taxes for the first five years of its operations there, and then only levied them at 50 percent of the standard corporate tax rate for the next five (Barboza 2016).

That said, these types of deals that China has struck with many US and other foreign multinationals are likely winding down, as the country seeks to move away from its dependence upon manufacturing exports toward becoming a leader itself in technological innovation by providing support for homegrown brands and fostering consumption of products developed by Chinese companies. The country now seems to be embarking upon what a US congressional study has referred to as a project of "techno-nationalism" (Barboza 2016).

Recall how I mentioned earlier that China has recently initiated an ambitious 2025 plan aimed at becoming a world technological leader while seeking to wean itself off of foreign-made software and equipment. This shift brings issues of global trade into stark relief, and calls to mind our usual suspects in this story, the market fundamentalists. For the post–World War II era running up until the end of the 20th century, the US brokered, or shall we say, imposed, a trading regime on the nations of Europe and Japan, meant to create an international interdependent economic system that would serve to preclude any more European wars. It was a political regime whereby the governments of the US and its trading partners exerted influence over how their own corporations conducted business abroad, with an eye toward maintaining stability and independence (Lynn 2010, 2015).

In *Free to Choose* , Milton Friedman (Friedman and Friedman 1980) advanced the idealistic vision of a world market (implicitly drained of the onerous but very real element of the political in political economy) as one simply regulated by the eternal laws of supply and demand. But, in practice, this meant that elites who direct multinational corporations would have freer rein to govern international commerce as opposed to their (or our) elected leaders. Somewhat surprising, however, was the fact that then President Ronald Reagan, the champion of free market thinking, chose a more pragmatic approach to protecting American industries from competitive threats posed by ascendant Japanese electronics and automotive industries during the 1980s. However, it was Democratic President Bill Clinton during the 1990s who was instrumental in promoting and advancing the market fundamentalist vision for international trade, with his championing of the World Trade Organization (WTO) and in gaining most-favored-nation-trading status with China.

In the abstract, the market fundamentalist ideas about global trade have an undeniable appeal. In a practical sense, however, they run into trouble when held up to the light of global realities. One such critic who has consistently and incisively pointed this out over the last two decades has been Ralph Gomory, research professor at New York University's Sloan School of Business, who, interestingly, had roughly 30 years of corporate experience with IBM, where he eventually became director of research and senior vice president for science and technology. His co-authored 2001 book, *Global Trade and Conflicting National Interests*, ran severely across the grain of dominant economic thinking at the time, and was conveniently dismissed, if not derided (Gomory and Baumol 2000).

Gomory (2017) points out how economics textbooks unabashedly teach the virtues of free trade by assuming a world governed purely by market forces of supply and demand. However, he notes that the international economic system as it exists in reality contains a good measure of "mercantilism," wherein a country may employ the power and resources of government to advance and protect its own industries. This could involve providing various types of subsidies, infrastructure, even cheap labor to one's own favored industries intended to give them a competitive advantage over their foreign rivals. It best characterized the European world from the 16th to the 18th century. But, as has been the case in contemporary China, American corporations such Apple have actually benefited from all the subsidies, tax breaks, and infrastructure granted to manufacturers like Foxconn, because it means their final products are produced at lower cost, which means more profits for Apple.

As the US lost more of its manufacturing capacity to global competitors over the last several decades, Gomory (2011) has insisted that we have erroneously been encouraged to embrace an innovation delusion regarding how to successfully compete in the new economy of the 21st century; one said to be characterized by a flatter world of near frictionless trade and commerce (Friedman 2005). This perspective touts American innovation, advanced design, and cutting-edge R&D as the pathway to competitiveness. The idea here is that we simply move up the skills chain in the global division of labor and leave it for other countries to do the manufacturing and other lower level activities. Yet a near-exclusive focus on design, ideas, and R&D will never scale to the level of employment and economic activity necessary to balance trade and generate sufficient numbers of good paying jobs for citizens at home (Gomory 2011; Gomory and Sylla 2013).

Gomory (2011) points out that R&D represents too small a fraction a company's overall revenue to really have a large impact upon overall employment and trade deficits. From his own experience as head of research at IBM, five percent of revenues might be typical investment for a company in manufacturing. Additionally, the late Andy Grove, a founder and eventual CEO of Intel corporation—which became one of the world's leading manufacturers of semiconductors—raised concerns for many years that scaling up manufacturing and innovation frequently work hand in hand. From his own experience at Intel, Grove was keenly aware of the risks associated with scaling up manufacturing on the expectation of future revenues. Yet, once the electronics industry moved those processes abroad, oftentimes whole ecosystems of know how between suppliers and their customers (technology firms) would depart with them and eschew possibilities for applying manufacturing know how to future innovations in more advanced or related industries (Grove 2010).

The challenge is to figure out how to competitively adapt to a world that is half mercantilist and half free, knowing that there is no magic time machine to help us return to an earlier era and start again. China is moving up the skills chain with a new focus on developing its own hi tech industries, and, as noted, the US's big tech firms have been helping them do it in order to gain access to its markets. In fact, corporations in a range of industries (i.e., automobiles) have also been willing to comply with the government's stringent rules and demands in order to gain access to its vast consumer markets (Lynn 2015).

This larger discussion leads us to examine the stark reality of the issue of employment and our extremely profitable tech sector. Like big tech, big auto included some of the most highly profitable companies of its time. If we compare employment in the tech sector today versus the automotive sector that dominated US industry during the 1950s and 1960s, it is clear that auto generated substantially more jobs. In the late 1950s, General Motors boasted over a half million employees, and Ford, along with Chrysler, accounted for over 150,000 employees each (Madrigal 2017). Apple is the only company that comes close to them with 100,000 employees (Yahoo! Finance 2018a), but with only about 25,000 in its home region of the "Santa Clara Valley" (Madrigal 2017). Meanwhile, Facebook only has 30,000—not very much for a company valued at $500 billion (Yahoo! Finance 2018b).

WhatsApp, the messaging service acquired by Facebook, demonstrates the manner in which tech industry services are oftentimes readily scaled up (referring to the number of employees needed to service incrementally more users). WhatsApp only needed a small cadre of 50 engineers to service the 900 million users it had acquired by 2015 (Metz 2015). And yet, even during the golden era of auto manufacturing, the industry was already losing large numbers of jobs to automation. That reality represents a large part of the story of industrial and technological development. However, the reality that US tech firms do not generate significant numbers of jobs (especially at home) demands a reckoning. The 2016 election of Donald Trump represents (in part) a testament to this festering situation, if not any sort of remedy.

Consider one final example: Uber. Most of us are familiar with this ride hailing business, which is unique for a tech company in that it is situated squarely (even if we don't consider it as such) in the more traditional service sector that is generally very labor intensive. Uber has, for the most part, convinced us that it doesn't have any real employees: you know, who should be entitled to sick time, health insurance, unemployment insurance, retirement plans, paid vacation, and so on. Instead, they employ "driver-partners," or what are commonly referred to as independent contractors (Galloway 2018). They are emblematic figures in what is increasingly referred to as the "gig economy," a place where millions of new jobs are created, perhaps offering the enticement of flexibility for those who desire it, but in return generally offer no security, no control, and no stability (Graham and Shaw 2017; Manyika, Lund, Bughin, Robinson, Mischke, and Mahajan 2016).

Once again, it has been European countries and the European Union that have led the way, as policymakers around the world have struggled to craft rules for this growing segment of the world's labor supply based on short-term contracts rather than long-term employment. In 2017, the European Court of Justice ruled on a case against Uber, brought by a taxi group based in Barcelona, deciding that it is, in fact, a transportation business. In contrast, Uber has striven to define itself as a digital marketplace connecting drivers with riders (Alderman 2017). In fact, several European countries have taken action against the company. For instance, the city of London's transport authorities revoked Uber's license in 2017, but the company won an appeal to regain that license after agreeing to stricter government oversight that applies to more traditional taxi services (Satariano 2018a, 2018b). To provide some context of the wider significance of the EU case: in Spain, the home country of the taxi group that brought the case against Uber, the government reported in 2016 that 18 million temporary contracts were issued versus 1.7 million long-term jobs (Alderman 2017).

While Uber has faced limited scrutiny in the US (i.e., a ban in Austin, Texas), where business interests have had a much stronger hand in defining laws and public attitudes around freedom of contract, the California State Legislature has been working to change that. It proposes that Uber and other companies participating in the gig economy be required to treat workers as employees (Wood 2019). However, they have not received much encouragement from the Trump administration's National Labor Relations Board (NLRB), the government agency charged with enforcing US labor law with respect to collective bargaining and unfair labor practices. It released an advice memorandum on a related matter in 2019 affirming the status of Uber drivers as independent contractors and not employees, thus making them ineligible to unionize (Turner 2019).

A luxury brand that knows how to avoid paying taxes

Apple enjoys up to 90 percent of the profits in the entire smartphone industry, while only accounting for just about 12 percent of overall sales worldwide (Barboza 2016). Imagine we baked two pies, cut each into eight slices, and set them side by side. If one pie represents global smartphone sales, Apple takes one slice. For the other, representing all global profits in the smartphone industry, Apple enjoys seven of those slices! The company is incredibly profitable, and valuable, and as Scott Galloway (2017a) argues, the secret to their success revolves around Apple defining itself as a luxury brand.

Back in the late 1970s, Steve Jobs seemed to intuit the unique potential of Apple's products, as most computer products at the time were sold to techies or for business use and aesthetics were not remotely a consideration that factored into the early personal computer market. Even then, of course, the Macintosh line of computers was elegant and attractive, and stood out from the standard utilitarian basic metal boxes that housed most PCs. But, as Galloway (2017a) argues, a major turning point in Apple's evolution into a truly luxury brand occurred with the introduction of the sleek, portable, and ever-so-hip iPod. Here, unlike the personal computer, which sat on a desk in an office or back at home in one's bedroom, the iPod was wearable, a branded product that consumers could identify with, and more importantly be identified with, in public.

The trademark craftsmanship and elegant simplicity of design have stoked the desirability of Apple's products over the years, and Jobs deserves credit for imaging them in this manner, especially while other computer companies focused on the more utilitarian qualities of their own offerings. He also took the calculated risk, at a time of growing alarm about the future of brick-and-mortal retail in the face of online commerce, to launch Apple-dedicated retail outlets. In in anticipation of the project, Steve Jobs recruited former GAP CEO Mickey Drexler onto Apple's board of directors in 1999. Drexler remade the GAP throughout the 1980s and 1990s and transformed not simply its products but its stores and, with them, the overall branded experience that they provided customers, which drove the company through two decades of spectacular retail success. For their part, the Apple stores have come to function like iconic brand temples that, in major global cites, are situated next door to those of other luxury brands, with each aspiring to cultivate a unique consumer experience while generating an aura of desirability and exclusivity (Galloway 2017a).

So, if luxury and profitability fit hand in glove at Apple, what becomes of all those profits? The company is, after all, valued at around $1 trillion. Well, the company announced earlier in 2018 that it planned to buy back an additional $100 billion in stock, something that it tends to do more than any other corporation. When a company buys back stock it generally lifts its share price, thus rewarding investors who own it (Nicas 2018b). This most recent buyback occurred in the context of the Trump 2017 Tax Bill, which cut corporate tax rates from 35 to 21 percent, and offered a one-time rate of 15.5 percent to companies that agreed to bring back home untaxed offshore cash. Apple, Microsoft, and Alphabet (Google) collectively held $500 billion in offshore cash at the time (Manjoo 2017b). When Apple announced it would bring home most of the roughly $250 billion it held abroad, many wondered what it would do with all that available cash (Nicas 2018b). Wonder no longer.

Apple, probably more than any other company in recent history, has faced critical exposure over the creative and ingenious manner in which it has managed to avoid paying its fair share of taxes. In 2017, a huge leak of over 13 million financial documents, known as the "Paradise Papers," revealed the offshore financial dealings of politicians, celebrities, business leaders, and big corporations. The documents, leaked primarily by one offshore law firm, Appleby, reveal how Apple was able to avoid a 2013 European Union crackdown on controversial Irish tax policies and move most of its untaxed offshore cash, worth $252 billion by 2017, to the little-known Island of Jersey.

At the time of the crackdown, Apple had over $100 billion in offshore cash, most of which was held in Irish subsidiaries, and on which they paid almost no tax. And so the company sought the services of Appleby to find a suitable new home for all that cash. In the end, they chose Jersey, which is part of the Channel Islands and has strong links to the British banking system, but which makes its own laws and is not subject to European Union regulations (Paradise Papers Reporting Team 2017).

Apple, along with numerous other companies such as Facebook and Google, had been employing a tax shelter known as the "double Irish," which was highlighted in a major expose of Apple in 2012. That investigation also revealed how Apple, by putting a little office in Reno, was able to avoid California's corporate tax rate of 8.84 percent and instead pay the going rate in Nevada of zero (Duhigg and Kocieniewski 2012). It was followed up by a 2013 US Senate investigative subcommittee report that found Apple was "attributing billions of dollars of profits each year to three Irish subsidiaries that declared 'tax residency' nowhere in the world" (Drucker and Bowers 2017). This scheme allowed companies to collect profits through one subsidiary that has employees in Ireland, but then can route those profits to an offshore haven like Bermuda or the Cayman Islands. After a three-year investigation into the tax scheme, the European Commission ruled in 2016 that Apple must repay Ireland roughly $13 billion in unpaid taxes (Paradise Papers Reporting Team 2017). However, the Irish government provided a multi-year transition period for companies that had been employing the tax scheme, and also announced a new measure that expanded tax deductions for companies that move rights to intellectual property into Ireland. It appears likely that Apple utilized an Irish subsidiary to move intellectual property into Ireland, which should allow them $13 billion in tax deductions each year for the next 15 years (Drucker and Bowers 2017). Confused? So am I. But I'm sure you get the idea. To place it in perspective, Apple's accounts indicate that they made about $44 billion in 2017 outside of the US and paid only $1.65 billion in taxes to foreign governments, which amounts to a 3.7 percent tax rate (Paradise Papers Reporting Team 2017).

Scott Galloway (2018) has also pointed out that while (over the period of 2007 to 2015) the average S&P 500 company pays about 27 percent of its profits in taxes, the US's big tech firms pay at least 10 percent less than that overall—more like in the 15 percent range, although Facebook, by his calculations, seems to pay just a few percent. So, alas, something isn't only rotten in Cupertino, but the odorous fog seems to be spread more widely over Silicon Valley and up the US northwest coast to Seattle.

4 Amazon

Our Faustian bargain

For well over a decade, Amazon kept secret the number of people who had signed up for its $99 annual Prime membership. Then, in a 2018 letter to shareholders, Jeff Bezos celebrated the fact that the number had reached 100 million (Selyukh 2018). Not too surprising, as consumers generally have had a love affair with Amazon. It captures roughly half of every e-commerce dollar spent in the US (Streitfeld 2018). Three years in a row, between 2014 and 2016, Amazon was identified as the most reputable company in America, based on an annual survey of over 50,000 consumers conducted by the Reputation Institute (Strauss 2016). They appreciate its commitment to performance and innovation while providing excellent service. The company seems to have weathered the significant loss of trust and reputational damage experienced by our other big tech firms in recent years, dropping to a still enviable tenth place in the 2018 rankings (Valet 2018).

Jeff Bezos started the company in 1994, taking it public three years later. Reflections on the 20th anniversary of that event seem to clearly have vindicated his business model, which was widely questioned over many years. For instance, Warren Buffett, one of America's most well-known and respected investors, praised the "remarkable business achievement" that Amazon had become, while admitting that his investment group "missed it entirely," and did not believe Bezos would be able to "achieve on the scale that he has" (quoted in Sorkin 2017). As Scott Galloway (2017a) argues, key to Amazon's success has been Bezos' ability to sell investors on a vision of long-term growth over short-term profitability. A very difficult sell in the post-Reagan era, where short-term shareholder value and stock prices have been the ultimate, dare I say, the only, measure of success. As a testament to this extraordinary achievement, Amazon's market cap crossed the trillion-dollar milestone in September 2018 (Streitfeld 2018).

And so, Amazon has been the beneficiary of extraordinarily cheap capital. Investors purchased the stock in droves but did not seriously defect when growth without profitability ensued over many years. It seems the formula has been, "If we can borrow money at historically low rates, why don't we invest the money in extraordinarily expensive control delivery systems? That way we secure an impregnable position in retail and asphyxiate our competitors"

(Galloway 2017a: 34). Early on, Bezos drew inspiration from Walmart and its ability to deliver low prices to consumers by squeezing its suppliers. He also embraced a bold vision, aiming to one day become a giant in retail, as had once been achieved by Sears and later Walmart (Coll 2014).

Probably the most penetrating portrait of Jeff Bezos and the company he built is found in *The Everything Store* by Brad Stone (2013). Bezos comes across as a complicated character who is at times "nerdy, dreamy, prescient, and ruthlessly competitive" (Coll 2014). In-depth reports have portrayed an extremely competitive, hard driving, Darwinian workplace culture at the company's Seattle headquarters, home to its well-paid white-collar workforce, not to mention the at times disturbing portraits of working conditions in some of its warehouses (Nocera 2015). Neither Bezos' true intentions nor his endgame is easy to decipher, unless one takes a long view and carefully follows in his wake, surveying the wreckage as he navigates the company's competitive movements, always with an eye on some distant objective.

In the classic medieval German legend *Faust*, the main character, Dr. Faustus, makes a deal with the devil's envoy, Mephistopheles, wherein he sells his soul in exchange for knowledge (think books) and worldly pleasures (anything you wish to buy is a click away). Much like the now archetypal figure of Mephistopheles, Jeff Bezos seems to have brought out the collective Dr. Faustus in most all of us. This chapter explores the nature of the potentially Faustian bargain that we, collectively, have made with Amazon, and what it might bode for the future (Ramm 2017).

From white knight to marauder: Amazon's literary ambitions

When Amazon first ventured into the online retail book business during the mid-1990s, it provided a glimmer of hope for small publishers who bristled under the dominance of retail chains Barnes & Noble and Borders. After all, Bezos, who himself was trained as a computer scientist and spent his early career at a hedge fund, had married a novelist and professed a devotion to books and love of literature, envisioning the internet as a means to expand the possibilities by which both readers and publishers could flourish. He even hired in-house writers and editors and, in the early days, fostered a company atmosphere likened to that of a trusted and sophisticated independent bookstore. Bezos' first love was science fiction, which had inspired early aspirations to one day travel into outer space (Coll 2014). It should also be noted that he purchased (rescued) the *Washington Post* for a cool $250 million in cash in 2013, and has appeared willing to financially support the continuation of its high journalistic standards (Coll 2014).

However, it seems that books were incidental to Bezos' larger ambitions. Through his collaborations with Columbia University computer science professor–turned hedge fund manager (and Bezos' employer) David Shaw, he became fascinated by the potential of the internet to enable retailers to mediate between consumers and manufacturers on a grand scale. That's where the idea of "the everything store" emerged. However, Bezos shrewdly calculated that it would be wise to start with one product category and then expand outward to almost everything. So he evaluated 20 possible product categories around which to launch the company, including clothing, music, and office supplies. In the end, he settled on books, not for their cultural literary value, but because they were "pure commodities." A copy of any particular book in one store was the same in any other. Books were durable, easy to pack and ship, and hard to damage. Furthermore, with three million books in print, no single brick-and-mortar retailer could ever house them all under one roof. But an online bookseller could potentially secure access to and distribute virtually all of them (Coll 2014).

Within a decade Amazon had acquired a significant share of the market for books and began using its muscle to put the squeeze on its "commodity" suppliers. If publishers did not wish to make concessions to Amazon's demands for price reductions, the company could easily tweak its algorithms and reduce the visibility of the publishers' books, thus sending sales plummeting. An algorithm named Amabot was to eventually supplant all of those in-house writers and editors, replacing informed literary judgments and a quirky bookstore atmosphere with an aggressive march toward automation driven by customer generated data (Coll 2014).

The company was especially ruthless in its negotiations with those small and vulnerable publishers who may have initially looked to Amazon as a welcome alternative to the big retail chains. Named the Gazelle Project until in-house lawyers prevailed in renaming it the Small Publishers Negotiation Program, Bezos recommended that the company approach "small publishers the way a cheetah would pursue a sickly gazelle" (quoted in Streitfeld 2013).

Bezos was convinced that digital books could eventually emerge and triumph over physical ones. He was impressed with Apple's highly successful ventures into digital music, which greatly disrupted that industry. He then moved to enter the digital reading market in a race with Apple. In 2007, with the successful development of the Kindle reader, Bezos realized that he needed inventory, and pressured publishers to begin converting their physical books into digital form; however, he did so without ever revealing the pricing structure for this new line of products. He reserved that for public media events introducing the Kindle reader. The price would be $9.99—far below traditional list prices charged by retailers. And so, in effect, the publishers had unwittingly agreed to massive price cuts without ever really negotiating them. This move gave Amazon even more power over the publishing industry, while further threatening the viability of traditional booksellers (Coll 2014).

Several year later, in 2014, Amazon's contentious relationship with the book publishing industry flared up into public view once again. This time, it involved a large New York publisher named Hachette, which had the audacity to refuse Amazon's request for further price cuts in contract negotiations. While Amazon refused to comment publicly on the spat, Hachette stressed it was shipping book orders promptly, but many titles persisted in being listed as unavailable on Amazon's website. Hachette, which owns several small publishing houses and represents many (including somme renowned) authors, appeared to be on the receiving end of several not-so-subtle disciplinary tactics that conveyed a clear message as to who was in charge in this partnership (Streitfeld 2014).

One tactic appeared to be warning consumers that certain titles were delayed in shipping. This during a time in which Amazon was ramping up its Sunday delivery offerings and had been vigorously expanding its two-day shipping program. Another appeared to involve charging higher than expected prices on several Hachette titles, which could be purchased at, say, Barnes & Noble for several dollars less. Finally, in addition to the price increases, certain Hachette authors found their books were being undermined by Amazon aggressively recommending alternatives. One signature example was Marla Heller's *The Dash Diet Weight Loss Solution*, which was hit by all three of these strategies and dropped from the ranks of top 300 sellers on Amazon to as low as the top 3,000 (Streitfeld 2014).

Following the Walmart monopsony template

Concerns about Amazon's growing monopolistic control in the book industry expanding into other areas of online retail may obscure the real threat associated with its power, for, at least thus far, Amazon has delivered low prices to consumers. So low that many investors have been keenly skeptical of its business model of emphasizing growth over profitability. But the real concern raised by the growth of Amazon is not one of monopoly or oligopoly, where one or a few firms gain control over a market and then are free to dictate higher prices to consumers. Instead, the threat posed by Amazon lies in what is called monopsony power (Krugman 2014). In that case, the problem lies with a firm that has ability to dictate prices to its suppliers, which have little or no choice than to deal with the buyer (Lynn 2006). As we have mentioned, Jeff Bezos has been a great admirer of Walmart's success, and seems to be emulating its, well, monopsonistic tendencies in his own efforts to colonize much of the retail universe.

Economic journalist Barry Lynn, who over a decade ago began warning about extreme industry consolidation in the wake of the Reagan revolution, has identified how one or a few firms have come to dominate numerous markets including ones for raw materials (such as iron ore), heavy equipment manufacturing, banking, meatpacking, even eyeglasses. With this oligopolistic consolidation comes a power to control suppliers for a given market (Lynn 2006). In the case of big box retail, over the last several decades Walmart led the way (along with Target and now-defunct Kmart) in transforming the broader institutional structure of the economy itself. Through a process of *market making*, they have influenced virtually all activities associated with retail trade, from procuring product, identifying and forming partnerships with, and then defining the rules and standards for conduct of their global suppliers, to the shopping environment, pricing, and assortment of merchandise available on the shelves for the consumer (Petrovic and Hamilton 2006).

In so doing, they have fundamentally upended and transformed the decades-long relationship between once dominant manufacturers and their subordinate wholesale distributors and final retailers into a system where the retailer is king. This earlier *push* system, wherein manufacturers achieved efficiencies of scale through large-scale production runs, thereby minimizing costs but oftentimes generating massive surpluses that were eventually pushed onto retailers' shelves, has been replaced by a *pull system*, whereby retailers track consumer purchases, transmit this information up to manufacturers in the supply chain, who then must respond immediately and deliver just the right amount of product destined for retailers' shelves in order to meet changing consumer demand. Its accomplishment involved early adoption of the latest retail applications of new information technologies (IT), along with late 20th-century concentration in the retail sector, which in turn facilitated the widespread adoption of these changes throughout a reorganized and increasingly subordinate global supply chain (Bonacich and Hardie 2006).

Some have argued that this new system of *lean retailing* enthroned Walmart as perhaps the world's leading manufacturer in all but name (Lichtenstein 2006). Advancements in the use of IT systems served to transform the whole industry process of logistics, which had previously and simply meant the distribution functions undertaken by a firm that generally involved issues of transportation and warehousing. With the emergence of *lean retailing*, logistics has taken on the larger meaning of managing the entire system of supply chain relations (Bonacich and Hardie 2006). In Walmart's case, "the firm is also one of the world's most intrusive, jealous, fastidious micromanagers," whose aim has been "nothing less than to remake entirely how its suppliers do business . . . and turn them into extensions of itself" (Lynn 2006).

Monopoly and antitrust in an era of "always low prices"

One leading voice in the call to rethink current approaches to antitrust enforcement in this era of big tech platforms has been legal scholar Lina Khan (2017a, 2017b, 2018). Khan has taken special aim at the manner in which Amazon has accrued power in the age of e-commerce, and identifies several key and interrelated sources of such power enjoyed by big tech platforms. These include *gatekeeper* power, *leveraging*, and *information exploitation*. Not surprisingly, Amazon excels at exploiting all three, and does so in an integrated manner that amplifies its market power (Khan 2018).

Khan rightly homes in on Amazon's long-term business strategy as the original source from which it spawned such impressive market power. Two elements of that strategy are, first, its willingness to sacrifice profits for growth or market share, followed by its aggressive expansion into multiple lines of business. As we have already noted, Amazon's long-term business strategy has been no tightly held secret; but instead, Jeff Bezos has made it a cornerstone of the company's identity. Early public statements highlight how the company planned to grow, as Bezos emphasized in his first letter to shareholders, writing,

> We believe that a fundamental measure of our success will be the share-holder value we create over the *long term*. This value will be a direct result of our ability to extend and solidify our current market leadership position [measured by] customer and revenue growth.
>
> (quoted in Khan 2017a: 749)

Over the roughly two decades that the company's stock has been traded, losing quarters have been almost as frequent as profitable ones—and in those instances when the company actually showed a profit, the margins were exceedingly slim. Nevertheless, investors have supported Amazon in its quest for market leadership (dominance), and the company has consistently outpaced the growth of other online retailers, while major brick-and-mortar competitors, such as Walmart, Sears, and Macy's, have never been able to recoup loses they have conceded to Amazon through their own ventures into online retailing (Khan 2017a).

Furthermore, the company's willingness to accept losses with the rollout of its Amazon Prime loyalty membership program represents a powerful testament to this strategy. The program began in 2005, luring customers to join by offering unlimited two-day shipping for an annual fee of $79, which was raised to $99 in 2014. Over the years, Amazon bundled other services into the program, such as e-books and music/video streaming services. Prime can be credited as a main driver of Amazon's stock price and sales growth over the years; however, the company lost a great deal of money in order to gain a growing and loyal customer base. For instance, in 2011, it was estimated that the company actually lost $11 annually on each Prime customer. However, customers are estimated to increase purchases on Amazon by roughly 150 percent after becoming Prime members (Khan 2017a).

Khan envisions the *gatekeeper* role played by Amazon and other big tech firms that dominate today's internet platforms as likened to the powerful 19th-century railroads that connected customers with producer-suppliers.

> Because of their gatekeeper role, railroads had the power to discriminate, both among users and in favor of their own wares. These middlemen could tax farmers and oil producers who depended on their rails—or deny them a ride and sink their livelihoods.
>
> (Khan 2017b)

One example of how this power is exercised was captured in our discussion of Amazon's entry into and subsequent dominance over the market for books. Khan notes how Amazon has been known to flex its muscle when negotiating with book publishers by disabling their "buy-buttons," or even adjusting its algorithms in order to temporarily send their sales plummeting. It has also begun offloading portions of its shipping and other costs onto suppliers by raising fees it charges to list on its site (Khan 2018).

A second way in which Amazon and other tech platforms assert their power is through *leveraging*. Amazon is able to do so because it controls critical infrastructure, much like the railroads a century ago, that companies rely upon in order to reach consumers. It then uses that infrastructural resource to leverage its dominance and enter markets in direct competition with companies that rely upon it to reach final consumers, creating a conflict of interest where Amazon can readily issue preferential treatment to its own products and services (Khan 2017b, 2018). Here, an instructive case is that of Quidsi, once a rapidly growing e-commerce company that oversaw several subsidiaries, including Diapers.com, selling products in markets such as those for baby care, household essentials, and beauty products. In 2009, Quidsi's founders declined Amazon's offer to purchase the firm. Retaliation was swift and severe. Amazon cut prices for diapers and related products by up to 30 percent. Amazon software bots used to monitor price changes of competitors would trigger cuts every time Diapers.com cut its own prices. In 2010, it also rolled out Amazon Mom, a loyalty program offering two-day shipping and steep discounts on diaper products. Quidsi conducted analyses estimating that Amazon was on track to lose $100 million in diaper products alone over a single three-month period. Under this sort of pressure, Quidsi eventually sold out to Amazon, although Walmart had come in with a higher final bid. It seems that they may have feared further price retaliation had they sold the company to Amazon's rival. After completing the purchase, Amazon then progressively moved to raise prices and wind down its Amazon Mom loyalty program (Khan 2017a).

Another way in which Amazon has been able to leverage its power is through its growing delivery and logistics empire. First, the company has significant bargaining power in the delivery sector because it has become such an important customer. For instance, Amazon alone accounted for $1 billion of UPS' business in 2015. Such a presence gives Amazon extraordinary bargaining power with delivery companies—by some estimates receiving up to a 70 percent discount over regular deliver prices. What this seems to do is lead delivery companies to, in turn, attempt to recoup revenues by squeezing other smaller independent sellers, something which is referred to as the "waterbed effect" (Khan 2017a).

Furthermore, Amazon has consolidated its dominance over the delivery sector through its Fulfillment by Amazon (FBA) service, established in 2006. This allows participating merchants to store products in Amazon's warehouses, while the company packs, ships, and provides customer service on their orders. Ironically, it seems many independent sellers can secure better rates from FBA than they can from delivery companies such as UPS and FedEx, but in the end, their products are likely delivered to final customers using those very same companies (Khan 2017a).

Amazon's entry into fulfillment services has also been buttressed by its growing logistics empire, which includes physical infrastructure such as sorting centers, warehouses, semi-trucks, and truck trailers, even moving into container ships and planes. The company seems to be increasingly competing directly with UPS and FedEx, even as it is a vital customer of these firms. Ultimately, the company can leverage its dominance across online retail through its fulfillment service and growing logistics empire. In the end, sellers who use FBA have a better chance of showing up higher on Amazon searches than competitors who do not. And, yet, Amazon is positioned to use its logistics infrastructure to prioritize the delivery of its own goods over those sellers who use its FBA service (Khan 2017a).

Finally, Amazon is able to take advantage of *information exploitation* through its gatekeeper role as the platform through which so many sellers must reach final consumers. Because Amazon draws so much e-commerce traffic, many small merchants use its Amazon Marketplace service to attract customers. Third-party sellers account for around half of all the items sold on Amazon. Most are likely aware of the bind in which they are placed because they need Amazon to reach a broad customer base, yet Amazon is also a potential competitor for customer sales. Amazon seems to be using Marketplace as a kind of laboratory in which to identify new products and test new sales/marketing strategies. It collects vast amounts of information on the companies that use marketplace to sell their wares. It can then use that data to develop its own similar product lines and then directly compete with those same retailers for customer sales revenue. But it is never a fair fight because Amazon can deftly monitor and analyze the sales patterns of rival products, while it has the power to place its own replicas higher up in its search rankings. Meanwhile, the independent merchants who use Marketplace take on all the initial up-front costs and bear the risks associated with developing new products and bringing them to market (Khan 2017a, 2018).

Antitrust laws, as Khan notes, have been used earlier to prevent the kinds of power that Amazon and other big tech firms have amassed in recent years. However, the scope of antitrust enforcement has been narrowed in recent decades to focus almost exclusively on "consumer welfare," which in practice translates into technical questions over short-term price effects for consumers. These changes date back to the rise of the Chicago School revolution of the 1970s (surprise!), and have allowed these firms to amasses ever increasing market power over recent decades given their focus on "always low prices." However, a conundrum exists regarding the hypothetical potential embodied in a free and open internet that seems to have evolved along with dominant winner-take-all market platforms that provide the critical infrastructure of e-commerce (Khan 2017a, 2017b).

Tax avoidance as a core business strategy

In September 2017, Scott Galloway wrote,

> The most disturbing stat in business? Since 2008 Walmart has paid $64B [billion] in corporate income tax, while Amazon has paid $1.4B. This is

despite the fact that, in the last 24 months, Amazon has added the value of Walmart to its market cap [capitalization, or the value of the company]. The most uncomfortable question in business, in my view, is how do we pay our soldiers, firefighters, and teachers if a firm can ascend to $460B (#5 in the world) without paying meaningful corporate taxes[?]

(Galloway 2017b)

The question is even more profound today, as Amazon's market cap crossed the $1 trillion milestone one year after Galloway's post. Furthermore, the Institution on Taxation and Economic Policy reported that in 2017, Amazon paid zero federal income taxes on its reported $5.6 billion of US profits. It paid an effective federal tax rate of 11.4 percent in the five years before that. It then doubled its profits in 2018, and paid no federal income taxes once again. Finally, Amazon projected that it would receive an additional $789 million one-time tax break as a result of the Trump Tax Bill, which provides a grandfather clause for companies that have postponed tax liabilities from prior years (Gardner 2018, 2019; also see Shephard 2018).

It seems that tax considerations have been baked into the Amazon business model, and Bezos' exceptionally strong aversion to paying taxes (no one likes paying them) fits with his libertarian outlook. One might think of Amazon as a Silicon Valley company. However, in making his move into the mail-order business, Bezos was keen to minimize the company's tax exposure, which meant looking for an attractive city in relatively smaller state, as the company would have to charge taxes on customers who lived in any state where they had a business presence. Apparently, he even considered locating the company on an Indian reservation near San Francisco in order to tap into the region's tech talent without having to worry about paying taxes in California. Allowing customers to avoid paying taxes can provide a pricing advantage of as much as 10 percent (more typically 5–7 percent) over brick-and-mortar competitors, which is very significant given the low profit margins in much of the retail sector (Elkind and Burke 2013).

The legal struggle over taxing e-commerce has its origins in the 1980s when mail-order houses were able to take advantage of selling tax free to customers in states where they did not have a physical store. While customers were technically obligated by law to self-report and pay tax to their home states, almost no one did (well, someone might have).

The states were eager for a test case to force out of state businesses to collect sales tax. The key case in this instance involved office supplier Quill Corp. Because the company's corporate headquarters was located in North Dakota, the state demanded that the company begin collecting taxes on customers who resided in the state. The case led to a landmark 1992 US Supreme Court ruling in the company's favor. The court ruled that forcing distant sellers to collect sales tax in thousands of local jurisdictions would pose undue burden on the sellers and violates the commerce clause of the Constitution. A company would only have to collect taxes from customers if it had a substantial physical presence, or "nexus," in their state. The Quill ruling and struggles over the meaning of nexus would define much of Amazon's tax strategy for the foreseeable future (Elkind and Burke 2013).

When Banes & Noble, the dominant retail bookstore chain in the 1990s, began selling books tax free online, Amazon complained in court that it was exploiting an unfair method of competition known as "entity isolation." Barnes & Noble had established its online business as separate legal entity. Walmart and Target also initially employed this strategy with their online businesses, but all three eventually abandoned this approach and shifted to a "bricks-and-clicks" strategy to take advantage of in-store pickup (something Amazon would eventually do, but we're not there yet). Amazon, for its part, employed this entity isolation strategy with a vengeance as it rapidly expanded beyond books to, well, everything. It would assign ownership of its massive fulfillment centers to separate legal subsidiaries owned by the company (Elkind and Burke 2013).

Online retail has significantly impacted state coffers given its dramatic growth over the past two decades. Overall, sales taxes account for almost 25 percent of general revenue collected by states, and certainly more in that majority of states that levy them (General Sales Taxes 2018). And so, in the early 2000s, the heads of the states' tax departments banded together forming a national group called the Streamlined Sales Tax Project with the aim of simplifying the sales tax system and then convincing Congress to pass a law that would force out of state business to collect. But the process quickly got bogged down in negotiations over endless details. And, once businesses became involved, they soon began jockeying over provisions that might advance their own private interests. For its part, Amazon proved willing to take part in such a process that generated years of inaction and delay, with its public position being that it supported a "federal solution" that would require every company to collect (Elkind and Burke 2013).

At one point, in 2008, Bezos complained that local tax collection was so complicated that it imposed an "undue burden" on his company. However, by that time, Amazon had already launched a service that was collecting sales tax for over 2,000 merchants that used its website, including Macy's and Target (Elkind and Burke 2013).

A few states got wise to the fact that the search for a federal solution seemed to be going nowhere. In fact, it was a *Dallas Morning News* reporter named Maria Halkias who was struck by Amazon's defense against an "Amazon law" passed in New York State, in which the company argued that it did not have warehouse in the state. She contacted the Texas comptroller's office about an Amazon warehouse that was located near the Dallas/Fort Worth airport, which even had a sign out front reading AMAZON.COM. The state comptroller subsequently presented Amazon with a bill for $268 million in back taxes, penalties, and interest, noting in its letter, "We have included a pre-addressed envelope for your payment convenience" (Elkind and Burke 2013). In response, Amazon announced it was shutting down the warehouse and pulling out of

Texas altogether, citing the state's "unfavorable regulatory climate" (Elkind and Burke 2013). Really? In Texas?

In the Texas case, the state comptroller had help in the form of a cavalry of sorts, known as the "Alliance for Main Street," a multistate advocacy group that fought to level the playing field for local businesses that paid their fair share in taxes against Amazon and other online cheats. This group was funded by the likes of brick-and-mortar giants such as Sears, Walmart, and Best Buy, which were getting creamed by Amazon due to the state tax burdens that befell them but not the online giant. So they wrapped themselves in the mantle of "mom and pop" businesses which they had pretty much put out of business in the first place. This, combined with major efforts in California, eventually led to a deal where Amazon would eventually start collecting taxes in exchange for a couple of new warehouses and a write off of the original $268 million it owed Texas.

While it pulled its warehouses out of several states that tried to collect on it, and forged special bargains with others, such as South Carolina, Amazon eventually came to rethink its overall business strategy, and today has embraced the bricks-and-clicks strategy of its rivals while it has ramped up its rapid delivery programs, wherein it needs warehouses close to its customers. And so the company eventually joined its rivals in supporting a federal solution embodied in the Marketplace Fairness Act initiated during the Obama presidency. Now that the company would have to collect sales tax in every state, it wanted to make absolutely sure that all those other e-commerce firms that do not have a physical nexus in all 50 states pay up as well (Elkind and Burke 2013). Amazon only began collecting sales tax in all 50 states in April 2017 (Shephard 2018).

You can't fight city hall, but you can bend it to your will: Amazon announces HQ2

Amazon's announcement in September 2017 that it planned to open a second corporate headquarters outside of Seattle set off a fierce bidding war among American cities desperate to land the tech giant. Dubbed HQ2, the company's wish list included close proximity to a major highway, on-site access to mass transit, an international airport nearby, all within a metropolitan area with at least one million in population. It also wanted data on traffic conditions, information about universities nearby, qualifications of local workers, and the quality of fiber optic internet connections and cell phone service, as the total number of new employees at the site could reach 50,000. It also was looking for a city with a diverse population and ample recreational opportunities (Wingfield and Cohen 2017).

By January 2018, the field was narrowed down from over 200 to 20 finalists (Creswell 2018). Because the competition to land Amazon's new headquarters has been so fierce, cities have not only been touting the best of what they have available to lure the tech giant but have also been offering various tax and other incentives to sweeten the pot. However, it seems as though many of the contestants in this corporate-sponsored beauty contest chose to keep their incentive packages secret from their own residents and even members of their own city councils. Across the country in places ranging from New York to Chicago and Austin to Indianapolis, local residents and elected officials who were sworn to serve them remained in the dark about the incentive packages the mayors of their cities, oftentimes in coordination with local business groups, such as the chamber of commerce, offered to bring Amazon's HQ2 home. And while it is understandable that contestants would not want outsiders to have access to the details of their bids because it could place them at a competitive disadvantage, doing so places those city leaders who do not have access to the bidding process in a precarious dilemma with respect to representing their constituents without knowing what kinds of future liabilities they may be committing to in the process (Creswell 2018).

Yet some packages were revealed during the bidding process—as a result of political pressure or obtained through public records requests—and these offer a window into the, at times, massive financial bets city and state officials, along with their allies in the business community, have made with the future tax bases of their states and cities (it should be noted that the chamber and other related economic development groups tend not to have the same types of reporting and transparency requirements that apply to city governments). For instance, Maryland offered $8.5 billion in tax incentives and infrastructure projects, and the state of New Jersey offered $7 billion in tax credits and other incentives on behalf of Newark's bid (Creswell 2018).

The bidding war got so out of hand that urbanist researcher Richard Florida (Creswell 2018; Smith 2018), who was a member of the board that developed the bid for Toronto, which made the list of 20 finalists, eventually resigned from the project. Florida also circulated a petition calling on Amazon and the 20 finalists to put an end to the bidding war for HQ2. In formulating the petition, he surveyed roughly 100 prominent urbanists from across the political spectrum and found that almost everyone immediately singed up. The lack of transparency, as well as a general sentiment that financial incentives are somewhat marginal to the core infrastructure and other fundamentals that characterize a region's potential to attract new economic development, reflect important reasons why these experts called for a halt to the bidding war (Smith 2018).

However, Amazon is not the only tech company to hold such sway over US cities. Big corporations and especially tech firms have increasingly been able to take advantage of cities across the country that are struggling to support growing needs for affordable housing along with overstressed and undermaintained transportation systems and wider infrastructure. Increasingly, local officials, desperate for investment, are finding themselves bending to the will of tech interests at times over wider civic responsibilities (Manjoo 2018c).

Local institutions, including newspapers and other media, along with small businesses, have undergone decline with respect to a wider digital media environment that prioritizes the national over local issues. In fact, it has been upstart tech firms that first identified and successfully leveraged this new environment to their advantage, with Uber being a leader on this front. The company's founder, Travis Kalanick, made it a conscious business strategy to descend upon countless cities without first gaining permission for its new ride hailing service from local governments. While vociferous resistance quickly emerged in many cities, particularly among taxi services and drivers, the company was armed and ready to deploy its riders and supporters in a public relations war with city leaders, and even was successful in standing down the mayor and city council in New York City in 2015. Others soon followed suit, and thanks to what has become known as "Travis' Law," many of us now find our cities besieged by e-scooters, which may come as a great pleasure and convenience to some while causing agitation and dismay among others. But there was likely no deliberative process between citizens and their elected officials to pave the way (Manjoo 2018c).

Meanwhile, back to the bidding war. In November 2018, Amazon announced that it would be splitting its second headquarters between Crystal City, a Virginia suburb of Washington, D.C., and Long Island City, in Queens, New York. The *Atlantic*, echoing a chorus of critics, asked, "Did the world's smartest company really need 13 months, and applications from 238 cities, to reach the striking conclusion that it should invest in New York and D.C.?" It then offered this sobering statistic: "Every year, American cities and states spend up to $90 billion in tax breaks and cash grants to urge companies to move among states. That's more than the federal government spends on housing, education, or infrastructure" (Thompson 2018). By February 2019, Amazon had canceled its plans for Long Island City after receiving harsh criticism and negative publicity around these very issues from a vocal group of progressive politicians and activists, along with some union leaders (Goodman 2019).

Other people's taxes and how Amazon plans to acquire them: government contracts

A report by the Institute for Local Self-Reliance in 2018 sheds light on a largely unnoticed but growing segment of Amazon's market growth strategy: their efforts to capture public sector spending. You know, that for which they do not seem to pay their fair share of taxes. The report notes how in 2017 Amazon was awarded a contract by "U.S. Communities, an organization that negotiates joint purchasing agreements for its members, many of which are local governments. It's received virtually no media coverage, and yet it opens the way for billions of dollars in public spending to shift to Amazon." This national contract provides "cities, counties, and schools with office and classroom supplies, library books, electronics, and more" (Mitchell and Lavecchia 2018).

According to the Institute's report, the terms of the contract depart from established norms in public procurement and lack adequate safeguards for protecting taxpayer dollars. First, their analysis suggests that the Request for Proposal (RFP) was not written in a way to illicit multiple bids, as has been customary practice, but seems to have been written with one company in mind: Amazon. In fact, the company's bid was the only one that received a high score in the ranking process, with the other four contenders falling hopelessly short of the mark. It seems that Amazon won the contract without having to compete on price and without offering a volume discount, normally the case, for the $5.5 billion in sales revenue the contract is expected to generate over the next 11 years. Instead, the contract follows Amazon's dynamic pricing model (Mitchell and Lavecchia 2018).

In pitching the contract, Amazon assured public officials that they will still be able to make purchases with local businesses, but they will simply need to do so through Amazon's Marketplace platform. In effect, the company will be able to use its leverage with the over 1,500 jurisdictions that have adopted the contract to corral its competitors into using its platform. This includes handing over 15 percent of their revenue to Amazon and having to abide by the company's terms of use on the platform. An examination of emails and redacted documents indicate that final terms and conditions were rewritten by Amazon in what seems like efforts to mold the contract toward the company's standard commercial terms of service. The final contract even sets up the means by which Amazon can potentially challenge future freedom of information requests for documents relating to the contract, something that goes against the principle that citizens should be able to see how the government is spending their money (Mitchell and Lavecchia 2018).

In recent years, Amazon has made securing public sector spending part of its larger growth strategy. For instance, in 2016, the company hired Anne Rung, who was a top federal procurement officer during the Obama administration, to head its government division (Mitchell and Lavecchia 2018). Furthermore, it has made significant inroads into defense contracting, with its Amazon Web Services (AWS) having won a $600 million contact in 2013 to provide cloud service for the CIA (Martineau 2018).

In 2018, Amazon embarked on a quest to earn a much bigger prize. This time it involved a $10 billion winner-take-all contract, spread over ten years, to provide the Defense Department with 21st-century cloud computing capability, helping it incorporate AI into its data analysis and to provide real-time data to solders in the field. Once again, the bidding process seems to have placed Amazon as a clear front runner, as other competitors have balked at the process, and IBM and Oracle have registered protests with the US Government Accountability Office. They are particularly critical of the fact that the project will be awarded to only one contractor. They argue that this approach raises risks that such a system is less reliable than one involving multiple vendors because it increases the risks for total failure. Experts seem to agree (Martineau 2018).

The project, nicknamed JEDI (for Joint Enterprise Defense Initiative), contains numerous restrictions and requirements that, practically speaking, seem to point to a very select few tech giants, with only one viable leading candidate. Among them are requirements that the winner have the "infrastructure to transition approximately 3.4 million Pentagon users and 4 million devices to the cloud, [and] generate at least $2 billion a year from cloud services," something that Google is unable to do, and it has dropped out, although the company's public pronouncement emphasized uncertainty that the work would "align with [its] AI principles." The bid also seems to disqualify traditional defense contractors, as the winner must derive most of its revenue from sources other than defense contracts (Martineau 2018).

Finally, shortly after introducing a new low-cost online service in 2016—supported by AWS—that could recognize faces and other objects in images, Amazon began pitching the technology to local law enforcement around the country. While the US military and intelligence services have used facial recognition technology for years, the move by some local level law enforcement agencies to employ it for more routine forms of policing has raised alarms among privacy advocates. In fact, the ACLU, along with a group of more than two dozen civil rights organizations, sent a letter to Amazon CEO Jeff Bezos, asking that the company stop selling its Rekognition system to local law enforcement, citing its potential for abuse. Over 180 million adults in the US are in facial recognition data bases that can be searched by law enforcement. And with Amazon's market leverage and ability to expand its widespread adoption, such a move could prove a tipping point for its adoption by law enforcement without sufficient time for public debate (Wingfield 2018).

Surveying the wreckage in retail

As noted at the outset of this chapter, a key to Amazon's success has been its access to cheap capital, as Bezos sold investors on a vision of long-term growth over short-term profitability (Galloway 2017a). Furthermore, over recent years, the company has been able to leverage its less well known, non-core, but highly profitable cloud-services business, Amazon Web Services (AWS) and, more recently, its rapidly expanding advertising business (yes!), Amazon Media Group (AMG), to keep prices low for its main online retail business and continue investing in its logistical capacities. Amazon invests in ways that competitors simply cannot afford, because they, as opposed to Amazon, need to generate profits from their retail operations (Del Rey and Molla 2018; Masters 2018). So, the company continues to rack up huge advantages over its retail competitors. Furthermore, as we noted in exploring antitrust concerns about Amazon, the company is not simply developing its logistical capacities to compete directly with its retail rivals, but it is also increasingly providing the infrastructure to both service their needs and turn them into subordinate partners—for instance, through its Fulfillment by Amazon (FBA) service.

Amazon's growing supremacy in logistics, which is supported by advances in AI, robotics, and various forms of automation, is breathtaking in in its scope and ambition. Perhaps Walmart is the only competitor that has the (not very likely) chance of keeping up with them. Scott Galloway (2017a) surmises that Amazon's ambitions go something like, "What can we do that gives us an advantage that's hugely expensive, and that no one else can afford?" (39). For instance, its ambitions to reduce shipping times to two days, and now one day, have been extremely expensive. But that's the point. The company's logistics arsenal now includes drones, Boeing cargo planes, tractor trailers, and trans-Pacific freight services (Galloway 2017a). As Lina Khan (2017a) documents, Amazon's move to vertically integrate its retail business into a delivery and logistics empire has involved a $13.9 billion investment in building warehouses between 2010 and 2017. As of 2016, the company had opened more than 180 warehouses. By 2016, it had leased over 40 jets, and had announced plans to acquire thousands of branded semi-trucks. There is a growing sense that the company is not just partnering but also competing directly with UPS and FedEx (Khan 2017a). Amazon also seems to maintain a low profile regarding its growing number of warehouse facilities, not simply to avoid negative publicity about working conditions, but also to play down the extent to which it has expanded its robot workforce through automation ("Amazon's Robot Workforce" 2016; Galloway 2017a).

Not surprisingly, the rest of retail is struggling. A 2017 report by the World Economic Forum (2017) projects that e-commerce penetration into wider retail will grow from about 10 percent to over 40 percent by 2026, albeit with significant variation depending upon product category. *Fortune* reported that by 2017 Amazon was capturing over 50 percent of online sales growth in the US, with the company accounting for over 40 percent of all online revenue (Gajanan 2017). Galloway (2017a) refers to Amazon as the "Prince of Darkness for retail" (29), as the company's fortunes are inversely correlated with the rest of the sector. It's a zero-sum game. During the time period 2006–16, Amazon's stock price rose a mind-boggling 1,900 percent. Meanwhile, Sears, JCPenney, Best Buy, Macy's, and Target declined 95, 83, 49, 46, and 15 percent respectively. Walmart gained a meager 2 percent (Galloway 2017a).

The stock market research firm Bespoke Investment Group has actually developed a "Death by Amazon Index," which tracks the "performance of the companies most affected by the rise of Amazon.com" (Sommer 2017). The index tracks over 50 companies such as Barnes & Noble, Costco, Best Buy, GameStop, Macy's, Nordstrom, Sears, Target, CVS Caremark, Rite Aid, and Walmart. That list may well continue to shrink over the coming years. Toys "R" Us was perhaps the best known company caught up in a wave of retail bankruptcies during 2017 (Corkery 2017a). With well over 5,000 store closings in that year, covering a wide range of retail categories, the job losses rivaled the devastation that occurred in the depths of the Great Recession of 2008. With roughly one in ten American workers employed in the retail sector, its ongoing transformation may have dramatic social and political consequences (Corkery 2017b, 2018a).

While 2018 witnessed a continuation of the trends in retail decline, with some slowing and hopeful signs of adaptation, the big historic bankruptcy for that year involved Sears. The company, which filed for bankruptcy protection after 132 years in business, was referred to as the Amazon of its day by the editorial board of the *New York Times*. They note how Sears harnessed two of the great distribution/communication networks of its day—the railroads and the

United States Postal Service. In 1900, the famous Sears catalog reached 20 million Americans out of a US population of 76 million and ran as many as 1,500 pages carrying over 100,000 items (Corkery 2018b; Editorial Board 2018).

Sears had been in decline for many years, and perhaps e-commerce provided the nail in the coffin to seal its demise. Meanwhile, many of the survivors are looking for ways to push back against the Amazon threat, which is evolving to compete with brick-and-mortal retail on its own terrain; for instance, through the innovative and experimental AmazonGo convenience shop. In response, several top retailers are in the process of testing robots to stock shelves and cut labor costs, as well as develop new apps that allow shoppers to ring up items on their smartphones, which would further automate the checkout process. And while these types of innovations may raise new privacy concerns in the US, retailers in China are moving ahead with similar experiments even more rapidly. For instance, a company called Bingo Box has started a chain of over 100 unmanned convenience shops, where shoppers simply use their phones to, first, key in a code and enter the stores, then scan the items they wish to purchase, and, finally, are allowed to exit through an automatic door that unlocks once they've made payment. Meanwhile, in the US, Walmart has begun testing out a line of robots that can scan aisles looking for items that are mislabeled or out of stock, and then report back to workers who restock the shelves and apply new labels. The grocery chain Kroger, along with other retailers, has been testing out a mobile scanning service to supplement its existing cashier and automated checkout services (Wingfield, Mozur, and Corkery 2018).

While AmazonGo may still be in the experimental phases of development, Amazon's entrance directly into the retail grocery sector through the acquisition of Whole Foods in 2017 raised significant alarm and speculation among competitors and industry observers. In fact, the merging of these two companies, or, really, the absorption of one by the other, comes not without great symbolic irony, as captured by media writer John Herrman. Back in the mid-1990s, iconic CEO John Mackey described Whole Foods as "a mission-driven business." The company was part of distinctive trend during the 1990s and 2000s that involved an expanding cadre of "community minded" and "compassionate" corporate employers aiming to serve a growing chorus of affluent and conscientious consumers, who viewed their purchases as lifestyle choices in moral-ethical terms. Furthermore, the 1990s was a decade in which manufacturing employment underwent serious decline, while the service sector, in general, and retail, in particular, experienced significant growth. One hopeful story accompanying this shift was that service work could be upgraded to offer career paths that would provide stability, dignity, engagement, and perhaps professional development. Workers were no longer just employees; instead, they became "team members" (Herrman 2017).

In contrast, the Amazon experience is about "clicking a button that initiates a mysterious process carried out by teams of invisible laborers and automated processes and results in a package at your door within two days" (Herrman 2017) This process is orchestrated from a corporate office characterized by a harsh and competitive workplace culture, and involves a multitude of complex and invisible supply chains that swiftly guide products into Amazon warehouses that have also been criticized for the harsh working conditions under which their oftentimes subcontracted workforce toils, before the plain brown box with the smiley face lands on the customer's doorstep. And, for his part, Mackey, the eternal libertarian, may not be all that different from Bezos despite his oft-professed commitment to being pro-worker, as he has remained vehemently anti-union over the years (Herrman 2017).

Anti-union and secretive seem to characterize the way in which Amazon views its warehouse-distribution center operations. This side of the business has experienced dramatic growth over the past decade. The company had roughly 30,000 employees in 2010, but has grown to well over 600,000 today, far outnumbering any of its big tech rivals. And as its warehouses continue to expand and swell with employees (and robots), journalistic exposés from the US and UK continue to dribble out stories of extremely harsh working conditions that include relentless focus on productivity targets, which move ever higher, timed bathroom breaks, intrusive supervisory surveillance, and workers pushed to their physical limits, with some driven to emotional exhaustion, even breakdown (Hamilton and Cain 2019; Lieber 2019; Selby 2017; Zahn and Paget 2019). Of course, the company generally does not acknowledge these reports as valid or reflective of prevailing conditions in its warehouses (McCracken 2019).

In fact, back in October 2018 Amazon announced it was going to raise the minimum wage for its hourly workers to $15. This, coming within weeks after Senator Bernie Sanders' proposed legislation, the "Stop BEZOS Act," which would force large employers to pay the cost of federal assistance received by their employees. While the company claims that the move was not in response to Sanders' proposal, it will certainly help them recruit workers in competitive labor markets. Subsequently, Amazon has also come out in support of raising the federal minimum wage to $15 for all hourly workers, which would roughly double it (McCracken 2019). Just think of the pressure this would place on its brick-and-mortar competitors, such as Walmart, with all those retail employees, as Amazon, having no storefronts, pushes toward ever greater levels of automation in its warehouses.

While unions generally welcomed Amazon's move to raise pay for its hourly employees (McCracken 2019), unionization drives persist at the company's warehouses in the US and UK. For instance, the GMB union recently organized a London meeting with leading investment and pension fund managers having stakes in the company to advocate for better working conditions throughout Amazon's 17 warehouses in the UK, which employ over 25,000 workers (Farrell 2019). Along similar lines, organizing efforts in the US have also focused on working conditions as the primary reason why some employees desire union representation, with the relentless focus on productivity being a central concern (Sainato 2019).

Meanwhile, automation rushes forward on multiple fronts, and if the retail service sector is looking less promising as a source of future job growth, well, major employment growth in manufacturing appears increasingly less likely to make America great again, for the news coming out of China does not bode well for the prospects of putting lots of Americans back to work in factories. As China looks to move up the skills chain in manufacturing, while it is also adapting to a significant decline in the numbers of those entering the workforce having limited education and, therefore, are more likely candidates for factory work but can now garner higher wages, automation is key to that strategy. While just a decade ago auto manufacturing was fairly low-tech and labor intensive, recent assembly plants established in China by major US manufacturers Ford and General Motors are state-of-the-art operations replete with multitudes of robots carrying out much of the assembly work. In the case of Ford, one manufacturing operation is accompanied by an R&D center and test track that rivals others the company utilizes in North America and Europe, with its top executives offering assurances that they will be able to protect its intellectual property in the process (Bradsher 2017).

Back in the US, the steel industry is an instructive case highlighting the role of automation in accounting for the roughly 400,000 jobs it lost between the early 1960s and early 2000s. For instance, the overall number of steel shipments did not decline during this period but were accounted for by a new technological advance known as the minimill. In fact, outside of some truly significant job losses due to globalization and, especially, outsourcing to China in the early 2000s, it appears that automation is the culprit that looms ever larger on the job loss front (Miller 2016).

New forecasts predicting wider job loss across a range of sectors due to AI induced automation seem to grow increasingly commonplace. For instance, *Recode* reported on a recent industry study by research firm PwC estimating that "nearly 40 percent of jobs in the US may be vulnerable to replacement by robots in the next fifteen years" (Glaser 2017). The jobs identified as being most at risk are in transportation, manufacturing, and retail-related industries. Furthermore, it appears the US workforce is more likely to experience greater job losses due to automation than say, the UK, Japan, and Germany, due to the fact that a higher percentage of jobs here involve more routine types of tasks, which are more susceptible to automation. The study examined the types of tasks associated with various jobs in a range of industry sectors and then applied an algorithm to assess the "automatability" of those tasks and characteristics of the workers who perform them (Glaser 2017).

And while there are different views as to how all of this technological change will play out, and to what extent new forms of work, and even employment sectors, will emerge to replace older, obsolete ones, the sociologist in me remains mindful of how social, cultural, and political processes accompany and influence the nature of technological change in ways that make the future indeterminate (Boyd and Holton 2018; Mokyr, Vickers, and Ziebarth 2015). What is clear is that the direction, nature, and implications of future technological change demand robust public debate.

Meanwhile, back in the service sector, the future of e-commerce and brick-and-mortar retail seem to be converging in some respects, which likely means that some categories of traditional retail will remain viable but transformed into the foreseeable future. Amazon's acquisition of Whole Foods for $13.4 billion in 2017 is instructive (Saba 2017). It provides a significant step forward into what may become retail's emerging "multichannel era," where "integration across web, social, and brick and mortal" becomes crucial (Galloway 2017a: 44). Shipping provides Amazon with enormous advantages over competitors, but it also represents its greatest expense. Whole Foods' hundreds of stores have enabled Amazon to establish a physical presence in countless affluent urban centers, where its most valuable customers live. The company can utilize Whole Foods to provide a delivery hub for Amazon Fresh's lagging grocery business, and also to imagine wider experiments in the multichannel universe. For instance, Whole Foods could function as a transit hub for Amazon's broader retail operations facilitating pickup, delivery, and return operations (Galloway 2017a).

As Galloway (2017a) observes, physical retail isn't disappearing, but as the middle class shrinks, so does the physical retail infrastructure that once served it. For instance, while many of us may believe we are witnessing the death of the mall in America, what is really happening is that the valuable mall properties serving high-end consumers are thriving, generally speaking, while those serving middle- and lower-income neighborhoods are a dying breed. Today, "Forty-four percent of total US mall value . . . now resides with the top hundred properties, out of about a thousand malls" (Galloway 2017a: 44).

As the World Economic Forum (2017) report forecasts, over the next decade physical stores will still drive most of the revenue for large multichannel retailers, but the sector will bifurcate into high engagement, interactive, exploratory consumer focused outlets offering typically higher-end product categories (i.e., consumer electronics, appliances, etc.) and low-engagement, typically routinized products and services that will likely employ the most thoroughly automated systems and robotics and de-emphasize human labor (Wingfield 2017).

Major retailers are responding to this new multichannel era, and there is no question that Amazon's move into brick-and-mortar has meant their experiments have a renewed sense of urgency. For instance, Target has taken on a costly new strategy to situate itself in the heart of retail's multichannel future. They have plans to open roughly 30 smaller stores in city centers and near college campuses with a narrower focus on young, urban consumers. Here they intend to facilitate the range of multichannel options increasingly expected by consumers. They can order online and pick up in store, or have items shipped directly to their homes. Meanwhile, the new stores are more carefully curated and staff salaries were raised to bolster morale and help to provide a more satisfying customer experience. The stores also accept customer returns of items purchased online (Corkery 2018a).

In other instances, grocery retailers Walmart and Kroger have been experimenting with Amazon Fresh "click and collect" style services where customers place orders online and then schedule time slots to pick them up in person (Corkery 2018a). Home Depot seems to have found a measure of success in this new era of multichannel, and perhaps garnered the confidence of investors, as already 40 percent of its online sales are picked up at its over 2,000 stores (Saba 2017).

In the end, America (and, increasingly, Europe and the wider world) seems to have made a Faustian bargain with Amazon and Jeff Bezos, which places our consumer selves at the heart of the story while putting off a potential day of reckoning for the wider consumer economy and the workers that populate it for another day. Bezos, for his part, has even made intimations about the need for a universal basic income one day to compensate for the potential employment wreckage coming to retail (Galloway 2017a). He probably knows better than anyone else just what we are in for. Oh! Sorry, but I've got to go. That was the doorbell, and I believe there is a package waiting for me.

Part II

Pushing back the state

Privatization and corporate predation

Now that we have surveyed the dominant role of big tech in contemporary life, it is important to understand the historical context out of which it emerged and to highlight several key institutional transformations that have accompanied societal changes over recent decades. A fundamental distinction, essential to our understanding societal organization at the broadest level, follows the dividing line between state and market. This section explores the historical nature of the relationship between state and market, its recent evolution, and current manifestations of that dynamic that serve to organize institutional life throughout various societal realms. Key expressions of evolving state and market relations are highlighted and illustrated by focusing on dominant trends in our political-economic history over recent decades, including the ideological movement celebrating and leading to greater emphasis on free markets, deregulation, and privatization of growing sectors of society, all the while highlighting the growing presence, power, and influence of the corporate sector in directing public life and institutions.

5   Corporations and the state

Legal–political environment

The state, in relation to the market, and particularly corporate segments thereof, operates in a context of increasing complexity, and the transformation and evolution of its boundaries, capabilities, and functions, reflect the invisible nature of political, economic, and other forms of organized power (Sjoberg 1999). The vastness and scale of today's multinational corporations allows them to operate, in some respects, beyond the scope of the state's regulatory influence, while they clearly depend upon robust state and international institutions in order to enjoy stable legal–political environments for their operations. The corporation, with its limited liabilities (Hansmann and Kraakman 2001), is fundamentally a creature of the state, despite the fact that the state is regularly called upon to cope with externalities that are invariably the product of this legal–political arrangement.

The corporation is not a recent entrant on the American scene, but instead its inception roughly parallels that of the nation. As legal historian Adam Winkler (2018) points out, early settlers during the colonial period derived rights and duties from the charters of British corporations—such as the Virginia Company of London and the Massachusetts Bay Company—that first attempted to gain a foothold in North America. These early charters even influenced the way in which framers thought about the Constitution and the Bill of Rights. Beginning around the turn of the 19th century, the US became a leader in the growth and development of the corporation. For a century or more thereafter, most corporations were small and locally or regionally chartered at the city or state level. Furthermore, community or social interests were commonly included in those charters, which, in turn, were subject to periodic review and renewal. By some accounts, the limited liability corporation permitted investors to pool capital, make long-term investments, and potentially operate on a scale and scope of production and distribution capacity that contributed to the growth of the US economy during the first century of the nation's history and beyond (Gomory and Sylla 2013).

That long history, however, has been accompanied by periods of concern, even alarm, over the power and privileges enjoyed by corporations (Gomory and Sylla 2013). These emerged at the outset, during the 1790s, as well as during the late 1830s and early 1840s, a time of economic crisis. More significantly, the Gilded Age of the late 19th century, with its industrial Robber Barons and their Wall Street financiers, sparked popular populist movements intent on checking the power of corporate interests over American economic and political life. It was during this time that business interests, spearheaded by the Southern Pacific Railroad Company, made significant strides in asserting the rights of personhood for corporations—albeit based on dubious interpretations of the celebrated 14th Amendment, which was intended to secure the rights of newly freed slaves and offer them protection from discrimination (Winkler 2018).

Reactions against growing corporate power culminated in the trust busting activities of President Theodore Roosevelt and the passage of antitrust laws and corporate regulations. While Roosevelt's approach was to allow for large corporations to dominate specific industrial sectors but face significant regulation, later critics, including the renowned lawyer and eventual Supreme Court Justice Louis Brandeis, called for them to be broken up altogether (Yergin and Stanislaw 2002). These alternate views on corporations both found accommodation and synthesis during the New Deal era of reform under President Franklin D. Roosevelt. The Great Depression of the 1930s also witnessed the publication of the landmark work *The Corporation and Private Property*, by Adolf Berle and Gardiner Means (1932), who argued that the 20th-century corporation was affecting a change to American capitalist-democratic society that was as significant as the transition from feudalism to capitalism in Europe centuries earlier.

Given their contemporary relevance and legitimacy today, legal scholars Hansmann and Kraakman (2001) wrote at the turn of the 21st century that the core features of business corporations had become so widely accepted as to mark the end of history for corporate law—notwithstanding the 2010 Supreme Court's *Citizens United* ruling granting unlimited free speech rights to corporations. These features include legal personality, limited liability, transferable shares, centralized management under a board structure, and shared ownership by contributors of capital. Furthermore, since Milton Friedman's (1970) landmark statement regarding the social responsibility of business, a growing consensus about the goals and purposes of the corporation emerged such that even though corporations should be operated to serve the ends of society in general, the best way to achieve those ends is for corporate managers to be accountable, directly speaking, exclusively to shareholders. And corporate law has evolved in such a way as to shield managers and shareholders from direct legal challenge by interests in the wider social order. This is reinforced by a growing movement toward complete autonomy of the economic sphere from other societal systems and institutional domains.

Over recent decades, the power and autonomy of the corporation has been significantly advanced throughout the inter—or supra—national arena where multinational and transnational corporations (MNCs and TNCs) have enormous influence in shaping the rules and standards associated with the global economy. Political scientist and activist Susan George (2015) argues that corporate interests, oftentimes represented by executives from large corporations, their proxies and lobbyists, have been quietly active in directing official policy on the international stage, influencing and shaping institutions of international cooperation, law making, and standard setting, and of course, treaty formation. They have been forging a type of illegitimate authority across the global economic and political landscape. The ultimate ends of these corporate interests seem to be deregulation, freedom and autonomy from government oversight, weakening of labor standards and worker's rights, and finally the privatization of government services.

Corporate predation on the state

On the domestic front, the state's role has been further compromised by what James Galbraith (2008) refers to as growing predation on the part of powerful elites throughout the corporate sector. While corporations came to enjoy widespread institutional legitimacy, protection from the state, and also a good measure of autonomy from its regulatory commitments and public purpose, they have remained unsatisfied. In fact, Galbraith (2008) argues that they have used their enormous power and influence to resist much of the regulatory functions and prerogatives of the state, while in recent years they have successfully assumed (wrestled away) significant lines of state activity and the profits that come from captive markets supported by taxpayer dollars.

Corporate interests are not necessarily directed toward reducing the state. Instead, some simply wish to control it and to channel its lines of activity toward their own profit making endeavors. These corporate interests regularly sound the rallying cry that efficient markets (versus wasteful governments) should be called upon to deliver public services to sovereign consumer citizens, while diverting our attention from the pools of captive taxpayer generated profits over which they seek to gain control. Galbraith (2008) points to how they have achieved their aims in arenas such as health care, education, and retirement planning, although not complete control. We will examine some of these sectors, among others, in greater detail shortly. He argues that cumulative effect of these efforts has been the gradual creation of a kind of corporate republic, although the extent to which the project has come to complete fruition invariably depends upon ongoing political dynamics.

Effective predators invariably cultivate healthy prey, an idea that Galbraith ascribes back to the early 20th-century economist and social critic Thorstein Veblen. We the public, as citizens, must rely upon such healthy prey in the realm of government (and oftentimes in nonprofit and other sectors) to work on our behalf and serve the public good. However, our public servants are oftentimes beholden to, or under persistent threat from, said predators in their efforts to serve the common good. Perhaps nowhere has this been more evident than in the realm of health care.

6 From the not-so-Affordable Care Act to the opioid crisis

An overdose of corporate influence

When it comes to health care, the US has been an outlier among advanced industrialized nations foremost due to the absence of universal health coverage. In spite of the fact that overall health care costs in the US are extremely high, where roughly 17.1 percent of GDP is spent compared to, say, 8.8 percent for England, overall health outcomes are far worse (Mossialos, Wenzl, Osborn, and Sarnak 2016). This industry represents an enormous and roughly $3 trillion market in the US. As late as 2011, the health care industry employed over 21 million people, or roughly 15.7 percent of the US workforce (Moses III, Matheson, Dorsey, George, Sadoff, and Yoshimura 2013). This highly profitable sector, with its complicated public and private dimensions, was the focus of the legislative efforts that eventually became known as Obamacare, or the Affordable Care Act (ACA).

It was perhaps the most well-known open secret that the health care industry would define the boundaries of debate about how this legislation would be written, and would bankroll key politicians and those who provided council in the process (Angell 2015). The power of the health care industry players and their lobbyists to shape the contours of the politically possible cannot be overstated. Depending upon the way in which the data are constructed, the overall health care industry sector's lobbying efforts stood at just over $500 million in 2015 (these numbers peaked at roughly $550 million in 2009, the year in which the ACA was negotiated by Congress). Health care leads all sectors in lobbying contributions, with the finance, insurance, and real estate sectors coming in second with roughly $481 million in lobbying efforts in 2015, followed by energy and natural resources at roughly $322 million (Open Secrets 2015). All that lobbying serves to protect an important investment, as Dr. Elisabeth Rosenthal, physician turned longtime health reporter and correspondent, has incisively documented, sector by sector, how our health care system has been transformed over the past few decades from a "caring endeavor to the most profitable industry in the United States." Increasingly, the "logic of commerce," as opposed to "scientific guidelines," drive treatment, all talk and flashy PR touting "innovation" and "patient-centered, evidence-based care" aside (Rosenthal 2017: 4–5).

In the lead up to the 2008 presidential election, Democrats were besieged by constituents whose lives had been devastated by health issues related to either having no or insufficient coverage to handle medical expenses, and who faced a system that was geared toward denying health insurance to those most in need and extracting maximum and exorbitant payments from those who received care without sufficient coverage. Journalist Steven Brill (2013) has introduced unfamiliar Americans to the now-infamous hospital chargemaster—a complete listing of all of a hospital's billable items at highly inflated prices, which then are negotiated downward by insurance providers, but in many cases, not for individual patents without health insurance coverage. In fact, during the 2000s, unforeseen medical expenses, frequently incurred by families who had some medical insurance coverage, became the number one precipitating event leading up to bankruptcy among the middle class (Warren and Tyagi 2003).

In spite of their general hesitation to take up major health care reform since then First Lady Hillary Clinton spearheaded a failed campaign to do so during the 1990s, Democratic candidates, including an initially reluctant Barack Obama, were compelled to take up the cause once again. However, as the prospects of reform moved into serious consideration, under the championing of newly elected President Obama in 2008, the art of the possible had moved significantly rightward, with former Republican Governor of Massachusetts Mitt Romney's plan (Romneycare) providing the template. There would be no serious consideration of a not-for-profit, single-payer system. Democratic Senator Max Bacus, chair of the Senate Finance Committee, which drafted the health care reform legislation, became the single largest recipient of health care industry political donations (McGreal 2009).

As a precursor to the negotiations and eventual passage of the ACA, we need look no further than the Medicare Prescription Drug, Improvement, and Modernization Act, signed into law in 2003 by then Republican President George W. Bush. As conveyed by Steven Brill (2015) in his widely heralded account of the complex negotiations and political maneuvering involved in the evolution and passage of the ACA, a major figure involved in the passage of this legislation was the then Democrat-turned-Republican congressional representative from Louisiana, Billy Tauzin. He was instrumental in passage of this drug bill, which, in the end, provided increased funding for Medicare to pay for prescription drugs, but did not permit the government agency to negotiate with drug companies over prices. Shortly after the bill's passage, Tauzin took a job as the pharmaceutical industry's (PhRMA) leading lobbyist, earning roughly $2 million a year. Nice work if you can get it! Tauzin was to feature largely in legislative negotiations over the ACA in his industry's efforts to get out ahead of any such legislation. He was apparently noted for citing the adage, "If you're not at the table you're going to be on the menu" (Brill 2015). This time PhRMA held out for a continuation of the law forbidding Medicare from negotiating lower drug prices, along with a stipulation forbidding Americans from importing drugs from other countries (i.e., Canada) that do in fact negotiate substantially lower prices with pharmaceutical companies, and they also sought to kill any significant research on comparative effectiveness of drugs, as negative results could damage sales of profitable products. In the end, while

Tauzin and his allies tried to persuade Congress that the passage of the bill could be very costly to their industry, leading PhRMA CEOs were touting the highly profitable prospects of the ACA to Wall Street analysts (See Brill 2015).

Throughout the process in which the ACA legislation was being negotiated, the various sectors of the health care industry were armed and ready to unleash a barrage of attack ads for or against the legislation, depending upon how it all played out. The health insurance industry felt especially vulnerable about the prospects of reform, as depending upon how final legislation was crafted, they stood to lose or gain significantly. And when a chorus of conservative attacks began to rise in synchrony, proclaiming the proposed reform a "government takeover," the president's new strategy was to vilify the insurance industry. He then began to speak of insurance reform rather than health care reform: a move that implicitly represented the threat that the reform law might narrow in scope to focus on a prohibition against health insurers excluding preexisting conditions without the universal mandate that all citizens be covered under the law, which could have proven disastrous for the industry. Hence, the largest for-profit health insurers put together a war chest of $86 million for the lobbying organization America's Health Insurance Plans (AHIP), which deftly passed it along to a US Chamber of Commerce political action committee that would generate attack ads—free of AHIP fingerprints—if the legislation turned in an undesirable direction (see Brill 2015).

The insurance industry's attack ads in waiting are reflective of a wider problem faced by those seeking health care reform, which is that vested, monied interests made the prospect of incorporating cost controls into the legislation well nigh impossible. This sticking point emerged early on in the process during an otherwise celebratory congressional health care summit held in June 2008, months before Obama was first elected president. While such aims as the need for broader coverage and more preventative care generated broad consensus and support, key policy experts pointed out just how formidable cost controls would be to achieve. For instance, Peter Orszag, an economist who was head of the Congressional Budget Office (CBO) at the time, summarized the issue as one where such policies that target cost control invariably affect some health care–related entity's income and profits directly, which would lead them to hire lobbyists to fight against the legislation, whereas the benefits that might accrue to the general public from such initiatives tend to be experienced in a vaguer, more diffused manner. Nothing like the threat to a corporation's profitability serves to focus the minds and resources of those to whom its profitability and stock price have been entrusted.

This synopsis seems to have played out in the case of Romneycare in Massachusetts, upon which the ACA was ultimately modeled. Like Romneycare, the ACA was based on a three-legged stool approach to coverage that included no exclusions for preexisting conditions, a universal mandate for individuals to purchase health insurance, and subsidies to assist those who could not afford the cost of insurance. Jon Kingsdale, who was in charge of Romneycare, conceded that they had made the compromise to go for universal coverage and deemphasize cost containment in order to garner broad political support while limiting organized opposition. But, once such legislation gets passed, cost containment becomes a daunting challenge (see Brill 2015).

Ultimately, there no was no serious effort to control costs incorporated into the final legislation for the ACA. As the Massachusetts experience highlights, virtually universal coverage has been achieved for the citizens of the state; however, costs have steadily increased, and coverage has become increasingly expensive. The state ranks highest in health care spending per capita, and such spending has come to consume over half the state's budget, placing severe strains on other necessary state functions such as education, public safety, human services, transportation, and so on (Angell 2015).

And yet there have been accusations that the whole affair represented a government takeover, as opposed to a corporate one. The idea of labeling health care reform as a government takeover was seized upon by Republican pollster Frank Luntz, and it became a rallying cry for the anti-Obamacare movement that railed against the legislation (Brill 2015). However, the legislation was really all about the government providing subsidies for many citizens to purchase health insurance on the private market in a system that is, yes, very complex and bureaucratic, much more so than Medicare—the government administered single-payer system that covers Americans age 65 and over.

For Americans under age 65 there would be no public option to choose government-sponsored insurance that might compete with private insurance providers. Instead, the private insurance companies won a captive market delivered to them by the government, much of which is to be subsidized by taxpayer dollars even as costs continue to increase for the foreseeable future. And other major players in related health care sectors, such as the pharmaceutical companies, medical equipment suppliers, and of course the purportedly nonprofit (and for-profit) hospitals, stood to enjoy even more robust and increasingly profitable markets than the "villainous" insurance companies. For instance, while roughly three-quarters of America's hospitals are run as nonprofits, a seemingly benign situation, the profits of these nonprofits generally rival or exceed those of the for-profits. In fact, one of the ways in which the larger hospital conglomerates generate substantial profits and are able to pay their top executives multimillion-dollar salaries is by relentless and aggressive expansion, acquiring large networks of physicians, driving out competition, and then bullying insurance companies into paying exorbitant prices due to their dependence on such consolidated dominant market players (see Brill 2015; also see Longman and Hewitt 2014).

While the ACA has succeeded in providing desperately needed health care coverage for many Americans who had been left stranded without it, it has also left individual citizens (more perplexed than utility maximizing) to cope with this complicated amalgam of public and private dimensions of our health care system. Limited political choices led to a Romneycare-style plan, which involves enormous and cumbersome complexity compared, say, to the way in which Medicare provides universal coverage for citizens over 65. This involves creating user accounts and verifying identity, earnings and income tax verification to determine eligibility for subsidies, and then the need to browse available insurance plans to comparison shop. Surveys of those running assister programs during the initial enrollment period for the ACA reported that many individuals sought assistance due to such reasons as their own limited understanding of the law, the complexity of sorting through the plan choices, and lack of understanding of basic health insurance terms (such as "deductible"; Pollitz, Tolbert, and Ma 2014). Economist and *New York Times* columnist Paul Krugman (2013) characterizes the administrative morass enveloping the ACA as "kludge": an organizational structure that addresses problems in a clumsy and inefficient manner (see Teles 2013).

The problems leading to initial failure of the launch of the ACA website are legendary. And while the government deserves significant blame for the confusing organizational structures through which planning, coordination, and implementation transpired, their private sector counterparts who fumbled incompetently, and of course requested generous cost overruns to be sent to their coffers along the way—firms such as the lead contractor for the build, CGI Federal, an American branch of its parent company, CGI Group, a multibillion-dollar operation based in Montreal, Canada (see Browning 2013)—walk about ideologically and politically unscathed. CGI Federal grew through mergers to achieve its long-term vision of becoming embedded in the US government agencies it serves, in spite of its less than stellar history in fulfilling federal contracts. Such is the irony of a world in which those who try to make government work for its citizens end up making unpalatable compromises to ward off their ideological foes that in the end lead to even more bureaucracy and "kludge" than had they been free to proceed without all the resistance.

Speaking of resistance: The election of Donald Trump in 2016, after two terms of a Democratic Obama White House, meant that the Tea Party-inspired, anti-Obamacare, anti-government crusaders finally had an ally who could lead them into battle and slay the dragon of government-run health care once and for all! Well, be careful what you wish for. At the time of the ACA's passage in 2010, more Americans disliked it than supported it. And that dislike grew stronger over ensuing years. However, a January 2017 poll indicated for the first time that more Americans thought favorably of the law than those who thought it was a bad idea (Sanger-Katz and Park 2017). Trump's election, followed by the Republican effort to repeal Obamacare, served to shift the tide of public opinion in favor of the law. In fact, health care became a major campaign theme among Democrats during the 2018 mid-term election season—something that they had studiously avoided during the previous four election cycles in which Republicans ran on "Repeal and Replace" (Sanger-Katz 2018). With over one quarter of working adults having a pre-existing health condition, the issue of health care unseated the economy and jobs as the most prominent motivating issue for voters in 2018 (Santhanam 2018).

The opioid crisis fueled by addiction to corporate profit making

Not only has the US struggled mightily in comparison to other industrialized nations over how to forge an effective and affordable path to ensuring that all citizens enjoy adequate health care coverage, but has been doing so in the context of a massive public health crisis associated with the opioid epidemic. Not surprisingly, we are sure to find the usual suspects have been involved in exacerbating the crisis. And it is daunting. According to the Centers for Disease Control and Prevention (CDC), From 1999 to 2017 over 700,000 people died from drug overdose deaths, of which close to 400,000 involved some type of opioid (CDC 2018). These also seem to have contributed, along with suicides (which are often related), to recent and surprising declines in overall life expectancy in the US (Dwyer 2018).

Opioid consumption in the US far outstrips that of any other country. Several key factors account for the nation's opioid epidemic, which emerged back in the late 1990s. At that time major pharmaceutical companies began aggressively marketing their drugs as safe and effective for treating pain, with scant evidence to support those claims. Furthermore, doctors came under pressure from patient advocacy groups and government to treat pain more aggressively with medications. This was combined with the fact that many physicians at the time were being absorbed into large integrated health systems and were confronted with increasing pressures to process higher caseloads of patients efficiently. They also experienced pressure from patients to treat their pain more aggressively. Once increasing numbers of patients became addicted to opioids, many then transitioned to more potent drugs such as heroin and illicit forms of fentanyl, and a burgeoning illicit drug trade moved in to fill those needs and peddle further use. Research indicates that most heroin users in treatment began their journey into addiction with painkillers (Lopez 2017).

By 2019, Purdue Pharma, controlled by the powerful Sackler family and maker of the popular opioid OxyContin, settled with the state of Oklahoma in a lawsuit targeting at least a dozen opioid manufactures for contributing to thousands of overdoses and deaths, a precedent setting case followed closely in several other impacted states. The state claimed that pervasive marketing tactics employed by these companies significantly contributed to a devastating public health crisis surrounding overdose and addiction (Santhanam 2019). Yet more than a decade prior to the Oklahoma settlement, a confidential 2006 US Justice Department report revealed details of how executives at Purdue Pharma had actually become aware of "significant" abuse of OxyContin shortly after its introduction in 1996 (Meier 2018). While George W. Bush administration Justice Department officials could have brought felony charges against top executives at Purdue, the government chose to settle its case instead (Meier 2018).

When the Food and Drug Administration (FDA) approved OxyContin in 1995, they also basically gave the company permission to claim the drug was less appealing to drug abusers due to its longer acting formula. Internal documents revealed how the company seized on this point as a "principal selling tool." This would be central to its marketing campaign and the company trained sales representatives to promote the drug as less addictive in their appeals to doctors. Yet, within months of the drug's approval, reports to the contrary began trickling in, including studies published in medical journals, internet searches of chat rooms revealing its illicit use, and articles from local newspapers from a variety of states and locales in the US and Canada highlighting illegal sale and abuse of the drug on the black market. Over time, documented email reports from the field by sales representatives also indicated how they felt the company was facing a growing credibility issue. All the while, top executives seemed to either ignore or greatly downplay the significance of these reports. As part of the 2007 settlement, top executives pleaded guilty to only misdemeanor charges and were hit with over $600 million in fines—small potatoes for a multibillion-dollar company (Meier 2018). In fact, recent lawsuits by the attorneys general of Massachusetts and New York reveal that at the time of the 2007 guilty plea, the Sacklers had begun setting up a new company for the purposes of selling generic opioids should OxyContin become engulfed in the crisis. That company, Rhodes, eventually garnered a greater share of the US prescription opioid market than Purdue, surpassing it in 2016. Internal company charts and diagrams also revealed that as the crisis continued to worsen, Sackler family executives seized upon the lucrative possibility of selling treatments for opioid addiction (Hakim, Rabin, and Rashbaum 2019). What a marketing plan. Step 1: hook patients on a product specially marketed for being less addictive, and then, once they are addicted, Step 2: market new products to treat the addiction, which shouldn't have occurred in the first place.

These more recent revelations also highlight and document in much greater depth how back at the time of OxyContin's approval in the late 1990s, Purdue helped forge an industry marketing campaign funding "front groups" to influence the public and inform physicians about an "'epidemic' of untreated pain," the safety and benefits of opioids, and the minimal risk of addiction they posed. Of course, these groups operated under the mantle of being "unbiased" sources of information promoting the latest medical research (Hakim, Rabin, and Rashbaum 2019).

While Purdue Pharma may have become the poster child for the opioid crisis, another band of culprits may just loom larger in exacerbating it. These are the drug and medical supply distributors, among which are some of the very largest American companies you have probably never heard of (Fortune 2019). They have been hard at work hobbling the government's capacity to curtail the crisis, with their crowning achievement being successfully disarming the Drug Enforcement Agency (DEA) in its battles to thwart the unlawful distribution of prescription narcotics for illicit use, as revealed in a 2017 *Washington Post* and *60 Minutes* investigation (Higham and Bernstein 2017).

With hundreds of millions of pills being dealt and/or consumed illegally, the DEA's little-known Office of Diversion Control moved into action by first shutting down internet pharmacies. They then observed that pain management clinics were springing up all over South Florida and supplying voracious cus-tomers from surrounding states. At this point the agency decided upon a strat-egy whereby they would target the massive wholesale drug distributors that kept the pharmacies well stocked with opioids. They were able to do so based on an interpretation of the Controlled Substances Act of 1970, requiring drug companies to report large or suspicious orders. In very serious cases, the DEA could issue "immediate suspension order(s)," and freeze a drug company's oper-ations (Higham and Bernstein 2017).

The DEA eventually brought cases against 13 drug distributors. Generally, these enforcement actions were triggered by extremely large and/or suspicious orders. Among those cases, were actions taken against two massive distributors during 2007–8. One was McKesson, the fifth largest corporation in the US, which settled and paid a $13.2 million fine. The other was Cardinal Health, which ended up paying a $34 million fine (Higham and Bernstein 2017). Very small change for companies that today enjoy sales revenues in the hundreds of billions of US dollars.

In order to pursue its cases against the big distributors, careful legal argu-ments had to be crafted by Diversion Control's legal office. And if the phar-maceutical industry and its large distributors were going to defend themselves against overzealous government regulators and enforcement agents, why not simply hire away former DEA and Justice Department officials to help them support the cause? How about the lawyer who crafted the legal arguments for the Office of Diversion Control's enforcement actions in the first place? Well, in 2011, he joined a Washington D.C. law firm and began representing the drug companies and became the industry point person on key legislation that eventually pared back the DEA's enforcement authority. Since 2000, the indus-try and the law firms representing it have hired away well over 50 former DEA and Justice Department officials (Higham and Bernstein 2017).

Furthermore, they targeted Congress with intensive lobbying efforts and campaign contributions of roughly $100 million between 2014 and 2016 to support the Ensuring Patient Access and Effective Drug Enforcement Act and related legislation. In so doing, they enlisted Congressman Tom Marino of Pennsylvania, a former county and federal prosecutor, whose district was heav-ily impacted by the opioid crisis, to spearhead the legislation. His overtures to then Attorney General Eric Holder encouraging meetings with industry executives were reported to set off alarm bells within the DEA. The industry and their congressional allies claimed that the intent of their legislation was to clarify ambiguities in the drug law, while they wished to establish a more collaborative relationship with agency officials on enforcement (Higham and Bernstein 2017).

Over time, it seems a growing sense of defeat loomed over the DEA. An exodus of agents cashing out along with effective industry lobbying on the part of former colleagues made the agency more cautious about its enforce-ment actions. Furthermore, a change of leadership at the top signaled a more industry friendly approach. When Attorney General Eric Holder, who had earlier publicly opposed the industry friendly legislation, eventually stepped down, his replacement, Loretta Lynch, came on board more willing to work cooperatively and collaboratively with the industry. After settling into the new post, her office informed Congressman Marino that the DEA had met with 300 industry representatives. By the time that the bill finally passed, it seems the DEA and Justice Department had become resigned, however reluctantly, to its passage, which it did on unanimous consent, without objection or debate, and President Obama eventually signed off as well (Higham and Bernstein 2017).

The legislation favored industry corrective action plans over what some would call effective enforcement. In fact, immediate suspension orders on the part of the DEA plummeted from 65 in 2011 to only eight in 2016. One vocal critic of the legislation and the industry's efforts to thwart effective enforcement, John J. Mulrooney II, who had been chief administrative law judge at the DEA, wrote about what he views as the DEA's greatly diminished capacity to suspend operations of a drug company running afoul of federal law. This, all coming to pass while the opioid crisis rages on (Higham and Bernstein 2017; Mulrooney 2017). The legislation provides a potential incentive for companies to simply ignore their responsibilities to monitor suspicious sales of opioids, knowing that should they be caught they can simply provide action plans for how they will move toward compliance, avoiding sanction in the process (Mulrooney 2017).

By the way, Tom Marino, the Pennsylvania congressman who spearheaded the drug industry friendly legislation, was later nominated by President Trump in 2017 to be the White House's "Federal Drug Czar," which would have landed him an important role in helping to direct the government's response to the opioid crisis. Unfortunately, the *Washington Post—60 Minutes* report led to his withdrawal from consideration (Oprysko and Montellaro 2019).

In the end, lawsuits on the part of state attorneys general in New York, Vermont, and Washington State, supported by the DEA, may turn the tide in the battle with the drug industry over stopping the flow of opioid sales for illicit use and dealing. In this instance, the target is Rochester Drug Co-Operative (RDC), another massive drug distributor. While these companies by law are supposed to act as gatekeepers, given they potentially have extensive information about the nature of the sales made by the pharmacies they supply, RDC is accused of simply ignoring the red flags that should have alerted them to suspicious activity, and really at times finding ways to enable that activity in order to keep the sales revenue gushing in. It seems that some in Congress have also come around to seeing the problem, but it is very late in the game. As one example among many, congressional hearings have revealed how a drugstore operating in rural West Virginia was at one point receiving a combined 9,000 pills a day from industry giants Cardinal Health and McKesson (Hakim, Rashbaum and Rabin 2019; PBS Newshour 2019).

Now that we have had some introduction to the power of corporate interests interfering with the implementation of health care reform and exacerbating the opioid crisis, next we turn to the broader ideological fog that has enveloped the Predator State over recent decades.

7 Ideological backdrop

Attacks on state bureaucracy

Aiding and abetting the evolution of the Predator State has been a fervent ideological movement of resistance to the role of government involvement in any activity outside of security functions of the state (military and police), the main target of which has been the New Deal consensus of the post–World War II era. This movement came into its own during the 1980s, with the Thatcher administration in Britain, along with the Reagan administration in the US (Meek 2014). It persisted through the Clinton era of the 1990s, was reinvigorated during the presidency of George W. Bush through the early to mid-2000s, and largely survived the aftermath of the financial crisis of 2007–8 and the response by the Obama administration well into the second decade of the 21st century and the Trump era.

The rise and fall of Keynes, Galbraith, and the welfare state

Earlier in the 20th century, in the aftermath of the Great Depression of the 1930s and two devastating world wars, people in Western industrialized nations looked to institutions of government for security against the harsher features of the capitalist system.

The Great Depression of the 1930s and mass unemployment highlighted a colossal failure of that system. Devastation at the end of World War II left tens of millions in Western Europe without enough food, countless displaced persons, a depleted and mostly destroyed industrial base, and a beleaguered private sector with little capacity to mobilize capital and investment toward rapid recovery. After so much sacrifice and bloodshed in the war effort, a return to economic depression was unthinkable, and so government answered the call to rebuild society, move toward full employment, and stabilize the overall economy. Hence, the mixed economy was born, which while still capitalist in nature with a robust private sector, the role of government in ensuring that capitalism would provide growth, stability, and security was firmly in place. Furthermore, by the aftermath of World War II, the command and control economy of the Soviet Union, with its system of state planning, had come to enjoy widespread admiration and respect throughout Western Europe (Yergin and Stanislaw 2002).

For instance, in Britain, the government took on a greatly expanded role during World War II, and did so with great effect and efficiency of industrial production, all achieved through careful planning. The labor coalition that won power after the war implemented a vision of government that was far more responsible for the welfare of its citizens. In following the famous Beveridge Report—which was to achieve global influence—they fought to conquer the five giants of want, disease, ignorance, squalor, and idleness (unemployment). They established the National Health Service, institutionalized a system of pensions, provided support for education and housing, and made a commitment to ensuring full employment. By 1945, the British welfare state was born. Furthermore, the British nationalized enterprises in key sectors of the economy. These state-owned corporations were run not by direct government involvement, but through government-appointed boards of directors (Yergin and Stanislaw 2002).

In the American context, the onset of the Great Depression raised concerns about the excesses of capitalism, market failures, greed, and financial manipulation, all of which came crashing down in October 1929. Linked to this were abiding concerns about the rise of corporate trusts, or large concentrations of economic power, that often involved merged entities controlling large swaths of a single industry, with railroads and banks being some of the early culprits, as these threatened to crush the world of small-scale, independent enterprise (Yergin and Stanislaw 2002). As a result, the New Deal policies under President Franklin Roosevelt during the 1930s would lead the country into a new era of expanded government involvement in the economy. This involved initial attempts at direct involvement in the economy on the part of the government in collaboration with business and labor, as epitomized by the National Recovery Administration (NRA). However, the thrust of these efforts that put the government in direct control of select economic sectors were eventually scaled back into regulatory efforts, or a set of rules and a process of rule making to ensure that powerful business interests would be limited in their potential abuses of power, and instead would operate more fairly and equitably. Thus was born the modern regulatory state in the US context (Yergin and Stanislaw 2002).

By the latter half of the Great Depression the US government had significantly adopted what has come to be known as a Keynesian approach to managing capitalism, which allowed it to address economic problems, broadly speaking, but do so in a manner that avoided overly intrusive actions into the economy by focusing on the larger macroeconomic picture and utilizing fiscal policies of government spending. Nevertheless, James Galbraith (2008) points out that the legacy of the New Deal and its successors created a set of institutions that are neither wholly public (government) nor private (business) in nature, but that are actually a hybrid of the two, remain partially hidden or difficult to discern, and that support through government largesse the smooth functioning of several important sectors of economy and society including the military, agriculture, health care, and higher education, to name a few. To this should be added what historian Jason Scott Smith (2006) argues was an essential, if misunderstood, legacy of New Deal public works programs, emblemized by the Public Works Administration (PWA) and the Works Progress Administration (WPA), that reflected not simply massive jobs programs but, more fundamentally, state-sponsored economic development, which generated a lasting and positive legacy on the American economy.

The revolutionary ideas set forth by 20th-century British economist John Maynard Keynes—whose work represents the foundation of Keynesianism—were received in a world that was undergoing a Great Depression with seemingly no end in sight. Furthermore, the legacy of classical economic thought available to economists and policy makers offered no solutions to the economic problems of the times, particularly that of the desperately high levels of unemployment in industrialized nations, except to wait out the storm of economic devastation and allow for the supposedly "natural order" upon which the economy rested to apply its cleansing effects all in its own due course. Keynes' (1936) masterpiece, *The General Theory of Employment, Interest and Money*, critiqued the received wisdom that markets, left to their own devices in balancing out supply and demand, would deliver full employment. Instead, Keynes argued that economic life was chronically unstable, and that periodically private, market-based investment in the economy was insufficient to deliver robust economic activity and generate full employment; therefore, public investment, financed by government spending on public works and so on would fill the void by creating jobs and stimulating demand for goods and services that would lead the economy back to full employment. This seemingly simple, yet revolutionary, idea took hold across Western industrialized nations during the post–World War II era and government interventions into the larger economy were seen as essential for the success and stability of capitalism. Keynes' solution was one that still allowed for a fairly decentralized market economy, thereby helping to save capitalism from the perils of socialism and *itself* (Yergin and Stanislaw 2002).

But the post-war era was not simply about rebuilding capitalist economies and buttressing the welfare state. Instead, it unfolded under the long shadow of the Cold War and the political and military tensions between the US (along with its Western allies) and the Soviet Union. And while, as political theorist S.M. Amadae (2003) argues, the Cold War was waged externally as an economic competition and military standoff, it also led to an internal ideological and political battle against the forces of Marxism, communism, and other varieties of authoritarian rule. Rational choice liberalism was a political philosophy that emerged from the despairing critiques made by such 20th-century economists as Joseph Schumpeter (1942) and Friedrich Hayek (1944), who feared that any form of government-initiated collective action was by its very nature despotic. Their critiques of collectivism fundamentally challenged aspirations for an expanded public sphere where citizen welfare could be advanced through collective action.

A narrowly self-interested, rationally calculating, independent actor became the focal point of democratic theorizing and the object of enlightenment aspirations for democracy and human freedom as envisioned by rational choice liberalism. In the process, notions of "the public interest" and the "general welfare" had come to be met with extreme skepticism, while citizen sovereignty came to be replaced by consumer sovereignty. In such a schema, market sovereignty does not simply complement democratic politics; it supplants it (Amadae 2003)!

Ironically, during the time in which the seeds of rational choice liberalism had merely grown into tender shoots, our own American Keynes of sorts, Canadian-born economist and statesman John Kenneth Galbraith, was busy advising US presidential administrations and influencing the public imagination about the nature of the post-war economy—through his numerous popularized best-selling works on American capitalism—in ways that contravened such basic assumptions associated with rational choice liberalism, such as citizen-consumer sovereignty, individual freedom, and consumer choice. Galbraith's most powerful ideas were ones that challenged such notions and those of classical economic thought. For instance, in *The Affluent Society*, Galbraith (1958) challenged the classical economic notion that the private market rationally allocates resources based on the preferences of sovereign consumers. Here, he noted the *social imbalance* between a saturated market for privately sold goods and services while the provision of public goods (clean air, parks, schools, etc.) remained insufficient. To this he added that corporations' marketing and advertising efforts were actively and successfully manipulating consumer preferences.

In *The New Industrial State*, Galbraith (1967) continued to challenge basic foundations of classical economic thought and its idealized sovereign consumer. For him, the great corporations of the day had come to dominate much of the economic landscape. These massive entities, and their *technostructure* of top managers, scientists, engineers, and other professionals, were involved in a new type of planning system focused on mastering technology and the complex bureaucratic-organizational systems in which they were embedded. In fact, in a later book, published at the end of his career, *The Economics of Innocent Fraud*, Galbraith (2004) chides corporate elites (the CEOs) about their unwillingness to acknowledge the fact that they (somewhat like government officials) manage large bureaucracies. Galbraith, much like Keynes, was a supporter of capitalism, but not one based upon a nostalgic fantasy of a simpler bygone era, but of one based upon a reality that reflects institutions, vested interests, and organized power.

Keynesianism had become so apparently triumphant during the heart of the post-war era that, in 1965, *Time* magazine placed Keynes on their cover (the first time it had done so for a nonliving person), attributing America's growing affluence to its embrace of the late economist's political-economic philosophy (Parker 2005). Yet William Domhoff (2013), in *The Myth of Liberal Ascendency*, reminds us that Roosevelt's New Deal policy initiatives that gained support from labor unions and liberal sympathizers enjoyed an important but short lived window of opportunity in American history to advance progressive political change. In fact, by 1938, Republicans had gained a significant number of seats in Congress and joined forces with Southern Democrats to create a durable coalition to resist progressive legislation on unions, civil rights, taxes, and business regulation. Furthermore, as mobilization for the war ensued, corporate executives (often referred to as dollar-a-year men, as many returned their salaries and benefits to the government during their temporary years of sacrifice) were brought in to manage the War Department, and worked with conservative allies in Congress to dismantle New Deal programs and institutions. Roosevelt's liberal staffers, the New Dealers, became alarmed at how the potential for corporate interests to capture the state and its regulatory apparatus was being realized, much to their chagrin and growing marginalization (Parker 2005).

Even with its hold on political power somewhat subtly yet firmly in its grasp, the business community did come to accept aspects of a Keynesian approach to public policy, and governing more generally, during the post-war era. Amid the war, a new organization, the Committee for Economic Development (CED), having 50,000 business executive members, encouraged corporations to accept a broadly Keynesian approach to the relationship between government and the wider economy. The CED became a powerful moderating counterweight to the more staunchly conservative National Association of Manufacturers, while also significantly tempering the influential US Chamber of Commerce's anti-Keynesian stance over subsequent decades. And so, by the 1950s, a business or military Keynesianism emerged wherein government efforts to manage the economy were fundamentally driven by military-strategic goals, and the corporate sector was left to manipulate private consumption—through advanced marketing and advertising techniques—in the private sector. Throughout the 1950s corporate leaders begrudgingly accepted Keynesian management of the business cycle, as corporations enjoyed substantial profits which were increasingly concentrated among the largest firms, with those in defense-related industries enjoying the highest profit margins. On the political scene, Cold War conservatives routinely trotted out the "communist" label to denigrate liberal candidates and social programs, while readily questioning the loyalty and patriotism of those who stood in the way of militarized government spending (Parker 2005).

By the 1970s, the post-war economy was running into strong headwinds emerging from multiple sources such as the growing burden of deficit spending associated with the war in Vietnam, the spike in oil prices in 1973 (and again in 1979) tied to the oil producing nations of OPEC, the move by the Nixon administration to lift the dollar from the gold standard and subsequent devaluation of the US dollar, growing foreign competition faced by American corporations accompanied by declining profits, all of which were in some respects linked to a new phenomenon coined stagflation, where higher levels of unemployment coincided with increasing inflation. Over the course of the 1970s, Galbraith and the Keynesians ceded power and influence to monetarist economist Milton Friedman and the conservatives.

Friedman's monetarist approach came to dominate economic and policy circles, and served to delegitimize Keynesian fiscal approaches (government borrowing and spending to stimulate the economy) in favor of an emphasis on the Federal Reserve's efforts to control interest rates and the money supply (Parker 2005). By 1979, the Federal Reserve initiated its first major rise interest rates, which peaked in 1981 at near 20 percent. Inflation was swiftly and brutally defeated, claiming among its casualties manufacturing industries in the upper Midwest US (Galbraith 2008). These monetarist ideas were championed by libertarian conservatives during the 1970s, as Friedman wedded them to an almost messianic campaign against liberal government spending and interventions into the economy. Such ideas were embraced by a resurgent conservative business community during the 1970s that was chafing under declining profits and perceived excesses of government regulation and union influence in political affairs (Parker 2005).

Conservatives were able to build upon an emerging political alliance with disaffected white, middle-income, and especially factory workers, many of whom rebelled against political gains of the civil rights and other activist social movements of the 1960s and which continued into the 1970s. This resurgent and rightward oriented power shift in the business community was reflected in the growing centrality of the Business Roundtable (in contrast to the CED), which by the latter half of the 1970s was becoming a central player in corporate policy planning networks (Domhoff 2013). The US Chamber of Commerce was also spurred into taking more aggressive political action and lobbying efforts, drawing inspiration from the now-infamous Powell Memorandum. Written by Lewis F. Powell, who had been a board member of Philip Morris on the eve of his appointment to the Supreme Court by President Richard Nixon, the confidential memorandum advocated for greater political activism on the part of the business community to counter the influential consumer advocate Ralph Nader and his advocacy group, Public Citizen. Conservative think tanks also emerged with swelling budgets used to promote free enterprise and resist government regulation of business. The National Chamber Litigation Center was founded in 1977 and became an enormously influential business advocacy organization, having racked up an impressive record of winning Supreme Court cases over the intervening decades (Winkler 2018).

Conservative President Ronald Reagan, who was first elected 1980 after having been governor of California for eight years, was actually viewed as a political outsider, even by his own Republican Party. He emerged during an era in which a crisis of confidence loomed over the institutions of the post-war economic system and the Keynesian revolution that had reigned over Western industrialized economies for many decades. For his part, Reagan unashamedly professed ideas that ran counter to New Deal America, loudly proclaiming that government was the problem, not the solution, to what ailed the American economy. Instead, the solution lay in the magic of the market and free enterprise, which could best be unleashed by rolling back government involvement in the economy and in people's lives, especially their pocketbooks at tax time. Even as Reagan's favored supply side economic policies, intended to dramatically reduce taxes (especially on the wealthy), created the fiscal disaster of government deficits unheralded in US history, he still oversaw a major transformation in the way Americans (and much of the world) came to view the proper scope of government's role in the economy with respect to regulation, taxation, spending, and even welfare state programs (Hoopes 2011; Yergin and Stanislaw 2002).

Reagan had a strong ally across the Atlantic in British Prime Minister Margaret Thatcher, who came to power in 1979—a time in which virtually all of the infrastructure and much of the economy in Britain was in state hands. Thatcher was arguably more ideologically fervent in her political-philosophical views and more aggressive in her actions than was Reagan. This shopkeeper's daughter was deeply influenced by the Austrian economist Friedrich Hayek and his wartime classic *The Road to Serfdom*, which asserted that (any) centralized economic planning links socialism to communism, and ultimately Nazi-style fascism. Thatcher got right to work breaking up unions and privatizing large swaths of once state-owned British industry, doing so with a missionary's zeal. She believed that privatization would bring with it market virtues of competition and efficiency, thereby making British industry more competitive at home and abroad. It would also (in theory) turn Britain into a nation of small shareholders in their nation's industries (which failed to materialize). The most significant outcome, argues author James Meek (2014), of Thatcher's privatization initiatives that were followed through upon by subsequent liberal administrations is that they have turned Britain into a private (as in privatized) island. They have not only privatized historically public services, such as water and public utilities (with foreign corporations and their government subsidizers getting in on the act), but more significantly have privatized the de facto authority to tax British citizens, or at least those who depend upon water, electricity, public transportation, and other essentials.

The transformation in the terms of political discourse and debate surrounding the role of government in the private economy has been profound in the US as well, for it was Democratic President Bill Clinton who declared in his 1996 State of the Union address that "the era of big government is over" (Yergin and Stanislaw 2002: 341). Clinton, who represented those who came to be known as New Democrats, embarked on a campaign to reduce the federal deficit as the best way to spur economic growth. He did so with enthusiastic support from his Wall Street advisers, particularly Robert Rubin, head of the President's National Economic Council, not to mention Alan Greenspan, chairman of the Federal Reserve Board, appointed by Ronald Reagan. More recently, two-term Democratic President Barack Obama campaigned for office by enthusiastically celebrating the market for its ability to allocate resources, maximize production, and promote (ensure) human freedom more generally. Obama has been referred to as a Chicago (as in University of Chicago) liberal with a social conscience (Leonhardt 2008).

Weakening the countervailing power of the state

While a new era of skepticism about government's role in the economy as provider of, or regulator-referee over, the provision of goods and services may have been born out of a disillusionment that shook several decades of faith that government would ensure capitalism's smooth functioning and generally serve the public interest, it also weakened the capacity of government to act as countervailing power and ensure the fairness of markets and act as a guardian of consumer and citizen interests. Moreover, it has also given way to the rise of corporate (super) predators who feast on the public largesse by providing a range of services either once assumed to be the purview of government, or in taking advantage of limited government oversight and regulation of their activities. Some have come to thrive on, or seize, sets of perverse incentives to transform their activities into merely self-serving profit making, while distorting the larger public purposes to which they have been entrusted.

The regulatory regime that had been in place during the post-war era was well captured by John Kenneth Galbraith (1952) in his *American Capitalism*, where he explained that the great expansion of state activity, mainly in the form of regulation and other legislation, was associated with the rise of a countervailing power to curtail the abuses of economic power that accompany the rise of big corporations; and hence, free market competition was no longer an adequate and autonomous mechanism for regulating economic activity (Yergin and Stanislaw 2002). During the immediate post-war decades union growth had benefited from New Deal labor reforms and facilitated bargaining for higher wages and benefits for many workers. Federal regulations and antitrust laws, mainly put in place from the late 19th century through the New Deal 1930s, remained on the books and were generally enforced (Gomory and Sylla 2013; also see Reich 2015, especially ch 18).

By the mid-1970s, a movement toward deregulation and subsequent embrace of privatization began to undo America's trust in the government to manage and oversee the economy and utilize the tools of judicial antitrust enforcement. A new crop of economists came to question both the need for, and the efficacy of, government regulation of the economy. They argued that regulation was oftentimes cumbersome, costly, rigid, distorted the market, and stifled innovation. Many praised competition as the cure for markets that were said to be natural monopolies. Furthermore, they raised fears about regulatory capture, wherein regulators oftentimes become beholden to those very corporate interests that regulation was intended to restrain (Yergin and Stanislaw 2002).

A note on antitrust and the rise of big tech

The Reagan 1980s marked a watershed moment in the government's approach to antitrust, which today resonates structurally with the rise of big tech. The shift was spearheaded, once again, by Chicago School market fundamentalist thinking, this time led by Robert Bork. Since the 1960s, he and others had been chipping away intellectually at the economic structuralist approach to antitrust law and enforcement. This longstanding viewpoint was inspired by Louis Brandeis, who, in a classic 1914 essay, "A Curse of Bigness," argued that large-scale enterprise needed to be curtailed in order to preserve industrial liberty, asserting that economic, social, and political goals should inform antitrust (Crane 2018).

By the late 1970s, the Chicago revolution, laid out in Bork's (1978) classic manifesto *The Antitrust Paradox*, had transformed the Supreme Court's thinking on the matter, even citing Bork in 1979, as it argued (astoundingly) that the late 19th-century Sherman Act was intended as a "consumer welfare prescription" (quoted in Crane 2018: 7; also see Khan 2017a). This consumer welfare approach dramatically narrowed the scope of antitrust enforcement to questions of short-term price effects on consumers. Other historical concerns such as "negative impact on worker wages . . . squeezing of suppliers, fragility in the supply chain, reduction in innovation, and constraints on personal liberty and democracy—sit in the background, behind the consumer-based frame" (Dayen 2017b). The Reagan administration's 1982 merger guidelines enshrined this approach into policy at the Antitrust Division of the Justice Department (Khan 2017a).

The Reagan revolution, inspired by the Chicago School economic thought, also served to decouple the critiques of bigness commonly leveled at both business and government, wherein the latter became the sole target, while the former emerged in politics, law, and culture largely unscathed. As legal scholar Daniel Crane (2018) argues, this shift has come to reveal some intriguing political fissures around antitrust where the Reagan era consensus is now under increasing attacks from both the left wing of the Democratic and the right wing of the Republican parties.

So, here we see the Reagan era roots of big tech. As we have already introduced a range of questions regarding monopoly and big tech, one argument that enabled these companies to remain in the good graces of government regulators and the public at large has been their success at being perceived as good for consumers. For instance, contrast big tech with big telco (cable companies), which consumers love to hate, and note until recently how the government has supported net neutrality rules that treated broadband internet service providers as common carriers required to treat internet traffic equally (Bogost 2017a). Ironically, even in a world of net neutrality, we still have big tech toll booths and gatekeepers managing access to most of the content that is delivered through broadband, but they have been able to shift the costs and abusive treatment onto competitors/clients, leaving consumers with the (illusion) of a free and open internet (Bogost 2017b).

Today, even the *Wall Street Journal* has acknowledged how big tech firms dominate their respective industries the way Standard Oil and AT&T dominated their markets earlier in the last century (Ip 2018). These companies, which controlled more than 80 percent of their respective markets in their day, are not so different from big tech in terms of the extent of their dominance.

However, big tech has benefited from the Reagan revolution. In fact, recall how Lina Khan (2017b) likened the dominance of Amazon to the 19th-century monopolistic railroads, especially in how they use (and potentially abuse) their gatekeeper roles. The railroad analogy holds petty well for all of big tech. And, as we are coming to see, increasingly the US government, as well as individual states, are now reconsidering the applicability of a narrow consumer welfare standard, and pursuing antitrust investigations (Dayen 2017b; Lohr 2019a; Lohr, Isaac, and Popper 2019).

Over the late 1970s, 1980s and beyond, the government came to withdraw or relax many regulatory restrictions over economic activity, thereby deregulating numerous industries in the process. Industries such as airlines, railroads, telephone companies, finance, public utilities, and electricity, were wholly or partially deregulated over this time period (Yergin and Stanislaw 2002). Lo and behold, by the mid-2000s, economic journalist Barry Lynn was among the first to sound the alarm about a new rise of monopoly dominance over economic markets. In one key work, *Cornered*, highlighting the problem, he seems to have assembled an exhausting array of consolidated industries including appliances, athletic shoes, internet search engines (obvious today), semiconductors, LCD glass displays, bottles and bottle caps, electronic components, credit cards, professional services, sunglasses (production and retail outlets), online booking, cable/internet, commercial banking, and publishing (see Lynn 2010 fn 23: 258; also see Dayen 2015; Grullon, Larkin and Michaely 2019). Recall that Facebook has acquired over 90 companies since 2007. Meanwhile, Google has acquired over 270 companies in roughly the past 20 years (Wu and Thompson 2019).

This larger trend of industry consolidation seems to be related in certain respects to a decline in the number of public corporations over the past 40 years. These are generally defined as companies whose ownership is spread over numerous investors who own shares traded over some type of stock exchange. It has been argued that one possible cause underlying this trend is that it has become easier for small firms to be acquired by larger ones rather than to grow organically (Kahle and Stulz 2017). This trend coexists with another, having very different implications, whereby it is easier, in principle, for a new business to contract out for many of the elements or functions that used to require significant capital investment and made it necessary for firms to go public in order to grow significantly (Davis 2016). The growth of venture capital funding has also played a role in this shift.

The urge to privatize

Given the ascendant ideology fusing markets and human freedom—recall, fervently championed by Margaret Thatcher in the UK—it follows that privatization of government services would be the next logical step. While privatization can simply involve selling government assets, it also encompasses the notion of bringing market forces of competition to the provision of services either directly provided or overseen by government. In recent decades, government contracting and procurement activities have shifted toward greater inclination to outsource to corporations and business, generally speaking, entities that are assumed to have superior experience and capabilities to deliver best value at the lowest cost. Therefore, today, at all levels of government, particularly at state and local levels, outsourcing and privatization have become increasingly the norm.

Unfortunately, as James Galbraith (2008) argues in *The Predator State*, our government has increasingly come to resemble as a corporate republic of sorts, whereby the norms, customs, and practices of the corporation have seeped into the functioning of the executive branch. Corporate CEOs generally are less patient and accustomed to dealing with a range of interests, values, issues, and stakeholders when making decisions; instead, they tend to home in on narrowly defined cost-benefit scenarios. Given this corporate mentality and how it caters to business interests, critical criminologists have urged us to consider how the state needs to be scrutinized more closely not simply for explicit acts of commission, but also a range of explicit–implicit acts of commission and omission, when it comes to crimes, harm, and wrongdoing (Kauzlarich, Mullins, and Matthews 2003).

Within weeks after entering office in January 2017, President Trump, making good on his campaign promise to break the grip of bureaucracy and "drain the swamp," had assembled teams to aggressively scale back government regulation. The mission was carried out primarily outside of public view in many instances by political appointees with industry ties and potential conflicts of interest. Journalistic investigations, interviews, and public record requests revealed that some appointees were brought in to review regulations their previous employers had endeavored to weaken or eliminate. Some appointees were actually lawyers who had represented corporations against the government and its regulatory agencies; others were staff members of political dark money groups, while still some others had come from industry-financed organizations opposed to environmental rules. As reported by joint investigators at ProPublica and the *New York Times*, industry influence was apparent at the Education Department, the Interior Department, and the Environmental Protection Agency (Ivory and Faturechi 2017).

While the US welfare state has always been administered with a significant role for the private sector to play in the provision of government services, privatization has been carried forward on dramatically new levels in recent decades. Moreover, the movement toward privatization has, significantly, been accompanied by an ever greater role for corporate sector elites to actively intervene in the shaping of policy debates regarding the nature of the services to be provided and deemed best to serve the public, now increasingly understood to mean the customer or the consumer.

8 Privatization of the military and the rise of corporate warriors

As noted earlier, the US government embraced a business or military Keynesian approach to managing the economy during the post-war era. This led to the rise of what President Dwight D. Eisenhower warned the country about in his 1961 farewell address to the American people: the military-industrial complex, which represented an amalgamation of corporate interests with those of the military and security establishments. It is the invisible hand, not of Adam Smith's virtuous market, but of corporate interests that increasingly guides, directs, and feeds off of the limitless taxpayer resources made available to the government security apparatus (Bartlett and Steele 2007). The growing embrace of privatization over recent decades has only fueled the extent of military-security-related privatization, culminating in the US involvement in Iraq being heralded as the first contractors' war. It accompanied the amazing transformation, and makeover of, an industry once tarnished with a dark and nefarious reputation (Hagedorn 2014).

Backdrop: the Cold War era

Former *Wall Street Journal* staff writer Ann Hagedorn (2014) recounts the history of this industry to which America outsourced so much of its security and other related operations during the wars in Iraq and Afghanistan. Plain and simple, old fashioned mercenaries, the dogs of war, have emerged, rebranded, as central beneficiaries in the privatization movement in recent history. She points to the highly secretive Special Forces Club (SFC) as one of the most important centers of gravity in the evolution of the industry. Inauspiciously located on a small winding street in central London, the SFC has been a gathering place primarily for British and American special agents who carried out clandestine work during World War II as well as in more recent theatres of conflict. Prominent among its members are those veterans of the British Special Air Service (SAS), who carried out covert operations behind enemy lines during World War II and inspired the American equivalent Office of Strategic Services (OSS), a forerunner to the CIA, whose seal hangs prominently in the SFC.

Former members of SAS, which has been renowned for its counterterrorism and counterrevolutionary expertise, laid the groundwork, and cultivated the marketplace, for mercenary activities in the early Cold War era. These unconventional soldiers were employed by multinational corporations and directed at arm's length by British and American intelligence agencies. They were involved in toppling regimes, reinstating exiled leaders, and at times eliminating rebel groups that threatened secure access to valuable natural resources including diamonds, gold, and oil, with the bulk of operations focused on the contested regions of Latin America and Africa during the Cold War. The dramatic growth of asymmetrical, or unconventional, wars and conflicts at the outset of the 21st century only reinforced the demand for such services.

The movement toward military privatization also included an ironic twist of fate through the development of LOGCAP, the US Army's Logistics Civil Augmentation Program, and the Army's experiment in utilizing private firms for logistic services to bypass the Abrams Doctrine, otherwise known as the Total Force Policy. This policy, enacted in 1973, was intended to make it more difficult for politicians to take the country to war because it required that both active and reserve military personnel be treated as one integrated force, and thereby would mean the disruption of a much broader swath of American lives should the nation go to war, thus ensuring fuller political engagement and awareness on the part of the public in time of war (Hagedorn 2014).

With LOGCAP setting the stage for further privatization of military support services, in 1992 then President George H.W. Bush's Secretary of Defense, Dick Cheney, commissioned Halliburton's Brown and Root to study the benefits of privatizing a range of military support services. Cheney, who would eventually become Halliburton's CEO, received a positive report from Brown and Root affirming many of the potential advantages of privatization. In turn, the government awarded the company a five year LOGCAP contract to run support operations for the US military in Haiti, Somalia, the Balkans, and Kuwait (Hagedorn 2014).

LOGCAP contracts expanded dramatically under Democratic President Bill Clinton during the post–Cold War 1990s, where civil war broke out in the former Yugoslavia, creating a humanitarian crisis as thousands of Bosnian Muslims were being slaughtered by Serbian military forces. As Clinton denounced the "ethnic cleansing" and exhorted US and international action to stop it, he found limited public support at home and resistance by military leaders to carrying out airstrikes against Serbian forces, as fears of being drawn into another Vietnam in a land that held limited US strategic interest loomed over the debate. The solution to overcoming this impasse was for the US military to enlist PMSCs that would provide weapons and training to bolster the Croatian army, which was eventually able to force peace negotiations with the Serbs (Singer 2003).

The use of PMSCs by the president under LOGCAP enabled the US to maintain a presence in the Balkans for years beyond the initial conflict and to avoid having to call up thousands of reservists, as these companies provided logistics support and other military services to help maintain the peace with their overseas presence barely noticed by the American public. This success prompted then Vice President Al Gore to highlight LOGCAP as a model of good governance: a tribute to the Reagan legacy of privatization indeed (Hagedorn 2014; also see Singer 2003).

The turning point: Iraq war

The most dramatic acceleration in the transformation of the US military's use of, and dependence upon, PMSCs occurred shortly after the 2003 invasion of Iraq. In the lead up to the war one major debate that emerged revolved around the need for US troops to occupy Iraq in order to maintain the peace post-invasion. This led to some very public and embarrassing disagreements between those in the military who claimed that the occupation would require several hundred thousand US troops and those strong supporters of the war in the Bush administration who claimed that number to be well under 100,000 troops. Shortly after the seemingly successful invasion and overthrow of Saddam Hussein's Baathist regime, the head of the Coalition Provisional Authority (CPA), charged with overseeing the peace and supporting efforts to rebuild the nation, issued orders intended to De-Baathify Iraqi society (Gordon 2008). These unilateral orders meant an extremely broad swath of former members of the Baath Party would be banned from employment in government services, while also dissolving Saddam's security and intelligence forces, including the armed forces. This left hundreds of thousands of Iraqis unemployed, many of whom had extensive military training, all ripe for turning to the growing insurgent movement in Iraq (Chandrasekaran 2006). At this juncture, the prospect of the administration admitting its serious miscalculations regarding the securing of post-invasion Iraq was apparently a political impossibility. Instead, the solution was to turn increasingly to PMSCs and privatize the struggle to win the peace in Iraq, making it truly the first contractors' war (Hagedorn 2014).

And so, a wide range of functions came to be outsourced during the war in Iraq, including such activities as logistics support, operational support and training, intelligence gathering, reconstruction work, escorting convoys, and armed security (Scahill 2007). Eventually, the number of private contractors would exceed conventional military personnel, with billions of dollars in profits to be made during the war. Halliburton's subsidiary KBR would earn a cool $40 billion in Iraq. Even the head of the CPA, Paul Bremer, was a private civilian contractor, charged with overseeing the military occupation of Iraq and the presence of over 60 military and security companies, along with almost 20,000 employees from a myriad of nations around the world (Hagedorn 2014).

The challenges of overseeing and coordinating so many private military companies in Iraq was highlighted by one particular tragic incident in Fallujah, when in March 2004 four American civilians, working for the then unknown company Blackwater, were killed by a group of Iraqis who burned and then hung the bodies from a bridge over the Euphrates River (Gettleman 2004). It brought worldwide media attention to the stark reality of the widespread use of private military contractors in Iraq. This tragic event was a catalyst for the US government to provide a coordination hub for all of the security contractors working in Iraq, as it turned out that employees working for a different private military company had sent warning that the victims not travel on the particular road along which they ultimately passed through Fallujah that day, but the warning never made it through to the men. And so, the Pentagon and CPA devised Project Matrix, which would be awarded to a private firm that would ultimately be charged with creating and managing a coordination center for over 50 PMSCs in Iraq. The project winner would take on this herculean task while the CPA would officially be dismantled and shut down, leaving behind a large complex of PMSCs to oversee the reconstruction of Iraq, an audacious exercise in privatized nation building (Hagedorn 2014).

Aegis Defense Services Ltd., the company that eventually won the Project Matrix contract, turned out to be emblematic of the transformations characterizing the evolution of the PMSC industry over recent decades, as well as the ways in which elites can create, manage, manipulate, and transform corporations and other forms of enterprise to serve their evolving goals and interests. Originally conceived as a maritime security company, Aegis was founded in late 2002 by several investors, among whom was its CEO, Tim Spicer. His resume included graduating from an elite British training academy for army officers, working as an assistant to the UK's director of special forces, managing public relations for the British army in Bosnia, and commanding a battalion in Northern Ireland. He had also started (and failed) several private security companies prior to the Aegis venture, among which were Sandline International, which represented a bridge between Aegis and one of the most significant offspring of the SAS, a company named Executive Outcomes (EO; Hagedorn 2014; also see Campbell 2002).

EO was founded in 1989 by a former South African apartheid era military officer, who had held a leadership position in the country's Civil Cooperation Bureau, known for its work in efforts to destroy the anti-apartheid movement (Isenberg 1997). Some years later, a collaboration with a former SAS commander led to the establishment of an EO office in the UK. The company eventually operated in more than ten African nations, at times providing security services to governments or companies confronting rebel groups over control of mines or oil rigs, and so on. EO carried out such controversial activities as facilitating the shipment of illegal weapons into South Africa, working with the Angolan government to defeat (and allegedly slaughter) insurgents who had seized oil installations, and had bartered military services in exchange for natural resources. Its operations were shut down in South Africa in 1989 in response to Nelson Mandela's anti-mercenary law. Among the many holdings of the London conglomerate, of which EO was a part, was Sandline International, which boasted Tim Spicer as its CEO (Campbell 2002; Hagedorn 2014).

Spicer was seen as a pivotal figure in the industry, as Sandline represented a rebranded version of EO, one that was properly managed and more conventionally and publicly marketed its military services. The old term mercenary was out, and in was the new one of private military company (Campbell 2002). This was all part of a larger PR campaign to be promoted by a new industry group called the International Peace Operations Association. Of course, Sandline had its own history of scandal—which included shipping 30 tons of arms to Sierra Leone in violation of a UN arms embargo—but it represented an important transition in the industry leading to Aegis. Over several years, Aegis and other large firms had become embedded in American military-security efforts, with new subsidiaries, flashy websites, and sophisticated marketing and PR operations. Furthermore, as Aegis established a formal presence in the US and expanded its holdings, it populated its board of directors with highly prestigious members, such as a former chief national security advisor to President Reagan, and the grandson of Winston Churchill, who had been a longstanding conservative member of parliament in the UK. It also appointed Kristi Clemens—who was an appointee of President Bush in the Department of Homeland Security and had also at one time directed public relations for CPA head Paul Bremer in Iraq—CEO of the company's American branch, Aegis Defense Services LLC (Hagedorn 2014).

As word of Spicer's mercenary past spread, formal objections to the Aegis contract were raised. Numerous US senators sent a formal request to the secretary of defense urging that the Pentagon's inspector general conduct a thorough investigation into the award process. A leading expert on military privatization, Pete Singer, raised questions of whether the US government officials who awarded the contract were aware of Spicer's past (Sennott 2004). But more significantly, the most important objection to the contract was that the military was going to outsource a fundamental challenge in the use of PMSCs, and that was coordinating and overseeing the work of said contractors by issuing the largest private contract in Iraq, and on a cost-plus basis, no less. This meant that the more contractors spent, the more they would be compensated by the US government (Singer 2004).

Perhaps the event that most forcefully crystallized public attention on the issue of privatization of military and security services in Iraq was one that involved now-infamous Blackwater USA in the tragic 2007 Nisour Square massacre. Blackwater contractors, in the process of responding to an incident near the square on the outskirts of Baghdad, opened fire on a busy street, killing 17 Iraqi civilians and wounding many others. Reaction to this event included international meetings being called at such institutions (and agencies) as the United Nations, Amnesty International, and the International Red Cross. The US Congress held a bipartisan meeting of the House Committee on Oversight and Government Reform, with the focus being on the activities of Blackwater as a case study of sorts, and how they were reflective of the wider industry (Private Security Contracting 2007). The goal was to explore the need for oversight and to strengthen the legal framework in which it functioned. However, it became readily apparent that a political divide had emerged between liberals, several of whom ideally wanted to discontinue or set strict guidelines upon the use of PMSCs, and conservatives, who supported them as an invaluable asset for ensuring the nation's military objectives and security. This political divide, in all practicality, meant that no substantial action would be taken to monitor, control, and limit the role and influence of these private security companies for the foreseeable future.

The new reality

This inability of government to substantially set limits on the growth and role of PMSCs represents an important aspect of the context in which companies such as Blackwater, which came to be emblematic (the "hood ornament") of the industry, have evolved, and even thrived, beyond the theaters of Iraq and Afghanistan (Risen and Rosenberg 2015). In fact, in a manner somewhat analogous to how Silicon Valley's growth in the early post-war era was nurtured by government contracts, support, and collaboration, so has Blackwater, along with the private security industry, evolved into a multinational company operating on a global stage. For instance, Blackwater's infamous CEO, Erik Prince, has moved on to direct new efforts throughout Africa. His new firm, Frontier Services Group, has provided logistics support for natural resources explorations throughout the continent, receiving backing from a large state-owned Chinese investment company. It is no secret that China is eager to secure rich natural resources available in Africa, and they are fortunate to have the vast background and experiences of a former Navy Seal whose company, Blackwater, enjoyed US government military security contracts worth billions of dollars (Hagedorn 2014; Risen and Rosenberg 2015). Prince would later tempt President Trump with a proposal to privatize the war in Afghanistan (Lee, Kube, and Lederman 2018).

Back at home, through its extensive experience gained in Iraq and Afghanistan, along with its impressive operational capacity, Blackwater has made itself indispensable to the US government. While clearly a favorite of the Bush administration, Jeremy Scahill (2010) writes about how Blackwater found a new "sugar daddy" in the subsequent Democratic Obama administration. Its substantial investment in Democratic lobbyists aided a successful pivot over to the new administration. By 2012, the Obama administration's goals were to cut or downsize military expenditures, while more quietly shifting to a broader focus on security. In practice, this would mean an increased reliance on PMSCs, along with drones, Special Forces, and so on (Hagedorn 2014). And, yet, how has the company continued to receive lucrative government contracts amid a trail of investigations for serious crimes and other violations (murder, manslaughter, conspiracies, false statements) by Congress and other government agencies? By employing tactics that are commonly used throughout the mercenary-turned-private-security industry, most of which revolve around some sort of shell game. Blackwater has been put up for sale and/or undergone several name changes to keep winning government contracts, evolving into Xe Services LLC and then Academi (whose CEO had actually been that of Xe). Or, for instance, it opened military and law enforcement training centers in

North Carolina and then in the greater Chicago area, each of which took on a different name (Hagedorn 2014).

One longtime non-partisan watchdog characterizes the industry as functioning as a fifth branch of the military or a fourth branch of government (Hagedorn 2014). This triumph of PMSCs raises serious human rights issues on the global scene. Gideon Sjoberg (2005), a major concern of whose work addresses corporations and human rights, raises several related issues involving the use of a wider corporate control industry by governments, one of which involves avoiding public accountability, in that governments are able to carry out questionable activities at arm's length, outsourcing the dirty work to PMSCs. These corporate entities operate under a veil of secrecy, as corporations are known to carefully manage how and to what extent they reveal the details of their activities to public scrutiny. As we have seen, corporations oftentimes have the resources to shape public policy and purchase their clout through lobbying and careful cultivation of key members of boards of directors, advisors, and so on, so as to advance their narrow interests. Those narrow interests represent an axiom of classical economics, which is the maximization of profit. And, as Sjoberg emphasizes, these PMSCs emblemize a (perverse) variant of economist Joseph Schumpeter's notion of creative destruction as a source of capitalist growth and development. More destruction, and more mayhem, means more profits to be made!

International institutions have emerged to try and regulate the activities of PMSCs, albeit with limited success. First was the Montreux Document of 2008, an initiative led by the Swiss government and the Red Cross, that codified lists of best practices for PMSCs, and to which numerous countries have signed on. Next was the International Code of Conduct for Private Security Service Providers (ICoC), which outlines rules that ought to govern use of force and also vetting procedures for subcontractors. Hundreds of security companies have signed the code and it has received widespread support by states and nongovernmental organizations. However, it lacks a robust enforcement mechanism. Another approach advocates utilizing legislation modeled on the Foreign Corrupt Practices Act (FCPA) to regulate US-based PMSCs operating in the service of foreign governments, and to use its extraterritoriality provision to hold them accountable (Shah 2014).

The industry itself has also tried to establish its reputation and legitimacy through its own original International Peace Operations Association, which has been rebranded as the International Stability Operations Association (ISOA). The association retains its own high-powered Washington D.C. lobbying firm, holds annual meetings for the purposes of networking and marketing, and boasts a glossy magazine titled *JIPO*. It also has unveiled its own code of conduct about which industry critics are at best ambivalent (Hagedorn 2014). With spending on contracts and grants in Afghanistan and Iraq in support of operations reaching over $200 billion by 2011, it is estimated that at least $31 and up to $60 billion had been lost to fraud, waste, and abuse. Furthermore, a bipartisan congressional commission, formed in 2008, has concluded that agencies have come to over-rely on contractors, and sorely need to improve their operational capacities in the areas of acquisition management and contractor oversight (Commission on Wartime Contracting 2011).

The industry itself seems to thrive on what anthropologist Janine Wedel (2015) refers to as "the new corruption." Elites connected to PMSCs advance industry interests through activities that are typically legal, while the cast of characters involved "assume a tangle of roles in government, business, nonprofits, and media organizations" (Wedel 2015). In fact, she notes a growing trend over the recent past where retired military generals, who decades ago would have called it quits after serving their country, increasingly continue their service by advising military agencies or accepting membership roles on advisory boards, while simultaneously serving as consultants for defense and intelligence contractors (also see Wedel 2014).

It seems that over recent decades the phenomenon of C. Wright Mills' (1956) *Power Elite*, comprised of government officials, military officials, and corporate executives, who once assumed stable roles within their respective institutional sectors, has been morphing into a more complex and variegated cast of *influence elites*. By contrast, Wedel (2017) argues, this new cast of elites is increasingly "unmoored from particular sectors or organizations" (166). They are oftentimes more "flexible and global in reach," and "often operate informally and use formal and informal means interchangeably" (166–7). To achieve their objectives, said elites often use organizations that are more "flexible, mobile, malleable" even "short-term oriented" and "global in reach" to achieve their aims. In the end, these new elites can be "highly effective, while also less visible, less accountable, and more challenging to democracy" (169) than their earlier counterparts. While the corporate elite may have fractured in some respects (Mizruchi 2013; 2017), particularly with regards to what we might refer to as any sort of modern form of noblesse oblige, they have been successful in asserting power and influence toward narrower ends.

Speaking of which, we next turn to a major privatization occurring at home: that relating to prison operations and related services, which also raise serious questions for our democracy and human rights issues on the domestic front.

9 Privatization and the prison-industrial complex

The new Keynesianism

The operation of prisons by the for-profit sector has also become a fixture on the American landscape over recent decades. While there has always been a role for the private sector to participate in the provision of public services, its participation in prison-related industries was historically limited, with some modest advance being made in the late 1970s through early 1980s that included such activities as operating community treatment centers, and even building, and at times operating, short-term detention centers for illegal immigrants (Selman and Leighton 2010). However, throughout the 1980s and 1990s, analogies between the military-industrial complex and an emerging prison-industrial complex (PIC) were increasingly being drawn. Internationally acclaimed criminologist Nils Christie (1993) warned that a growing preoccupation on controlling crime would lead to an uncontrollable bureaucratic industrial expansion of the crime control industry. Meanwhile, journalist Eric Schlosser (1998), among others, identified the powerful interests that had come to define this evolving complex as a confluence of bureaucratic, political, and economic interests representing enormous influence directed toward continued spending on imprisonment and prison construction, generally speaking. These form a kind of iron triangle of interests that shape public policy and protect itself from public scrutiny and accountability (Selman and Leighton 2010). These forces link together the interests of government bureaucrats and officials, politicians, and typically corporate interests in growing the industry and locking the country into a course of action that can seem virtually (but not absolutely) irreversible, certainly not without some strong countervailing power to resist the momentum. For today, a plethora of large-scale organizations, both public and private, employing millions of people, now derive their revenues in some way from this complex (Douglas, Sjoberg, Saenz, and Embrick 2018).

Several historic and related transformations undergird the evolution of the prison-industrial complex, which actually includes a wide range of related industries and services related to a broader criminal justice-industrial complex (Selman and Leighton 2010). The PIC is actually built upon an incarceration binge which saw the US prison population grow from under half a million inmates in 1980 to over 2.3 million by 2008. Criminologists Donna Selman and Paul Leighton (2010) point to two major factors that led to the rise of the

PIC in general, and private prisons in particular, the first of which dates back to conservative reactions to the civil rights movement and Vietnam War-era protests of the 1960s. Out of this turbulent era came the conservative critique of the erosion of traditional values that fed a new (and generally coded) racial politics of the post-civil rights era in the 1970s focusing on the importance of cultural values, individual responsibility, and a renewed emphasis on punishment as a key deterrent of crime, and a severe questioning of the efficacy of rehabilitation on the part of neoclassical criminologists (riding the wave of market fundamentalist thought).

The backlash culminated in a "tough on crime, law and order" political ideological approach to winning political campaigns, first successfully utilized by Republican Richard Nixon to win presidential elections in 1968 and 1972, and then followed through by Republicans Ronald Reagan and George H.W. Bush throughout the 1980s into the early 1990s, aided by a growing media focus on violent crime. Democratic Party candidate Bill Clinton took up the tough on crime platform, winning the presidential election in 1992 and departing from a more exclusive focus by Democrats up to that point on issues of education, jobs, training, and rehabilitation. The party continues to struggle with that legacy to this day (Chozick 2015; Stolberg and Herndon 2019). This tough on crime focus at the national level was followed by the overwhelming majority of states that passed mandatory minimum sentencing laws for drug offenses and moved to abolish or severely limit parole (Selman and Leighton 2010).

The attack on rehabilitation and renewed emphasis on severe punishment as the primary deterrent of crime naturally led to the second factor setting the stage for the rise of the PIC: the dramatic growth in the prison populations during the 1970s into the 1980s, which was accompanied by few initiatives to build new prisons to hold the increasing inmate population. This culminated in numerous lawsuits connected to prison overcrowding, inhumane prison conditions, and rioting that affected the majority of states by the mid-1980s. The solution to the overcrowding problem was a massive expansion in state level prison construction such that corrections expenditures increased between 1980 and 1995 from roughly $7 billion to $40 billion. This expansion also occurred during what has come to be known as an era of deindustrialization in the US. With the loss of manufacturing jobs accruing, the rural prison economy became an important and politically viable source of economic development (Hallinan 2001; Selman and Leighton 2010).

However, the dramatic increase in prison privatization, and prison operations in general was also fed by the Reagan era anti-government ideology and celebration of privatization, specifically advanced through Reagan-initiated commissions exploring and ultimately advocating increased privatization of a range of government functions and services (the Grace Commission in 1982 and the President's Commission on Privatization in 1987). This outsourcing of prison operations had to overcome legal and philosophical challenges captured by the issues of whether privatization delegitimizes punishment by removing it from the legitimate authority of the state, and whether the public trust can be maintained by having private entities administer prisons in the service of profit as opposed to the ideal of justice and the broader political community (Selman and Leighton 2010).

Two companies in particular have emblemized and exploited the opportunities for private corporations to meet the demand for rising prison and detention space in the US. Corrections Corporation of America (CCA), established in 1983, and GEO Group, incorporated in 1984, emerged as dominant providers in this sector. Here, we point out two key aspects of CCA's success that highlight the confluence of the emergence of a PIC and the Reagan revolution in governing. First, the founders of CCA had a vision that reflected the shifting political tides of the times. They recognized that the appeal of prison privatization fit with growing attacks on big governments inept management and wastefulness in the provision of a range of public services, as well as with the celebration of free markets, and also the notion that increasing levels of incarceration were the appropriate "tough on crime" solutions to the nation's crime problems (Selman and Leighton 2010).

Next, the backgrounds of three cofounders of CCA highlight their public-private connections and involvements, along with their ability to leverage and work the three sides of the iron triangle of the PIC: the government bureaucratic/administrative; the political-legislative; and, of course, the private-corporate (Douglas and Saenz 2013). These corporate executives boasted significant resumes and connections that enable companies like CCA to thrive in the contrived market contexts that characterize government privatization. For instance, one co-founder, Tom Beasley, brought experience as Tennessee Republican Party chairman, and coincidently, CCA made its first big impression and hit the national media spotlight through its audacious bid to take over the entire state of Tennessee's prison system (Selman and Leighton 2010). Furthermore, co-founder Don T. Hutto was a former commissioner of corrections, first in Arkansas during the early 1970s and then in Virginia during the late 1970s. He then went on to become president of the American Corrections Association (ACA) during the mid-1980s, which overlapped with his involvement in CCA. Not surprisingly, as president of ACA, he was an advocate for privatization.

The CCA board has included numerous other well placed business/political operatives and servants over the years, all of whom helped to advance the company's interests in the "free market" for owner operator services in the privatized correctional and detention facilities arena. The company has been effective not simply in cultivating relationships with government officials, but has also been engaged in efforts to shape government policy though its involvement in the American Legislative Exchange Council (ALEC), a conservative group that acts as a clearinghouse of sorts for state legislators by creating policy proposals and drafting model bills to be introduced by those legislators with whom they network (Douglas and Saenz 2013).

CCA has depended upon federal contracts for its survival, and even government support to avoid bankruptcy, as the late 1990s saw it and other prison-based businesses experience declining profits. However, the aftermath of 9/11 provided a great boost to business for corporations like CCA and GEO, as budgets for increasing the number and capacities of immigrant detention centers increased dramatically, feeding what some have called the immigrant-industrial complex (Douglas and Saenz 2013).

Both private prisons and military support services should be viewed in a highly dubious light due to the fact that corporations providing such services have a built-in financial incentive to grow the business—and hence, grow the industry—given their narrow focus on shareholder value and the privileges of limited liability granted to investors (Sjoberg 2005). The PIC emblemizes many of the issues raised by Gideon Sjoberg (2005) regarding the wider corporate control industry, and as discussed in the context of private military companies, such as arm's length accountability, the problem of corporate secrecy and its impact on limiting public scrutiny and accountability, the profit induced pressures to grow the market, even if it runs against the public good, and the political clout exercised by these entities to shape public policy in the most narrowly profitable direction. It oftentimes requires advocacy groups and investigative journalists systematic and sustained efforts (over years) to raise public and political awareness enough to lead to actions turning back the tide of these privatization efforts (Wessler 2016). Even trying to account for the thousands of corporations involved in a multitude of sectors that sustain this complex is a daunting undertaking (Urban Justice Center 2018).

Journalist Shane Bauer provided one such landmark expose when he went undercover as a prison guard at the Winn Correctional Center in Louisiana back in the summer of 2016, reported in the pages of *Mother Jones* (Bauer 2016) and subsequently in a larger book format (Bauer 2018). The graphic and disturbing exposé highlighted what inevitably become core values at CCA (now CoreCivic) and, really, the wider private prison industry: a relentless focus on cost cutting in order to maintain profitability, which means low-wage, marginalized employment opportunities, miserly resources devoted to client care, and dangerous, dehumanizing conditions for prisoners and those who oversee them. Of course, in the for-profit prison business, those prisoners are the valued commodities.

After his prison exposé, Bauer was invited to speak with federal officials who had been undertaking a critical assessment of private prisons. This was followed by an announcement by the Obama administration that the Department of Justice was ending its contracts with private prisons. However, the mandate was short lived, as the incoming Trump administration, with then Attorney General Jeff Sessions, quickly moved to reverse it (Michaels 2018). Trump's crackdown on immigration has been a boon for private prisons, reinforcing a perverse trend in immigration detention where the number of immigrants arrested by ICE had fallen by half since the early 2000s—likely reflecting overall lower levels of illegal immigration—while the average daily population of US detention centers has almost doubled (Pauly 2018). Drawing on internal ICE reports from 2016, Madison Pauly (2018) of *Mother Jones* notes that of every 100 immigration detainees (over half of which have no criminal record), 32 are in private facilities run by the massive GEO Group, 21 are in CoreCivic (formerly CCA) facilities, and another 21 are in other private facilities.

Sociologists Karen Douglas, Gideon Sjoberg, and colleagues argue that because private prisons are now part of a wider massive industry complex upon which so many Americans depend for their livelihood, scaling it back represents a necessary but daunting task (also see Segal 2015). They document how the PIC and ancillary industries now include:

> the organizations charged with designing, building, and renovating prisons; the corporations that supply the industry with food and clothing and sundries; the corporations that equip the guards with protective gear and weapons; and the institutions that supply the prison industrial complex its labor. . . . The reality is that colleges and universities train a significant number of people that work directly in the system. Further, major corporations have a stake in the prison industrial complex not only in building and maintaining prisons and jails but also in their use of prison labor in making products. Beyond that, the food we eat, the clothes we wear, the banks that hold our deposits, the jobs that provide our livelihood, the colleges we send our children, or the ones in which we teach, are all supporting the prison industrial complex. Both Main Street and Wall Street are propping up the prison industrial complex. The system is simply part of the mainstream life of the United States.
>
> (Douglas, Sjoberg, Saenz, and Embrick 2018: 370, 373)

Are we practicing a form of criminal justice Keynesianism, much along the lines of the military Keynesianism that emerged during the early Cold War? With 5 percent of the world's population, but (almost) one quarter of the world's prisoners (Lee 2015), somehow, I don't think it would be comforting for the late John Kenneth Galbraith, or Keynes, for that matter, to bear witness to this perversion of the New Deal–inspired welfare state in our post-Reagan world.

10 Administering democracy and the non-prophets of civil society

The rise of the charitable industrial complex

The role of privatization, deregulation, and the achievements of the Reagan-Thatcher revolution have been accompanied by another highly significant development in the evolution of state and market relations, and that is the rise and growing significance of the third, or nonprofit, sector, and with it, the philanthrocapitalism of corporate elites, who have become its most relevant players.

This current era of philanthrocapitalism has parallels to the rise of big philanthropy dating back to the early 20th century, and the fortunes made during the Gilded Age. Here we see the emergence of such mega-foundations as the Carnegie Corporation (founded in 1911 and built upon an empire of steel) and the Rockefeller Foundation (founded in 1913 and built upon a financial empire). These tax-exempt private corporations, with legal-financial structures that would permit them to last in perpetuity, adopted open-ended missions such as "improving the human condition" (Barkan 2013). However, they immediately generated suspicion and hostility from both sides of the political spectrum (both the mainstream left and the right), raising questions about the vast private resources deployed toward achieving grandiose aims, with apparently no democratic input from the wider public as to the means or the ends of those pursuits.

Linsey McGoey, author of *No Such Thing as a Free Gift* (2015), reiterates these critiques of big philanthropy, and urges us to consider how the actions of our philanthropic elites mirror those of *big men* in a wide range of non-market-based folk or tribal societies, for these figures have utilized the power of gifts to generate reciprocal obligations on the part other big men, which, in turn, represented future sources of enrichment for themselves and their own favored communities.

Peter Buffett (2013), son and heir to a foundation largesse of perhaps the nation's most respected investor, Warren Buffett, speaks of the looming presence of a "charitable industrial complex" (CIC). Buffett employs such notions as "philanthropic colonialism" and "conscience laundering" in his efforts to capture some of the outsized ambitions as well as the internal anxieties that characterize members of this rarefied sector. The fundamental social issue he identifies is oftentimes revealed when he attends major philanthropic meetings where he witnesses heads of state, investment managers, and corporate leaders "all searching for answers with their right hand to problems that others in the room have created with their left." This charitable sector has been growing significantly over recent history, faster than either business or government sectors, with hundreds of billions of dollars at play each year, while employing millions of workers (almost 10 million as of 2012). As of 2013, there were over 60 private grant making foundations with assets over $1 billion, with high-tech industry wealth being a major source of growth (Barkan 2013; also see McKeever 2015; Salamon 2012, 2015).

The recent historical growth of the nonprofit sector accompanies a longer term dramatic rise in inequality in US society, which has been linked to the information technology revolution and the rise of vastly profitable global markets, among other factors (such as those associated with the weakening of labor unions and the countervailing power of the state). This structural transformation in our national and global political economy reflects a fundamental conundrum: those who are benefiting most from—and, in many respects, have engineered—this transformation are now actively involved in "doing good" for society, of course on their own terms.

Today's global elites, as Chrystia Freeland (2011) writes, are different from the rich of yesteryear in that they are increasingly highly educated, hardworking, globally connected, and fully deserving (in their own minds) winners of an exceptionally competitive global economic competition. In fact, their sense of entitlement is equally matched by their strong belief in meritocracy; sensibilities that were seriously affronted in the aftermath of the 2007–8 financial crisis. In spite of the $700 billion US government (TARP) bailout, elites, particularly in the financial sector, felt a deep sense of victimization and maltreatment by the Obama administration and its proposals to rein in the sector's excesses, as well as its efforts to restore a more historically fair and balanced level of taxation on its members. This was the time in which the CEO of Blackstone, a private equity firm, characterized an Obama tax proposal as "like when Hitler invaded Poland in 1939" (quoted in Freeland 2012: 243). However, even many former Wall Street supporters of the Democratic president were also deeply affronted by his proposals and turned against Obama, calling him "antibusiness" and even "socialist." One long-term Democratic supporter recounted for Freeland an exchange he had with a Democratic leader in Congress about pending tax reform legislation in which he said, "Screw you . . . the government won't get a single penny more from me in taxes. I'll put my money into my foundation and spend it on good causes. My money isn't going to be wasted in your deficit sinkhole" (Freeland 2012: 243).

Freeland also notes that increasingly the most coveted status symbol among this rarefied group is not found in ostentatious displays of material wealth (although this may still be important), but in the founding of a philanthropic foundation. Many relish the idea of actively managing such an institution to highlight the grand ideas they have for solving major social problems of the day. Furthermore, today's foundations are more likely to reflect the business approaches embraced by their elite sponsors, who are eager to get their hands dirty, solve problems, and value results as measured in business terms, such as ROI (return on investment).

Beginning in the 1980s Reagan era, management scholars began to take interest in the third sector, which was accompanied by a gradual blurring of the lines between philanthropy and capitalism itself, sparking a whole new vocabulary. For instance, the notion of "social entrepreneurship" came to spotlight how business models could be employed to foster innovative approaches and solutions to social problems. The idea of "social innovation" emerged to reflect new ideas generated to meet unmet needs, where said ideas could come from heroic individuals, social movements, or even market incentives. More recently, the idea of "impact investing" reflects the appealing notion that investments can be targeted to provide societal benefits while providing market returns. Unfortunately, in spite of all the excitement, investment fund managers had trouble identifying laudable and socially conscious businesses that could also provide these returns (McGoey 2015).

Some management scholars also pointed out how philanthropists could learn from venture capitalists, given they share similar goals and challenges. Both are in engaged in risk taking activities, and need to identify worthy recipients of limited funds in the hopes that those investments will pay off, whether it be financially or socially (McGoey 2015). Of course, the holy grail of all of this has been to fuse social good with business success (i.e., profits). Here, management scholars Porter and Kramer (2002), in their classic *Harvard Business Review* article, take up Milton Friedman's (1970) challenge regarding the social responsibility of business and the incommensurability between economic and social objectives by arguing that a convergence of these interests can be sought out in a company's competitive context, and leverage between the economic and the social can potentially be achieved.

As Linsey McGoey (2015) observes, "the value of pro-market solutions particularly during times of economic catastrophe has been one of the most common themes to emerge out of the 2008 collapse" (86). The true believers pressed on, and many of the marquee philanthropic events maintained vibrancy in the face of the global financial crisis. Of course, she notes that the price of admission can be steep, and willingness to pay may not secure one an invitation to some of the most desirable philanthropic events, be they TED conferences, the invitation-only Skoll World Forum, or the Milken Global Conference (yes, the former junk bond trader convicted of securities fraud, Michael Milken), among others. Elites with big ideas, eager to eliminate global problems such as poverty, hunger, and disease, come together in these exclusive and rarefied settings to save the world and enhance their social networks.

In addition to this contemporary "bottom line" approach to philanthropy, today's mega-foundations are different than those in the past (i.e., small philanthropy) in that they are more politically savvy and engaged, and are willing to lobby and finance political/public relations campaigns to support their pet solutions, all the while enjoying a weakened government sector with declining public resources and a political environment that celebrates privatization of public sector functions (Barkan 2013).

Less government, more governing!

In part, the rise to prominence of philanthrocapitalists has been aided by shifting notions regarding the nature of democracy and how democratic ideals can best be actualized—a transformation that, once again, dates back to the Reagan-Thatcher era of the 1980s. The demise of the Soviet system witnessed growing and enthusiastic support from the capitalist West, not so much for the fortification of the administrative state among post-Soviet societies as support for the institutions of civil society, which in narrow terms has come to be translated into the nonprofit or third sector (Nickel 2012). Meanwhile, notions of state and government, once potent entities, have been diluted into more nebulous yet multifaceted forms of governing.

Both US President Reagan and British Prime Minister Thatcher celebrated the resistance movements that emerged during the 1980s opposing the Soviet Union, especially the Solidarity movement in Poland led by its labor union organizer Lech Walesa. In fact, Thatcher met with Walesa in Poland in 1988, supporting his worldwide acclaimed union movement's resistance to tyrannical Soviet rule, an event that Walesa credits as being instrumental to their ultimate political victory. This people's movement that emerged out of civil society against a repressive government was celebrated by Thatcher, even as she opposed labor union movements in her own country, decrying them as part of the apparatus of a repressive state that had strangled the spirit of enterprise and free markets, which were essential for personal freedom in her worldview (Nickel 2012).

This celebration of civil society as the fertile soil in which tyranny was pushed back by everyday citizens throughout the former Soviet Union was the key point of departure through which Thatcher and others eventually came to define civil society in market terms. True to form, Thatcher viewed human freedom as dependent upon free markets and free trade. Therefore, any limitations upon the free market meant limitations on sacred human freedom and dignity. Furthermore, in good Hayekian fashion, any centralized state-initiated restrictions on market freedom (even if these are supported by the people and their labor union movements) represent a step down the slippery slope to communism and fascism. Therefore, democracy flourishes where free people engage in free exchanges, unhindered by the state, whose proper role is to merely preserve the institutional framework that enables these practices (Harvey 2005)

Globalization, and the intensification of social, cultural, and especially economic relationships and exchanges on a worldwide scale (Giddens 2000), accompanied by the fact that public officials must confront growing complexity throughout contemporary society, also represents a set of issues that have dovetailed with neoliberal or market-based rationales for an emphasis on civil society. Social theorist Anthony Giddens' (2002) notion of a "third way" took hold during this period, emphasizing a more fluid symbiotic relationship between the state and civil society. Furthermore, the rise and growing centrality of international governance institutions (IGOs), such as the United Nations, the World Bank, and the International Monetary Fund (IMF), became part of a focus on global civil society and global governance, which created or reflected tensions surrounding the administrative state's capacity to govern on all fronts (Nickel 2012).

During the 1990s, there was much excitement about the potential of civil society, as evidenced by movements (such as Solidarity in Poland) to lead the way toward democratic reforms, particularly among Eastern European nations emerging out of the long shadow of Soviet rule. Business leaders, politicians, and the heads of international minded foundations came to herald the democratic possibilities inherent in civil society–based organizations. US government agencies focused on international development, and private foundations, such as the Ford Foundation, provided generous grant money for scholars to propose projects both to research and develop global civil society. Universities, in droves, established study groups on civil society. And all these efforts emerged without really sorting out whether the term was more akin to Thatcher's market revolution or Poland's labor union–based Solidarity movement (Calhoun 1993).

As the 1990s progressed, deeper and abiding questions regarding the nature and meaning of civil society seem to have been settled by the simplifying assumption that civil society means NGOs (nongovernmental organizations, i.e., nonprofits) or the wider third sector in which they operate. This simplifying assumption makes sense once we consider that funding agencies and private foundations increasingly want recipients to "objectively" account (oftentimes in terms of some measure of ROI) for the presence, robustness, and growth of civil society in their annual reports. What better way to account for the heath of civil society (democracy) in any given territory or nation state than in determining the size of the third sector by counting up the number of NGOs (Nickel 2012)?

This transformation has been part of the widespread acceptance of governance, idealized by the notion of third sector NGOs (or nonprofits), and gradual demise (denigration) of historical liberal notions of government and the administrative state. This latter notion (see Rohr 1986) reflects a political order that was exemplified by the accomplishments of the New Deal order and beyond, relying on a formal bureaucratic administrative apparatus, expert professional managerial knowledge informing the operation of agencies and offices whose charges are granted by government statute (also see DuGay 2000). In the end, the laudable promise that democracy has been reinvigorated by empowered and active third sector NGOs rests significantly on the fundamental question: to whom are they accountable? The people? Or the people who fund them?

11 Education reform without educators and the philanthrocapitalism of corporate elites

Perhaps nowhere has the presence of the charitable industrial complex and the broader corporate agenda had greater impact over recent decades than in the area of education reform (Baltodano 2017; Hursh 2015; Ravitch 2014). Two recent historical developments that highlight the omnipresent role of philanthrocapitalism have been the widespread state-by-state acceptance of the Common Core K-12 education standards during the first decade of the 21st century, along with the push by many states to expand funding for charter schools. In each case, corporate elites, along with monied interests, played an outsized role in comparison to students' parents, teachers, and local communities, let alone education scholars, in determining the direction of education reform.

Making schools accountable to philanthrocapitalists

Common Core (or, Common Core State Standards) represents the latest development in a longstanding history of education legislation in the US. These date back to the Johnson administration's Elementary and Secondary Act of 1965 (ESEA), which introduced Title I funding to assist the academic achievement of students in poverty. The administration of this federal funding was left to individual states, in order to deflect any criticism over too much federal control over education—a concern that would inform subsequent education reform initiatives. While it was reauthorized several times over the latter half of the 20th century, it was not until the 1994 reauthorization, the Improving America's Schools Act (IASA) and House Resolution Goals 2000, which raised the ideas of a "core of challenging state standards," and the desire for a voluntary set of national standards, both of which served to highlight the public's distrust of a set of national education standards (Schneider 2015). More widely recognized has been President George W. Bush's No Child Left Behind (NCLB) reauthorization of ESEA. Its significant features involved the use of standardized testing to determine whether schools met annual yearly progress (AYP) targets, with those schools serving the neediest populations facing the risk of losing their Title I funding should they not meet testing goals. But NCLB was not successful in establishing federal standards.

The impetus for national education standards, opposition notwithstanding, has had its supporters over the years. One influential organization that has played a major role in nurturing their development has been Achieve, Inc., a nonprofit organization created by the National Governors Association (NGA) in 1996. Its board of directors is comprised of governors and business leaders, while its nonprofit status facilitates generous tax-deductible donations from corporations and philanthropies. Perhaps the individual most responsible for Achieve's creation was then IBM CEO Louis Gerstner, Jr., whose keynote address to the 1995 NGA annual meeting emphasized that the first priority for public education should be to set the highest academic standards and hold all involved accountable. To that end, in 2005, Achieve was instrumental in creating the network called the American Diploma Project (ADP), which encouraged states to align their standards, assessments, and graduation requirements toward college and career readiness. ADP was clearly a precursor to what would become Common Core (Schneider 2015).

In 2008, Achieve produced an ambitious report promoting a state-led common core of standards—a project that, in reality, would require millions (perhaps billions) of dollars to get 50 states to come together, agree upon, and implement such a set of standards. Later that same year, the NGA and Achieve participated in generating a broader shared report, *Benchmarking for Success*, promoting the development of an upgraded common core of shared state standards, and called for states to adopt them, to bring textbook and related media in line with them, and to hold schools accountable for ensuring that students achieved high levels of performance. Teacher and author Mercedes Schneider (2015) emphasizes how Common Core was never meant to simply encourage state standards, but ultimately to drive curriculum and assessment. So, just how was it possible to embark on such a massive and costly national educational reform campaign, where involving the federal government would have meant the kiss of death for the project? A campaign whose ultimate success was certainly in doubt from the outset, but that, in the end, was successful in enlisting all 50 states (which in reality meant only the states' governors and superintendents of education) to sign on to a set of standards that had yet to be written? Only by enlisting the man whom some have referred to as the unelected school superintendent of the country: Bill Gates.

Two education reform advocates (each of whom had at best made cameo appearances as classroom teachers over their careers) convinced Bill Gates to bankroll not simply the development of Common Core math and reading standards for K–12 grade levels, but more importantly, they funded an effective public relations campaign that overwhelmed any critical public opposition to the project, and which only emerged several years into its implementation (fueled in part by anti-federal government, anti–Obama, anti-corporate, Tea Party activism; see Elkind 2016). All in all, the Gates Foundation spent over $200 million on such efforts over roughly six years (Layton 2014). For instance, the Gates Foundation provided the Hunt Institute—affiliated with the University of North Carolina, and led by former Democratic Governor

Jim Hunt—with an outsized $5 million grant, which it used to coordinate numerous organizations (most of which also received Gates money) around the country in efforts to promote Common Core. They used a large portion of Gates money to hire a communications firm owned by a Democratic strategist to conduct polling, develop fact sheets, talking points, and even a messaging tool kit that could be useful in garnering support from key stakeholders such as teachers, parents, business leaders, and community groups (Layton 2014; Schneider 2015).

In fact, the Gates Foundation is one of a select few foundations, including the Broad and Walton Foundations, that have leveraged collectively a roughly $1 billion annual investment in education reform over the first decade or so of the 21st century that has achieved major influence over the debates about and ultimate direction of education reform in the US. This money has served to influence a host of (nonprofit) grantees who are obliged to adopt the foundations' policy objectives, while also influencing cash-strapped states and school districts, desperate for funds, many of which ultimately get tangled up in ill-advised obligations they adopt as conditions of these grant monies, which, in turn, generate swelling administrative costs of their own. These foundations also generate pipelines of administrative personnel, such as the Broad Foundation's Superintendents Academy, which provides six weeks of training for professionals in business, government, and military sectors to move into administrative positions in urban public school districts. Their strategic investments in personnel have paid big dividends at the federal level as well. They helped to create a virtual revolving door of personnel into the Obama administration's Department of Education, which was quietly but strongly supportive of Common Core (Barkan 2011).

In anticipation of the 2008 presidential election, the Gates and Broad Foundations funded their own $60 million campaign to get both political parties to sign on to their vision of education reform. Their campaign paid off handsomely when newly elected President Obama selected former Chicago Public Schools CEO Arne Duncan as head of the Department of Education. Not surprisingly, Duncan's surge into the national spotlight was made possible by a Gates Foundation $90 million grant for Chicago Renaissance 2010, a plan to turn around Chicago's failing public schools, which involved numerous school closings and consolidations, displacing students into other invariably low-performing schools, and disrupting neighborhood life and exacerbating problems of youth violence. Under Duncan, the DOE fully embraced the foundation community, even creating a position of director of philanthropic engagement. Furthermore, numerous top executives at DOE came from Gates, Broad, and various organizations they fund (Barkan 2011).

And so, the Obama administration's major education initiative, Race to the Top (RTTT), involved a competition among states for a slice of a $4.35 billion pie for those leading the way in education reform. And while the RTTT application did not explicitly require that states sign on to Common Core as part of the application process, they were expected to participate in a consortium developing high-quality standards (and to adopt those standards). Fortunately, states could submit their signed Common Core (commitment) memorandum of understanding as evidence of their participation. Furthermore, the Gates Foundation was heavily involved in supporting and funding the application process for those states whom they deemed preferred candidates for the funds— a hefty $250,000 investment per applicant (Barkan 2011).

While opposition (specifically to Common Core) has led to some significant rebellion throughout the states (Zernike 2015), for Gates, the long-term prospect of national one-size-fits-all standards for K-12 education opens up great possibilities for digital learning products to be developed on a massive national scale—a real enticement for software developers like Gates' Microsoft, as well as for Pearson, the world's largest education publisher (Layton 2014). These two companies announced a joint publishing venture in 2014 whereby Microsoft would load Pearson's Common Core classroom materials on Microsoft's tablets, enabling it to compete with Apple's iPad for supremacy in US classrooms and the tax dollars it represents. In a 2014 meeting with market analysts at major investment banks, top executives at Pearson pointed to Common Core as a major opportunity to build to scale their assessment and curriculum-based products and as an important reason why they committed heavily to major investments in North America. Pearson's commitment to scaling up actually began several years earlier when its nonprofit, the Pearson Charitable Foundation (PCF), began making grants that totaled over half a million dollars to one of the two organizations that hold the license for Common Core. Penguin group, a Pearson acquisition, is one of two companies (the other being McGraw-Hill) specifically named in the license as supplying Common Core examples (Schneider 2015).

The charter school bandwagon

Accompanying the movement to standardize K-12 education in the US, most recently through Common Core, has also been the push throughout numerous states to embrace relatively untested charter schools (even virtual ones at that). Since the early 1990s, over 40 states have developed their own charter school laws. Enrollment in charter schools doubled three times between 2000 and 2014 (Center for Popular Democracy 2014). Meanwhile, the total number of charter schools increased from about 2,000 in 2000 to 7,000 by 2017 (National Center for Education Statistics 2019).

Not surprisingly, where there is money to be made, the vultures will gather. Take, one prominent example, K12 Inc., virtual education company, and the investment banker, Michael Moe, who helped take the company public. He has spent over 15 years trying to transform the roughly trillion-dollar educational sector into a streamlined, profitable market, ripe for Wall Street investment (Fang 2011, 2014).

Moe has held several "Education Innovation Summits" over the past decade or so, which draw dozens of companies as well as former high-ranking state-level school officials and politicians looking to cash in on their careers in public service. He has been a board member of the Center for Education Reform, a pro-privatization think tank that produces policy papers and has invested significant dollars on state-level ad campaigns tarnishing those who oppose measures to expand school vouchers, as these enable students to take their state apportioned tax dollars to charters and other private schools (Fang 2011). In fact, there has been a movement among several states in recent years to expand vouchers for K-12 education, much of which has been lavishly promoted by tech and education tech companies via public relations and lobbying campaigns, apparently without much evidence of the effectiveness of these charter schools.

K12 Inc., which went public in 2007 and specializes in online education, has been riddled with a poor performance record, and even had its contracts terminated by several states (Fang 2014). However, it maintained promising and impressive growth prospects in the eyes of investors because of its competencies in lobbying new states for market access and in working closely with policy makers at the state level to pass legislation expanding virtual schools into new districts. This has been a core focus among numerous investment groups, along with their for-profit education company counterparts. And, as investigative journalist Lee Fang (2011) points out, philanthropy is the "Trojan horse" through which they achieve desired educational reforms. You see, we're not remaking education to serve our market driven, for-profit interests; we are simply committed to doing what is best for our nation's children.

Speaking of doing what is best for our nation's children, President Trump's selection of Betsy DeVos (sister of Blackwater-famed Eric Prince) in 2017 to head the Department of Education could not have sent a clearer message as to the administration's belief in the power of money and markets to reign over what were historically considered institutions held in the public trust. A *New York Times* story on the eve of DeVos' appointment examined her record of supporting for-profit charter schools in Michigan. It highlighted a recent instance where there was seemingly bipartisan political agreement that that schools in Detroit were in serious trouble, given a "chaotic mix of charters and traditional public schools that were the worst performing in the nation" (Zernike 2016a). Bipartisan legislation was put forward that would provide some greater oversight and set standards for opening and closing schools in the city. However, DeVos used her political influence to effectively resist any such proposal, arguing that any such oversight would lead to more government bureaucracy and limit the choices available to parents, who are best equipped to decide which educational opportunities they want for their children (Zernike 2016a).

The proliferation of charter schools in the 21st century seems to fundamentally contravene the purpose for which they were created in the first place. The original intention was to create a way for educators to experiment with innovative approaches to teaching and curriculum design, the ultimate goal of which was to foster successful innovative models that could help to improve public schools. In order to facilitate this experimentation, lawmakers exempted charter schools from many traditional regulations governing the public school system. In fact, a report issued by the Center for Popular Democracy in 2014 drew inspiration from a 2010 Department of Education inspector general's report to Congress raising serious concerns about the growing number complaints accompanying the rapidly increasing numbers of charter schools in the US, with oversight vulnerabilities being a major, if not the major, issue needing remedy. In fact, it seems that both supporters and detractors of charter schools now share concern over the limited oversight of these educational institutions, which have morphed into something quite strikingly different than early supporters envisioned. Even the Walton Foundation has donated serious money to the cause of making charters more accountable (Center for Popular Democracy 2014).

Betsy Devos has been an education philanthropist and lobbyist for decades but does not have a background working in the field of education. She and her husband, who is an heir to the Amway fortune, are extremely powerful and longstanding political operatives in Michigan. They were instrumental in lobbying for the 1994 law that established charter schools in the state. This enabled a wide range of non-government organizations to start charter schools that were supported by public funds but received little oversight. Detroit has the second-highest proportion of charter schools in the country, just behind New Orleans. Meanwhile, roughly 80 percent of the charters in Michigan are operated for profit, something that, combined with the unregulated environment, is cause for concern even among many charter supporters. At the time of DeVos' nomination by President Trump, over half of Detroit's students were attending charter schools, while practically none (under 1 percent) of the city's schools were given high grades (A or B+) by Excellent Schools Detroit, a major clearinghouse relied upon by parents. Federal reviews have found high numbers of charters to be among the state's lowest performing schools. Dozens and dozens of schools have opened and closed over the years, creating complicated choices for parents. It is not uncommon for some children to change schools frequently, while the highest performing schools tend to be out of reach for the poorest students in Detroit due to inadequate transportation. Adding to the confusion at the time was the fact that the state of Michigan had 45 different charter school authorizers and no clear and comprehensive set of criteria by which the schools would be judged (Gross 2017; Zernike 2016b).

Devos seems to have used her political might to resist moving toward improved and systematic oversight and accountability for charter schools in Michigan. In fact, she is probably even more dogmatic in her support for market fundamentalist approaches to education than even Milton Friedman himself ever was. It was Friedman who laid the intellectual groundwork for the school choice movement back in his 1955 essay, "The Role of Government in Education." Author and educator Mercedes Schneider points out the naivete inherent in Friedman's position, as the publication of his paper coincided with school choice initiatives in the South intended to preserve racial segregation.

The government and the courts subsequently endeavored for decades to curb these initiatives (Shneider 2016).

Friedman would see vouchers as the means to move away from a government system to a private one where parents could use the money for approved educational services meeting "minimal government standards" (see Schneider 2016: 29). What Friedman failed to foresee is how the reality of educational choice oftentimes tends to sit more with the for-profit entities delivering the services than with parents themselves, and that the perverse incentives surrounding, particularly, for-profit education seem to be leading to significant issues of financial fraud (Center for Popular Democracy 2014).

Now, let's place this discussion in a broader historical perspective. Economist Timothy Taylor reminds us that all the way back in 1776, Adam Smith, writing in *The Wealth of Nations*, perhaps the most revered foundational text embraced by market fundamentalists, advocated for the government to provide public education. While he did so partly on the grounds that educating workers would benefit the economy, he also emphasized the political benefits (dare I say necessity) of educating the people:

> The more they are instructed the less liable they are to the delusions of enthusiasm and superstition, which among ignorant nations frequently occasions the most dreadful disorders. An instructed and intelligent people . . . are more disposed to examine, and more capable of seeing through, the interested complaints of faction and sedition, and they are, upon that account, less apt to be misled into any wanton or unnecessary opposition to the measures of government.
>
> (quoted in Taylor 2017)

12 Looking forward

Confronting risk society by envisioning
a countersystem of care

This work began with an examination of how the largest tech firms have come to amass so much power and influence over our lives and our society, which should make us concerned and uneasy about the relationship these firms have forged with us and wonder whether they really represent and advance our ideals and values to the extent they seem to have claimed that they do. It also endeavored to place the rise of big tech in a larger context and to help us view the current scene as a reflection of a broader transformation in state and market relations dating back in large part to the Reagan–Thatcher era of the 1980s. This transformation also reflects more fundamental changes surrounding how spheres of governing have been transformed as well as who has become more entrenched in the governing process; namely, corporations, the elites who direct them, and corporate interests generally speaking

Throughout Part II of this book, questions were raised regarding some of the most profoundly consequential developments associated with the growing power and influence of corporations and their predations through the areas of health care reform, as well as key arenas of privatization associated with the security functions of the state including the military, security, and criminal justice sectors. It highlighted the rise of privatization throughout the military and security complexes, paralleled by similar developments throughout the criminal justice system, noting how the military Keynesianism of the post–World War II era seems to have been eventually accompanied by a new and disturbing form of criminal justice Keynesianism.

It also examined the movements to celebrate, renew, and advance democracy through the growth of nonprofits (or NGOs) and a strengthening of civil society, which was accompanied by the rise of philanthrocapitalism, much of which has been funded and directed by our fabulously wealthy tech and finance entrepreneurs, and has come to supplant traditional functions of government through new notions of governing. Also highlighted were efforts by philanthropic corporate elites to push for education reform that, in the end, have advanced (directly or indirectly) the privatization agenda and for-profit public schools. Unfortunately, these experiments to privatize America's schools have been most commonly pushed forward in poorer, urban school districts serving predominantly minority children.

While these transformations in state and market relations must be viewed critically, current institutional arrangements leave us hopelessly unprepared to deal with major societal risks we face moving forward. These include growing challenges associated with the US becoming a truly aging society in the context of emerging retirement and broader health crises; the persistence of poverty; employment uncertainty (much of which is driven by AI advances associated with tech); education and criminal justice challenges; and environmental and ecological threats. Adapting to present and future societal risks will require a rebalancing of market fundamentalism toward a more institutionally robust knowledge and caring society. Such a program is also complicated by two major ongoing challenges: one of which has been the neglect, and at times denigration, of the fact that we live in and depend upon a knowledge society (one that nurtures and institutionalizes the gifts of Athena), while the other points to the way in which dark money has so effectively permeated the public sphere and political processes in a way that single-mindedly advances a vision of a market society dominated by powerful monied interests, and, therefore, will prove especially resistant to a needed rebalancing of state and market relations

While this book has highlighted efforts to push back the state and the growing centrality of market-business-corporate activity in many traditional arenas of state action, we must heed James Galbraith's (2008) reminder that an enduring New Deal remains central, even if partially hidden, to contemporary economy and society. These beleaguered government supported institutions— be they in areas of health, education, military security, or housing—persist, and were instrumental in supporting the recovery out of the recession that followed the 20007–8 financial crisis, but will need to be fortified to deal with ongoing risks facing society.

The risks we must "care" about

The US, along with other industrialized nations (with Japan leading the way; Aral et al. 2015), is becoming a truly aging society. This reality, where a growing proportion of the population is aged 65 and older, is accompanied by looming retirement and broader societal health crises. As the US population ages, it seems those nearing retirement are increasingly less-well prepared to make the transition. One major reason is due to the now decades-long shift in private sector corporate pensions from once generous defined-benefit plans to now pervasive defined contribution plans, more commonly known as 401(k) plans.

Unfortunately, as defined contribution plans began expanding during the 1980s, they were intended to supplement traditional, employer-funded defined-benefit pensions. However, over time they become the replacement! In fact, The *Wall Street Journal* recently reported that the very corporate human resource executives who pioneered the 401(k) system back in the early 1980s now have serious regrets about their creation and how it has evolved. Over the years, corporations used the new system as a way to reduce costs and shed defined-benefit plans, and they succeeded in shifting retirement risk onto the shoulders of individuals (Hacker 2008). For instance, today those in the bottom half of earners between ages 50–64 typically have retirement assets of only about $25,000 (Martin 2017). In fact, it seems that less than 50 percent of private sector workers currently participate in some type of pension plan (Ellis, Munnell, and Eschtruth 2014).

While society is aging, there is a broader health crisis underway in the US, ironically, as indicated by recent declines in overall life expectancy, which medical experts view as a general barometer of the nation's overall health. Many of us in the West who witnessed the transition to capitalism by Russia and other nations that had been part of the Soviet Union during the 1990s were alarmed by similar trends. Declines in life expectancy seemed unthinkable at the time. In the case of the US, life expectancy dropped slightly in 2017 as part of the longest running decline in the country since World War I. Age groups that were significantly affected ranged from 25 to 54. Death rates from drug overdoses, especially from synthetic opioids, rose significantly over the last few years, while suicide rates, particularly among those living in rural areas, have risen over the past 15 years or more (Frej 2018).

Furthermore, while for many years now politicians seem to battle, at least rhetorically, over how to win over the middle class and shore up the American Dream, the persistence of poverty remains an underreported but sobering reality in the US. In fact, the United Nations monitor on extreme poverty and human rights recently embarked on a tour of the country, highlighting the serious economic and personal hardships facing those mostly forgotten Americans (Pilkington 2017a, 2017b). This tour only reinforces the significance of the work and broad social coalition being forged by Reverend Dr. William Barber, who has been leading a movement to revive Dr. Martin Luther King's 1968 Poor People's Campaign (Cobb 2018).

The problem of a declining middle class and issues of poverty loom large in ongoing debates about the future of employment, given rapid advances in AI that are driving automation in both the manufacturing and broader service sectors. First, in exploring the outsourcing of manufacturing, looking specifically at the case of Apple, notable has been the fact that so much of industry (not simply tech) has become dependent upon global supply chains and manufacturing, much of which are centered on China. However, as noted, China is moving up the skills chain and is automating its own manufacturing operations through broader advances in AI such that we may increasingly ask (trade wars aside): to what extent are Chinese robots doing the jobs that American companies used to hire US workers to do? In fact, these developments are central to China's larger aims to advance its own high-tech industry leaders. Furthermore, as was explored in some depth, the way in which Amazon is leading the way toward greater use of online (e-commerce) shopping, as opposed to in-person brick-and-mortar shopping services, is wreaking havoc in retail service sector employment.

Given the specter of large-scale job displacement in the years ahead, the idea of a universal basic income (UBI) has moved from the fringe to more mainstream discussion and experimentation, with some initiatives even coming from the tech sector itself (Cassidy 2015; Surowiecki 2016; Waters 2017). In fact, who knows better how future waves of technological advancements will likely impact employment than those involved in ushering them in? Numerous experiments are already underway around the globe (Weller 2017).

The extent to which advances in AI-driven automation take us down the road to a jobless future remains to be seen. However, related to the UBI question is one of anemic economic growth. For instance, a recent chairman of the Federal Reserve, Ben Bernanke (2016), raised the specter of "helicopter money," in reference to economist Milton Friedman's (yes!) facetious notion that the Fed could simply drop money from helicopters in order to stimulate the economy during times of slow economic growth and low inflation. A similar case was made in recent years by Adair Turner (2016), a highly respected British technocrat who became chairman of the country's Financial Services Authority when the financial crisis struck in 2008. Such a program, he argues, may be necessary to increase the purchasing power of individuals directly or to fund needed government infrastructure, which would help to alleviate the problem of slow growth and low inflation, or "secular stagnation."

Moving toward a framework of a caring society would also help us to confront serious and interrelated education and criminal justice challenges that we now face (Douglas, Sjoberg, Saenz, and Embrick 2018). While the original and noble intent behind charter schools was to provide small laboratories for experimentation in order to translate successes back into traditional public schools, the entire movement has been commandeered by a combination of profit-seeking interests along with others set on denigrating or simply scaling back government. The broader reform movement has had the greatest impact on predominantly poor, minority, urban school districts, whose students would really benefit from the kinds of educational opportunities that Bill and Melinda Gates, and really, most professional-class parents, seek to provide for their own children (Ravitch 2014).

Moreover, because of the way education is funded in the US, we really have a two-tiered system, where those growing up in poor, minority neighborhoods attend underfunded schools that have increasingly become heavily policed, high-security zones. This contributes to the school-prison-pipelines that feed the criminal justice complex, which has become part of the fabric of our post-industrial economy (Douglas, Sjoberg, Saenz, and Embrick 2018). While we must address broader issues of job displacement, the current form of criminal justice Keynesianism cannot be sustained morally or practically.

The criminal justice system drains needed resources away from education and other vital social needs. As state coffers have been further drained over the past few decades to pay for tax cuts, the cost of higher education has been dramatically shifted onto the family safety net, and many individuals now carry that debt burden well into middle age (Kuttner 2015). Furthermore, considering the array of aging, health, poverty, and employment risks we face, consumer capitalism can only feasibly, let alone morally, be sustained on top of the foundation provided by a caring society. A caring society cannot be forged as an afterthought to consumer capitalism. And we will need to stop kidding ourselves that such is the case.

Recall, our big tech firms are world-class tax avoiders. Neither they, nor the entrepreneurs and investors who garner so much of the nation's wealth, contribute the way other firms and wealthy individuals have in times past. The "Paradise Papers" revealed the extent to which so many wealthy companies and individuals utilize offshore havens to avoid taxes. This problem is truly global and will require international cooperation if it is to be effectively addressed. A cursory examination of the way in which wealth and taxation have diverged here in the US highlights some striking transformations. The top .1 percent of families now control 20 percent of the wealth in the US, a share that has doubled since 1985. Yet the top marginal tax rate has dropped from roughly 90 percent in the early 1960s to roughly 37 percent today (Tankersley 2019). While we can acknowledge the allure of wealth and high-end consumerism in contemporary society, as well as how liberals have learned to love the market in many respects, these values should not come at the expense of providing the basic infrastructure of a caring (just and decent) society. And don't just take my word for it. Abigail Disney, granddaughter of Roy Disney and heiress to the Disney family fortune, has been making a similar argument. While a committed philanthropist herself, she publicly supports a wealth tax and advocates for a world much less dependent upon philanthropy (Shapiro 2019).

Of all the risks mentioned thus far, the most serious long-term threats are associated with environmental and ecological challenges linked to climate change. Market incentives alone, especially as they are inscribed into the legal structure of the corporation, are simply not effective at anticipating and responding to long-term collective risks, but instead tend to focus efforts on narrowly, exclusively, maintaining profitability. As was discussed in relation to the privatization of military, security, and criminal justice functions of the state, the incentives for corporations to grow the business can lead to very unsettling outcomes for our values and our democracy (Sjoberg 2005). Holding them to at least minimal human rights standards on a global scale is a necessary project moving forward (Sjoberg 2009; Ruggie 2013).

In the case of ecological-environmental risk, as far back as the late 1970s, Exxon, for instance, was aware of the fact that the burning of fossil fuels was contributing to climate change, and lead scientists at the company briefed its top executives on the matter. In fact, they even later utilized NASA climate models to run cost estimates and plan for future drilling operations in the Arctic. However, by the early 1990s Exxon had joined the Global Climate Coalition (GCC), along with a host of other big oil companies, and hit upon a winning strategy for avoiding and delaying meaningful government action on the problem, which was to emphasize the uncertainty in the science around the issue, versus outright denial. This has proven to be a winning strategy over the years in convincing Americans that there is no scientific consensus on global warming. Sadly, for their grandchildren's futures (and ours), there is strong consensus. Over time,

Exxon and its partners at the GCC have found support in myriad groups and lobbyists funded by fossil fuel companies and those in related industries, with the Koch brothers and their numerous industry-linked groups perhaps being the most effective and influential of them all (McKibben 2018).

Furthermore, corporate-funded lobbies and organizations promoting market fundamentalist ideas have been extremely successful in their campaigns to denigrate the state, which in practical terms means an impoverished understanding of the fact that we live in and depend upon a knowledge society. The Trump presidency is emblematic of this. For instance, the president chose to appoint former Texas Governor Rick Perry to be his Secretary of Energy, one of several departments that Perry had at one time openly claimed he wanted to abolish. The overall intent seems to have been to run the department in way that catered directly to the interests of oil, gas, and other carbon-related industries. In fact, the new team at the Department of Energy showed little interested in even being briefed on operations and ongoing programs at the department, as Michael Lewis found in reporting for *The Fifth Risk* (2018). This seems part of a pattern where the administration has shown little interest in many aspects of the complex work carried out by key government agencies in assessing and managing a host of risks. It also is the case that the usual suspects lobbied hard to hold the president to his promise that he would exit the Paris Climate accords, which he did in 2017, leaving the US standing alone in its unwillingness to support the agreement.

While they seem to generally be on board in facing the threat of climate change, it is shocking how many of our libertarian tech moguls, especially those with backgrounds in engineering and science-related fields, seem to be oblivious to the broader knowledge society that provides the nurturing soil in which they enjoy the rewards of their remarkable achievements. The pillars of government, along with the scientific, research, and university complexes, are essential for the furtherance of the knowledge society. But perhaps our tech heroes and entrepreneurs live under a kind of Hayekian spell, enamored by their own successes in the market and simply assuming that anonymous market mechanisms will spontaneously drive civilization forward, and that the need for conscious planning (outside of their pet philanthropic foundations) and systematic, institutionally based systems of knowledge creation and risk assessment, economic or scientific, for that matter, are unnecessary (Davies 2017).

Now, on one particular front, vital national security concerns may be leading to a reassessment of the role of the state in supporting and advancing scientific-technological developments. Those who denigrate the state, and are even willing to adopt a cavalier attitude toward shutting it down for extended periods of time, still can rally behind it when national security concerns run high. The latest cause for alarm has been a new type of arms race emerging with China and the competition over who will construct the next generation 5G network linking computers and smartphones by connecting devices around the globe and dramatically advancing network capacity for AI-driven productive investments in robots, autonomous vehicles, back office and other service functions, and so on. In this context, the Trump administration has been lobbying political allies to ban the telecommunications giant Huawei and other Chinese companies from involvement in the network's development (Sorkin, Grocer, Hsu, and Schmidt 2019). They see the

> world engaged in a new arms race—one that involves technology, rather than conventional weaponry, but poses just as much danger to America's national security. In an age when the most powerful weapons, short of nuclear arms, are cyber-controlled, whichever country dominates 5G will gain an economic, intelligence, and military edge for much of this century.
>
> (Sanger, Barnes, Zhong, and Santora 2019;
> also see Sorkin 2019a; Medin and Louie 2019)

Is it time, once again, for a new round of military Keynesianism (Crawford 2018)?

In the end, a major obstacle to forging a caring society continues to be the fact that dark money and effective lobbying has permeated the public sphere and political processes in a way that advances a market society dominated by powerful monied interests—a vision that ensures long-term self-destruction, even while it may delay democratic reckoning over the near term (MacLean 2017; Mayer 2016). We really need right-leaning politics to stand in loyal opposition to the project of the caring society. Otherwise, we are left with gridlock and kludge (more complicated, debilitating, and unnecessary bureaucracy). In fact, that seems to have been a major aim of the well-financed business lobby–driven attacks by the political right: to undermine government's capacity to fulfill its functions and then use that as evidence to further denigrate it (Hacker and Pierson 2016). And, yet, there is a genuine role to be played by political conservatives of the right, as claims against the state can multiply and expand rapidly. Therefore, having a loyal (as opposed to disloyal) opposition that supports the general contours of the caring society, but takes into account long-term fiscal and resource allocative challenges, would prove to be a necessary and productive role. Well, it is always a possibility—perhaps more of a white tiger than a unicorn—but don't count on it!

The one major Achilles heel this dark money movement possesses is the fact that it represents a political-economic ideology consciously built on the interests of so few in relation to so many. That is why extremely effective planning, organization, and disciplined execution was necessarily achieved by a small cadre of the committed. Yet the growing deluge of women winning political office in the US is one potentially bright harbinger that the promise of a caring society may one day be fulfilled, for, as a general rule, women have historically been called upon to do most of the care work in society. Therefore, it seems more likely that growing numbers of women in politics will be more mindful and vocal about issues of caring. In following feminist economist Nancy Folbre (2009), we could say the founding fathers of market fundamentalism shared a collective blind spot in that regard. Now is the time for a market correction.

Furthermore, it seems younger generations are now more open to socialist ideas than earlier ones who lived through the Cold War. As the *Economist* highlights in a recent cover story, "The Rise of Millennial Socialism," roughly half of Americans in their 20s now have a positive view of socialism, though, in reality, they seem supportive of ideas that are not very radical in most parts of the advanced industrial world, such as universal health care (The Rise 2019). They also worry about growing inequality and how powerful vested interests and lobbying have shaped government policy in a manner that no longer serves the people. Yet they remain generally supportive of a market economy.

Finally, it seems corporate leaders are hearing messages of discontent among the electorate and are growing increasingly alarmed, as they face the ire of both the progressive left as well as the nationalist right. For instance, at the 2019 Milken Institute's annual conference, organized by Michael Milken, the once-famed junk bond trader, a major concern shared by attendees was the growing backlash against capitalism, fueled by extreme concentrations of wealth along with yawning inequality (Porzecanski, Tan, and Basak 2019). A number of Milken's speakers are on Bloomberg's Billionaires Index, one of whom was Ray Dalio, founder of Bridgewater, the world's largest hedge fund. Dalio recently published a widely circulated and incisive analysis of what ails contemporary capitalism, focusing on the wealth gap and how it has exacerbated inequality and is linked to the limited opportunities many now face as they struggle to achieve economic success amid declining education and health outcomes (Dalio 2019; Rushe 2019).

The most dramatic response, however, has come from the vaunted Business Roundtable, a lobbying organization drawing membership from the leaders of America's leading corporations, which in 2019 issued a statement on "the purpose of a corporation" (Business Roundtable 2019). In it they argued that companies should no longer exclusively focus on shareholder value—recall an idea that dates back to Milton Friedman's (1970) classic statement—and should focus instead on a wider circle of stakeholders including customers, employees, suppliers, and the wider community (Gelles and Yaffe-Bellany 2019; Sorkin 2019b). While more a statement than a concrete plan of action, it could represent an acknowledgement among business elites of a broader political-cultural shift taking place in society. Only time will tell.

Afterword

You're all Reaganites, and you don't even know it! Such was my introduction to graduate school at the University of Texas at Austin during the early 1990s, and my class in sociological theory with Gideon Sjoberg. While my classmates and I were affronted by his comment, somehow many of us sensed he was conveying an uncomfortable truth. Over many years, directly and indirectly, I have endeavored to make sense of just what he meant, while I have had the privilege of ongoing dialogue with Sjoberg over the past several decades. This book simply could not have been written without his support over the years, as many of the issues raised in it have emerged out of our shared scholarly interests and intellectual conversations, along with theoretical framing that derives from key insights he developed over the years.

Back in 1984, as Reagan was finishing up his first term in office, Sjoberg began sketching out the features of a growing critique of bureaucracy and state planning that emanated from various points of view along the political spectrum from left to right. He did so in the afterword of a co-edited work on *Bureaucracy as a Social Problem* (Sjoberg 1983). That general work was focused on how bureaucracy had become a central feature of 20th century life with the massive growth of large-scale organization throughout the industrial world in the aftermath of World War II. A major interest was how political power and organizational elites served to define the purposes of, and manner in which, large-scale organizations functioned in both public and private sectors.

Sjoberg's work also reflects abiding concerns regarding how this wider rational bureaucratic order functions to keep the class system in place, often making it well nigh impossible to move up from the lower rungs. A major source of insight emerged out of his applied research in San Antonio, Texas, working with mostly poor Mexican Americans, and out of which he co-authored an article on "Bureaucracy and the Lower Class" (Sjoberg, Brymer, and Farris 1966). He followed this up with later work focused on bureaucracy and "social triage," emphasizing how elite managers of large organizations, both public and private, often make decisions to sacrifice those who are marginalized in order to preserve the organization and advance its goals (Sjoberg, Vaughan, and Williams 1984).

In spite of this critical view of bureaucracy, Sjoberg, a child of the Great Depression, who grew up on a farm along the West Coast in what he defined as Steinbeck country, did not romanticize the past, appreciated basic technological developments that could make life easier (if not more complex), and supported the necessary efforts reflected in the New Deal of the 1930s that helped to make life more secure in a world that was dramatically changing. In fact, he often mentioned that a major interest he had in writing *The Preindustrial City* (1960) was that it provided an important framework for thinking about the industrial order that emerged over the course of the 20th century, and later in thinking about how that order underwent a new round of transformations in the late 20th into the early 21st century. He explored these later transformations through the lens of bureaucratic capitalism: a global rational-legal order, characterized by large-scale organizational entities that spanned the realms of business and government, wherein the former had achieved some measure of independence from the latter, while still fundamentally relying upon it to exist and persist (Sjoberg 1999).

He never explicitly stated it as such, but I had a sense that he was amazed at how "Reaganites" could simply wish away features of the modern industrial capitalist order as were so astutely described by John Kenneth Galbraith during the post-war era. In fact, it is surprising to me that I probably only gave Galbraith's work serious attention after having left graduate school, even though his books were on the shelves in my parents' house, some of which were likely purchased by my father, who became an aerospace engineer after serving in World War II, and others were likely from college coursework taken by older siblings during the 1970s.

Sjoberg's interests turned decidedly toward the corporation, and then finance capital, in the latter phase of his long intellectual career. By the 2000s, his theorizing about the need for a sociology of human rights had come into sharper focus, while attending not simply to the state as a potential threat and guarantor, but also the corporation (Sjoberg, Gill, and Williams 2001). He also came to write directly about corporations and human rights, and was especially concerned about privatization of military, criminal justice, and security functions of the state, given the secretive nature of corporations as well as the built-in incentives to grow the business (Sjoberg 2005, 2009).

Sjoberg has most directly influenced the formulation of this book, its analytical approach, as well as the use of journalistic case materials, though his longstanding development what I call a Pragmatist-Weberian understanding of the complex relationship between individuals and organizations (Sjoberg, Gill, and Tan 2003; Vaughan and Sjoberg 1984). We shared endless intellectual and wide-ranging conversations about this relationship. I believe that one reason he took an interest in me had to do with my background as a branch operations manager with a large Fortune 500 industrial supply corporation, which I pursued after earning a degree in engineering-management. It is understandable that many find the study of organizations to be abstract, dry, even boring. Yet, with the right framework, they become arenas of endless drama and intrigue.

They are also essential for understanding our lives, our world, and creating alternative futures. Sjoberg was keenly interested in the possibilities for creating alternative futures and developed a theoretical approach he coined "counter-system analysis" for doing so. Ever mindful of the problem of the "iron cage," now long associated with Max Weber, he felt that the vast complex organizational structure of society stifled reflectivity and made meaningful exploration of alternative futures, or pathways, extremely challenging. Countersystem analysis was intended to aid in that process (Sjoberg and Cain 1971; Sjoberg, Gill, and Cain 2003).

The search for alternatives begins with critique. This book seeks to illuminate how in the aftermath of the Reagan revolution, now 40 years in the making, we need to take critical stock of the way in which powerful interests have reformulated institutional life in ways that do not adequately serve the many, but more than adequately serve the few.

References

Akerlof, George A., and Robert J. Shiller. 2015. *Phishing for Phools: The Economics of Manipulation and Deception*. Princeton: Princeton University Press.

Alderman, Liz. 2017. "Uber Dealt Setback After European Court Rules It Is a Taxi Service." *The New York Times*, December 20.

Alter, Adam. 2017. *Irresistible: The Rise of Addictive Technology and the Business of Keeping Us Hooked*. New York: Penguin Press.

Amadae, Sonja M. 2003. *Rationalizing Capitalist Democracy: The Cold War Origins of Rational Choice Liberalism*. Chicago: The University of Chicago Press.

Amazon's Robot Workforce. 2016. "Amazon's Robot Workforce Has Increased by 50 Percent." *Talent Daily*, December 29.

Angell, Marcia. 2015. "Health: The Right Diagnosis and the Wrong Treatment." Review of America's Bitter Pill: Money, Politics, Backroom Deals, and the Fight to Fix Our Broken Healthcare System, by Steven Brill. *New York Review of Books*, April 23.

Arai, Hidenori, et al. 2015. "Japan as the Front-Runner of Super-Aged Societies: Perspectives From Medicine and Medical Care in Japan." *Geriatrics & Gerontology International* 15(6): 673–687.

Baltodano, Marta P. 2017. "The Power Brokers of Neoliberalism: Philanthrocapitalists and Public Education." *Policy Futures in Education* 15(2): 141–156.

Barboza, David. 2010. "After Suicides, Scrutiny of China's Grim Factories." *The New York Times*, June 6.

———. 2016. "How China Built 'iPhone City' With Billions in Perks for Apple's Partner." *The New York Times*, December 29.

Barkan, Joanne. 2011. "Got Dough?: How Billionaires Rule Our Schools." *Dissent* 58(1): 49–57.

———. 2013. "Big Philanthropy vs. Democracy: The Plutocrats Go to School." *Dissent* 60(4): 47–54.

Bartlett, Donald L., and James B. Steele. 2007. "Washington's $8 Billion Shadow." *Vanity Fair*, March.

Bauer, Shane. 2016. "My Four Months as a Private Prison Guard." *Mother Jones*, July/August.

———. 2018. *American Prison: A Reporter's Undercover Journey Into the Business of Punishment*. New York: Penguin Press.

Bell, Daniel. 1973. *The Coming of Post-Industrial Society: A Venture in Social Forecasting*. New York: Basic Books.

Benner, Katie. 2017. "Abuses Hide in the Silence of Nondisparagement Agreements." *The New York Times*, July 21.

Bernanke, Ben. 2016. "What Tools Does the Fed Have Left? Part 3: Helicopter Money." *Brookings Blogs*, April 11. Retrieved September 5, 2019 (www.brookings.edu/blog/ben-bernanke/2016/04/11/what-tools-does-the-fed-have-left-part-3-helicopter-money/).

Berle, Adolf A., and Gadiner C. Means. 1932. *The Modern Corporation and Private Property*. New Brunswick, NJ: Transaction Publishers.

Bernard, Tara Siegel, Tiffany Hsu, Nicole Perlroth, and Ron Lieber. 2017. "Equifax Says Cyberattack May Have Affected 143 Million in the U.S." *The New York Times*, September 7.

Block, Fred. 2008. "Swimming Against the Current: The Rise of a Hidden Developmental State in the United States." *Politics & Society* 36(2): 169–206.

———. [2011] 2016. "Innovation and the Invisible Hand of Government." Pp. 1–26 in *State of Innovation: The U.S. Government's Role in Technology Development*, edited by Fred Block and Matthew R. Keller. New York: The New Press.

Bogost, Ian. 2017a. "Net Neutrality Was Never Enough." *The Atlantic*, December.

———. 2017b. "Neutrality Can't Fix the Internet." *The Atlantic*, November.

Bonacich, Edna, and Khaleelah Hardie. 2006. "Wal-Mart and the Logistics Revolution." Pp. 163–187 in *Wal-Mart: The Face of Twenty-First Century Capitalism*, edited by Nelson Lichtenstein. New York: The New Press.

Bork, Robert H. 1978. *The Antitrust Paradox*. New York: The Free Press.

Bosker, Bianca. 2016. "The Binge Breaker." *The Atlantic*, November.

Boyd, Ross, and Robert J. Holton. 2018. "Technology, Innovation, Employment and Power: Does Robotics and Artificial Intelligence Really Mean Social Transformation." *Journal of Sociology* 54(3): 331–345.

Bradsher, Keith. 2017. "A Robot Revolution, This Time in China." *The New York Times*, May 12.

Brill, Steven. 2013. "Bitter Pill: Why Medical Bills Are Killing Us." *Time* 181(3): 16–55.

———. 2015. *America's Bitter Pill: Money, Politics, Backroom Deals, and the Fight to Fix Our Broken Healthcare System*. New York: Random House.

Browning, Lynnley. 2013. "Inside the Company That Bungled Obamacare." *Newsweek*, November 29.

Buffett, Peter. 2013. "The Charitable-Industrial Complex." *The New York Times*, July 26.

Business Roundtable. 2019. "Business Roundtable Redefines the Purpose of a Corporation to Promote an Economy That Serves All Americans." *Business Roundtable*. Retrieved August 28, 2019 (www.businessroundtable.org/business-roundtable-redefines-the-purpose-of-a-corporation-to-promote-an-economy-that-serves-all-americans).

Calhoun, Craig. 1993. "Civil Society and the Public Sphere." *Public Culture* 5(2): 267–280.

Campbell, Duncan. 2002. "Marketing the New Dogs of War." *The Center for Public Integrity*, October 30. Retrieved June 26, 2019 (https://publicintegrity.org/accountability/marketing-the-new-dogs-of-war/).

Cassidy, John. 2009. *How Markets Fail: The Logic of Economic Calamities*. New York: Farrar, Straus, and Giroux.

———. 2015. "Printing Money: A Radical Solution to the Current Economic Malaise." *The New Yorker*, November 23.

Center for Popular Democracy. 2014. "Charter School Vulnerabilities to Waste, Fraud, and Abuse." *Center for Popular Democracy*. Retrieved January 11, 2019 (https://populardemocracy.org/sites/default/files/FraudandMismgmt5-3-14%28FINALx3.0%29REV.pdhttps://populardemocracy.org/sites/default/files/FraudandMismgmt5-3-14%28FINALx3.0%29REV.pdf).

Centers for Disease Control and Prevention. 2018. "Understanding the Epidemic." *Opioid Overdose*. Retrieved August 6, 2019 (www.cdc.gov/drugoverdose/epidemic/index.html).

Chandrasekaran, Rajiv. 2006. *Imperial Life in the Emerald City: Inside Iraq's Green Zone*. New York: Alfred A. Knopf.

Chen, Brian X. 2018. "I Downloaded the Information That Facebook Has on Me. Yikes." *The New York Times*, April 11.

Chozick, Amy. 2015. "Crime, Clinton, and a New Era." *The New York Times*, May 1.

Christie, Nils. 1993. *Crime Control as Industry: Towards Gulags, Western Style*. New York: Routledge.

Cobb, Jelani. 2018. "William Barber Takes on Poverty and Race in the Age of Trump." *The New Yorker*, May 14.

Coll, Steve. 2014. "Citizen Bezos." *The New York Review of Books*, July 10.

Collins, Keith, and Gabriel J.X. Dance. 2018. "How Researchers Learned to Use Facebook "Likes" to Sway Your Thinking." *The New York Times*, March 20.

Commission on Wartime Contracting in Iraq, Afghanistan (US), United States. Commission on Wartime Contracting in Iraq, & Afghanistan. 2011. "Transforming Wartime Contracting: Controlling Costs, Reducing Risks: Final Report to Congress: Findings and Recommendations for Legislative and Policy Changes. Us Independent Agencies and Commissions." (https://cybercemetery.unt.edu/archive/cwc/20110929213815/http://www.wartime contracting.gov/).

Companies Appear. 2018. "Companies Appear to be Gaining Market Power." *The Economist*, July 7.

Condliffe, Jamie. 2018. "A Brief History of the Impact of E.U. Antitrust Fines on Tech Stocks." *The New York Times*, July 18.

Confessore, Nicholas. 2018. "The Unlikely Activists Who Took on Silicon Valley—and Won!" *The New York Times*, August 14.

Confessore, Nicholas, Gabriel J.X. Dance, Richard Harris, and Mark Hansen. 2018. "The Follower Factory." *The New York Times*, January 27.

Confessore, Nicholas, and Matthew Rosenberg. 2018a. "Spy Contractor's Idea Helped Cambridge Analytica Harvest Facebook Data." *The New York Times*, March 27.

———. 2018b. "Cambridge Analytica to File for Bankruptcy After Misuse of Facebook Data." *The New York Times*, May 2.

Conger, Kate. 2018. "Google Removes 'Don't Be Evil' Clause From Its Code of Conduct." *Gizmodo*, May 18.

Corkery, Michael. 2017a. "Toys 'R' us Files for Bankruptcy, Crippled by Competition and Debt." *The New York Times*, September 19.

———. 2017b. "Is American Retail at a Historic Tipping Point?" *The New York Times*, April 15.

———. 2018a. "Hard Lessons (Thanks Amazon) Breathe New Life Into Retail Stores." *The New York Times*, September 3.

———. 2018b. "Sears, the Original Everything Store, Files for Bankruptcy." *The New York Times*, October 14.

Cowley, Stacey, and Tara Siegel Bernard. 2017. "As Equifax Amassed Ever More Data, Safety Was a Sales Pitch." *The New York Times*, September 23.

Crane, Daniel A. 2018. "Antitrust's Unconventional Politics." *Virginia Law Review* 104: 118.

Crawford, Susan. 2018. "America Needs More Fiber." *Wired*, February 8.

Creswell, Julie. 2018. "Cities' Offers for Amazon Base Are Secrets Even to Many City Leaders." *The New York Times*, August 5.

Crupi, Anthony. 2018. "Despite the Thriller in Minny, Super Bowl Ratings Take a Tumble." *Ad Age*, February 5.

Dalio, Ray. 2019. "Why and How Capitalism Needs to Be Reformed (Part I)." *Economic Principles*. Retrieved April 8, 2019 (www.economicprinciples.org/Why-and-How-Capitalism-Needs-To-Be-Reformed/).

Dance, Gabriel J.X., Nicholas Confessore, and Michael LaForgia. 2018. "Facebook Gave Device Makers Deep Access to Data on Users and Friends." *The New York Times*, June 3.

Dance, Gabriel J.X., Michael LaForgia, and Nicholas Confessore. 2018. "As Facebook Raised a Privacy Wall, It Carved an Opening for Tech Giants." *The New York Times*, December 18.

Davies, William. 2017. "Elite Power Under Advanced Neoliberalism." *Theory, Culture, & Society* 34(5–6): 227–250.

Davis, Gerald F. 2016. *The Vanishing American Corporation: Navigating the Hazards of a New Economy*. Oakland, CA: Berrett-Koehler Publishers, Inc.

Dayen, David. 2015. "Bring Back Antitrust." *The American Prospect*, November 9.

———. 2017a. "Big Tech: The New Predatory Capitalism." *The American Prospect*, December 26.

———. 2017b. "The Rehabilitation of Antitrust." *The American Prospect*, December 22.

Del Rey, Jason, and Rani Molla. 2018. "This Is the Amazon Everyone Should Have Feared—And It Has Nothing to Do With Its Retail Business." *Recode*, July 26.

Dewey, Caitlin. 2016. "98 Personal Data Points That Facebook Uses to Target Ads to You." *The Washington Post*, August 19.

Domhoff, G. William. 2013. *The Myth of Liberal Ascendancy: Corporate Dominance From the Great Depression to the Great Recession*. Boulder, CO: Paradigm.

Douglas, Karen Manges, and Rogelio Saenz. 2013. "The Criminalization of Immigrants & the Immigration-Industrial Complex." *Daedalus* 142(3): 199–227.

Douglas, Karen Manges, Gideon Sjoberg, Rogelio Saenz, and David G. Embrick. 2018. "Bureaucratic Capitalism, Mass Incarceration and Race and Ethnicity in America." Pp. 365–388 in *Handbook of the Sociology of Racial and Ethnic Relations*, edited by Pinar Batur and Joe R. Feagin. New York: Springer.

Dreifus, Claudia. 2017. "Why We Can't Look Away From Our Screens." *The New York Times*, March 6.

Drucker, Jesse, and Simon Bowers. 2017. "After a Tax Crackdown, Apple Found a New Shelter for Its Profits." *The New York Times*, November 6.

DuGay, Paul. 2000. *In Praise of Bureaucracy*. London: Sage.

Duhigg, Charles. 2018. "The Case Against Google." *The New York Times*, February 20.

Duhigg, Charles, and David Barboza. 2012. "In China, Human Costs Are Built Into an iPad." *The New York Times*, January 25.

Duhigg, Charles, and Keith Bradsher. 2012. "How the U.S. Lost Out on iPhone Work." *The New York Times*, January 21.

Duhigg, Charles, and David Kocieniewski. 2012. "How Apple Sidesteps Billions in Taxes." *The New York Times*, April 28.

Dwoskin, Elizabeth. 2017. "Facebook's Willingness to Copy Rival's Apps Is Seen as Hurting Innovation." *The Washington Post*, August 10.

Dwyer, Colin. 2018. "U.S. Life Expectancy Drops Amid 'Disturbing' Rise in Overdoses and Suicides." *NPR Health*, November 29. Retrieved June 6, 2019 (www.npr.org/2018/11/29/671844884/u-s-life-expectancy-drops-amid-disturbing-rise-in-overdoses-and-suicides#mortality).

Editorial Board. 2018. "How Sears Was the Amazon of Its Day." *The New York Times*, October 15.

———. 2019. "How Silicon Valley Puts the 'Con' in Consent." *The New York Times*, February 2.

Elkind, Peter. 2016. "Business Gets Schooled." *Fortune*, January 1.

Elkind, Peter, and Doris Burke. 2013. "Amazon's (Not So Secret) War on Taxes." *Fortune*, May 23.

Ellis, Charles D., Alicia H. Munnell, and Andrew D. Eschtruth. 2014. *Falling Short: The Coming Retirement Crisis and What to Do About It*. New York: Oxford University Press.

Facebook's New Motto. 2017. "Facebook's New Motto: 'Move Fast and Please Please Please Don't Break Anything'." *Halting Problem*, May 21.

Fang, Lee. 2011. "How Online Learning Companies Bought America's Schools." *The Nation*, November 16.

———. 2014. "Venture Capitalists Are Poised to 'Disrupt' Everything About the Education Market." *The Nation*, September 25.

Farrell, Sean. 2019. "Unions Lobby Investors to Press Amazon Over UK Working Conditions." *The Guardian*, May 20.

Folbre, Nancy. 2009. *Greed, Lust, and Gender: A History of Economic Ideas*. New York: Oxford University Press.

Foroohar, Rana. 2015. "Why You Can Thank the Government for Your iPhone." *Time*, October 27.

Fortune. 2019. "Fortune 500." *Fortune*, Retrieved June 11, 2019 (http://fortune.com/fortune500/list/).

Fox, Justin. 2014. "How Silicon Valley Became the Man." *Harvard Business Review*, January 9.

Frank, Thomas. 1997. *The Conquest of Cool: Business Culture, Counterculture, and the Rise of Hip Consumerism*. Chicago: The University of Chicago Press.

———. 2000. "The Rise of Market Populism." *The Nation*, October 12.

Freeland, Chrystia. 2011. "The Rise of the New Global Elite." *The Atlantic*, January/February.

———. 2012. *Plutocrats: The Rise of the New Global Super Rich and the Fall of Everyone Else*. New York: Penguin Books.

Frej, Willa. 2018. "U.S. Life Expectancy Continues to Fall as Overdose and Suicide Rates Soar." *Huffington Post*, November 29.

Frenkel, Sheera. 2018. "Facebook's Privacy Changes Leave Developers Steaming." *The New York Times*, April 30.

Frenkel, Sheera, and Katie Benner. 2018. "To Stir Discord in 2016, Russians Turned Most Often to Facebook." *The New York Times*, February 17.

Frenkel, Sheera, and Nellie Bowles. 2018. "Facebook Employees in an Uproar Over Executive's Leaded Memo." *The New York Times*, March 30.

Frenkel, Sheera, Nicholas Confessore, Cecilia Kang, Matthew Rosenberg, and Jack Nicas. 2018. "Delay, Deny and Deflect: How Facebook's Leaders Fought Through Crisis." *The New York Times*, November 14.

Friedman, Milton. 1955. "The Role of Government in Education." (https://la.utexas.edu/users/hcleaver/330T/350kPEEFriedmanRoleOfGovttable.pdf).

———. 1962. *Capitalism and Freedom*. Chicago: The University of Chicago Press.

———. 1970. "The Social Responsibility of Business Is to Increase Profits." *New York Times Magazine*, November 13.

Friedman, Milton, and Rose D. Friedman. 1980. *Free to Choose: A Personal Statement*. New York: Harcourt. Inc.

Friedman, Thomas L. 2005. *The World Is Flat: A Brief History of the Twenty-First Century*. New York: Macmillan.

Funk, McKenzie. 2016. Cambridge Analytica and the Secret Agenda of a Facebook Quiz." *The New York Times*, November 19.

Gajanan, Mahita. 2015. "Young Women on Instagram and Self-esteem: 'I Absolutely Feel Insecure.'" *The Guardian*, November 4.

———. 2017. "More Than Half of the Internet's Sales Growth Now Comes From Amazon." *Fortune*, February 1.

Galbraith, James K. 2008. *The Predator State: How Conservatives Abandoned the Free Market and Why Liberals Should Too*. New York: Free Press.

Galbraith, John K. 1952. *American Capitalism*. Boston: Houghton Mifflin.

———. 1958. *The Affluent Society*. Boston: Houghton Mifflin.

———. 1967. *The New Industrial State*. Boston: Houghton Mifflin.

———. 2004. *The Economics of Innocent Fraud: Truth for Our Time*. Boston: Houghton Mifflin.

Galloway, Scott. 2017a. *The Four: The Hidden DNA of Amazon, Apple, Facebook, and Google*. New York: Penguin.

———. 2017b. "Bread Crumbs." *Daily Insights*, September 8. Retrieved October 4, 2018 (www.l2inc.com/daily-insights/no-mercy-no-malice/bread-crumbs).

———. 2018. "Silicon Valley's Tax-Avoiding, Job-Killing, Soul-Sucking Machine." *Esquire*, February 8.

Gardner, Matthew. 2018. "Amazon Paid Zero in Federal Taxes in 2017, Gets $789 Million Windfall From New Tax Law." *Institute on Taxation and Economic Policy*. Retrieved October 3, 2018 (https://itep.org/amazon-inc-paid-zero-in-federal-taxes-in-2017-gets-789-million-windfall-from-new-tax-law/).

———. 2019. "Amazon in Its Prime: Doubles Profit, Pays $0 in Federal Income Taxes." *Institute on Taxation and Economic Policy*. Retrieved May 28, 2019 (https://itep.org/amazon-in-its-prime-doubles-profits-pays-0-in-federal-income-taxes/).

Gelles, David. 2018. Tech Backlash Grows as Investors Press Apple to Act on Children's Use." *The New York Times*, January 8.

Gelles, David, and David Yaffe-Bellany. 2019. "Shareholder Value Is No Longer Everything, Top C.E.O.s Say." *The New York Times*, August 19.

General Sales Taxes. 2018. "The Urban Institute." Retrieved October 9, 2018 (www.urban.org/policy-centers/cross-center-initiatives/state-local-finance-initiative/projects/state-and-local-backgrounders/sales-taxes#revenue).

George, Susan. 2015. *Shadow Sovereigns: How Global Corporations Are Seizing Power*. Cambridge: Polity.

Gettleman, Jeffrey. 2004. "Enraged Mop in Falluja Kills 4 American Contractors." *The New York Times*, March 31.

Giddens, Anthony. 2000. *Runaway World: How Globalization Is Reshaping Our Lives*. New York: Routledge.

———. 2002. *The Third Way: The Renewal of Social Democracy*. Cambridge: Polity.

Glaser, April. 2017."The U.S. Will Be Hit Worse by Job Automation Than Other Major Economies." *Recode*, March 25.

Goel, Vindu. 2018. "In India, Facebook's WhatsApp Plays Central Role in Elections." *The New York Times*, May 14.

Gomory, Ralph. 2011. "The Innovation Delusion." *Huffington Post*, May 25.

———. 2017. "Why Americans Are Right to Rethink Free Trade." *PBS Newshour: Column*, August 14. Retrieved October 8 (www.pbs.org/newshour/making-sense/column-americans-right-rethink-free-trade/).

Gomory, Ralph, and William J. Baumol. 2000. *Global Trade and Conflicting National Interests*. Cambridge, MA: MIT Press.

Gomory, Ralph, and Richard Sylla. 2013. "The American Corporation." *Daedalus* 14(2): 102–118.

Goodman, David J. 2019. "Amazon Pulls Out of Planned New York City Headquarters." *The New York Times*, February 14.

Gordon, Michael R. 2008. "Fateful Choice on Iraq Army Bypassed Debate." *The New York Times*, March 17.

Graham, Mark, and Joe Shaw, eds. 2017. *Towards a Fairer Gig Economy*. London: Meatspace Press.

Granville, Kevin. 2018. "Facebook and Cambridge Analytica: What You Need to Know as Fallout Widens." *The New York Times*, March 19.

Grocer, Stephen. 2018a. "A Record $2.5 Trillion in Mergers Were Announced in the First Half of 2018." *The New York Times*, July 3.

———. 2018b. "The Tech Stock Fall Lost These 5 Companies $800 Billion in Market Value." *The New York Times*, November 20.

Gross, Allie. 2017 "Betsy DeVos' Accountability Problem." *The Atlantic*, January.

Grossman, Lev. 2014. "Inside Facebook's Plan to Wire the World." *Time*, December 15.

Grove, Andy. 2010. "How America Can Create Jobs." *Businessweek*, July 1.

Gruber, Johathan, and Simon Johnson. 2019. *Jump-Starting America: How Breakthrough Science Can Revive Economic Growth and the American Dream*. New York: Public Affairs, Hachette Book Group.

Grullon, Gustavo, Yelena Larkin, and Roni Michaely. 2019. "Are US Industries Becoming More Concentrated?" *Review of Finance* 23(4): 697–743.

Grynbaum, Michael M., and John Herrman. 2018. "New Foils for the Right: Google and Facebook." *The New York Times*, March 6.

Guangcheng, Chen. 2018. "Apple Can't Resist Playing by China's Rules." *The New York Times*, January 23.

Habermas, Jurgen. 1984. *The Theory of Communicative Action: Reason and the Rationalization of Society*, Vol. 1. Boston: Beacon Press.

———. 1987. *Lifeworld and System: A Critique of Functionalist Reason*. Vol. 2 of the *Theory of Communicative Action*. Boston: Beacon Press.

Hacker, Jacob S. 2008. *The Great Risk Shift: The New Economic Insecurity and the Decline of the American Dream*. New York: Oxford University Press.

Hacker, Jacob S., and Paul Pierson. 2016. *American Amnesia: How the War on Government Led Us to Forget What Made America Prosper*. New York: Simon & Schuster.

Hagedorn, Ann. 2014. *The Invisible Soldiers: How America Outsourced Our Security*. New York: Simon & Schuster.

Hakim, Danny, Roni Caryn Rabin, and William K. Rashbaum. 2019. "Lawsuits Lay Bare Sackler Family's Role in Opioid Crisis." *The New York Times*, April 1.

Hakim, Danny, William K. Rashbaum, and Roni Caryn Rabin. 2019. "The Giants at the Heart of the Opioid Crisis." *The New York Times*, April 22.

Hallinan, Joseph T. 2001. *Going Up the River: Travels in a Prison Nation*. New York: Random House.

Hamilton, Isobel Asher, and Aine Cain. 2019. "Amazon Warehouse Employees Speak Out About the 'Brutal' Reality of Working During the Holidays, When 60-hour Weeks Are Mandatory and Ambulance Calls Are Common." *Business Insider*, February 19.

Hanbury, Mary. 2018. "This Year's Super Bowl Commercials Are More Expensive Than Ever— Here's Your Complete Guide to All the Ads That Will Air." *Business Insider*, February 4.

Hansmann, Henry, and Reinier Kraakman. 2001. "The End of History for Corporate Law." *Georgetown Law Journal*: 439.

Harvey, David. 2005. *A Brief History of Neoliberalism*. Oxford: Oxford University Press.

Hayek, Friedrich A. 1944. *The Road to Serfdom.* Chicago: University of Chicago Press.

Hempel, Jessi. 2016. "Inside Facebook's Ambitious Plan to Connect the Whole World." *Wired*, January 19.

Hern, Alex. 2018. "Facebook to Stop Allowing Data Brokers Such as Experian to Target Users." *The Guardian*, March 29.

Herrman, John. 2016. "Inside Facebook's (Totally Insane, Unintentionally Gigantic, Hyper-partisan) Political Media Machine." *New York Times Magazine*, August 24.

———. 2017. "What Will Service Work Look Like Under Amazon?" *The New York Times*, July 18.

Higham, Scott, and Lenny Bernstein. 2017. "The Drug Industry's Triumph Over the DEA." *The Washington Post*, October 15.

Hjelmgaard, Kim. 2018. "Cambridge Analytica Active in Elections, Big Data Projects for Years." *USA Today*, March 22.

Hoopes, James. 2006. "Growth Through Knowledge: Wal-Mart, High-Technology, and the Ever Less Visible Hand of the Manager." Pp. 83–104 in *Wal-Mart: The Face of Twenty-First Century Capitalism*, edited by Nelson Lichtenstein. New York: The New Press.

———. 2011. *Corporate Dreams: Big Business in American Democracy From the Great Depression to the Great Recession.* Piscataway, NJ: Rutgers University Press.

Horwitz, Jeff, and Deepa Seetharaman. 2019. "Facebook Posts Strong Earnings, Revenue Growth." *The Wall Street Journal*, July 24.

Hughes, Chris. 2019. "It's Time to Break Up Facebook." *The New York Times*, May 9.

Hursh, David. 2015. *The End of Public Schools: The Corporate Reform Agenda to Privatize Education.* New York: Routledge.

Ip, Greg. 2018. "The Antitrust Case Against Facebook, Google, and Amazon: A Few Technology Giants Dominate Their Worlds Just as Standard Oil and AT&T Once Did. Should They Be Broken Up?" *The Wall Street Journal*, January 16.

Isaac, Mike, and Natasha Singer. 2017. "New Facebook App for Children Ignites Debate Among Families." *The New York Times*, December 4.

———. 2019. "Facebook Antitrust Inquiry Shows Big Tech's Freewheeling Era Is Past." *The New York Times*, July 24.

Isaac, Mike, and Daisuke Wakabayashi. 2017. "Russian Influence Reached 126 Million Through Facebook Alone." *The New York Times*, October 30.

Isenberg, David. 1997. *Soldiers of Fortune Ltd.: A Profile of Today's Private Sector Corporate Mercenary Firms.* Washington, DC: Center for Defense Information.

Is There a Concentration Problem. 2017. *Is There a Concentration Problem in America?* Conference Proceedings at the Stigler Center for the Study of the Economy and the State at the University of Chicago Booth School of Business. (https://research.chicagobooth. edu/stigler/events/single-events/march-27-2017).

Ivory, Danielle, and Robert Faturechi. 2017. "The Deep Industry Ties of Trump's Deregulation Teams." *The New York Times*, July 11.

Iyer, Bala, and U. Srinivasa Rangan. 2016. "Google vs. the EU Explains the Digital Economy." *Harvard Business Review*, December 12.

Johnson, Bobby. 2010. "Privacy No Longer a Social Norm, Says Facebook Founder." *The Guardian*, January 10.

Jones, Brandon. 2016. "What Information Does Facebook Collect About Its Users?" *Psafe*, November 29. Retrieved February 21, 2018 (www.psafe.com/en/blog/information-facebook-collect-users/).

Kafka, Peter. 2016. "Google and Facebook Are Booming. Is the Rest of Digital Ad Business Sinking?" *Recode*, November 2.

Kahle, Kathleen M., and Rene M. Stulz. 2017. "Is the US Public Corporation in Trouble?" *Journal of Economic Perspectives* 31(3): 67–88.

Kang, Cecilia. 2017. "Mark Warner: Tech Millionaire Who Became Tech's Critic in Congress." *The New York Times*, October 29.

———. 2018. "Turn Off Messenger Kids, Health Experts Plead to Facebook." *The New York Times*, January 30.

———. 2019. "F.T.C. Approves Facebook Fine of About $5 Billion." *The New York Times*, July 12.

Kang, Cecilia, and Sheera Frenkel. 2018. "Facebook Says Cambridge Analytica Harvested Data of Up to 87 Million Users." *The New York Times*, April 4.

Kang, Cecilia, and David E. Sanger. 2019. "Huawei Is a Target as Trump Moves to Ban Foreign Telecom Gear." *The New York Times*, May 15.

Kang, Cecilia, David Streitfeld, and Annie Karni. 2019. "Antitrust Troubles Snowball for Tech Giants as Lawmakers Join In." *The New York Times*, June 3.

Kauzlarich, David, Christopher Mullins, and Rick Matthews. 2003. "A Complicity Continuum of State Crime." *Contemporary Justice Review: Issues in Criminal, Social, and Restorative Justice* 6(3): 241–254.

Keynes, John M. 1936. *The General Theory of Interest, Employment, and Money*. London: Macmillan.

Khan, Lina M. 2017a. "Amazon's Antitrust Paradox." *Yale LJ* 126: 710.

———. 2017b. "Amazon Bites Off Even More Monopoly Power." *The New York Times*, June 21.

———. 2018. "What Makes Tech Platforms So Powerful?" *ProMarket*, April 5. Retrieved June 6, 2018 (https://promarket.org/makes-tech-platforms-powerful/).

Kivisto, Peter. 2004. *Key Ideas in Sociology*. 2nd ed. Thousand Oaks, CA: Pine Forge Press.

Klein, Naomi. 2001. *No Logo*. London: Flamingo.

Krugman, Paul. 2013. "The Big Kludge." *The New York Times*, October 27.

———. 2014. "Amazon's Monopsony Is Not O.K." *The New York Times*, October 19.

Kuttner, Robert. 2015. *Debtor's Prison: The Politics of Austerity Versus Possibility*. New York: Vintage Books.

LaForgia, Michael, and Gabriel J.X. Dance. 2018. "Facebook Gave Data Access to Chinese Firm Flagged by U.S. Intelligence." *The New York Times*, June 5.

Layton, Lyndsey. 2014. "How Bill Gates Pulled Off the Swift Common Core Revolution." *The Washington Post*, June 7.

Lee, Carol, Courtney Kube, and Josh Lederman. 2018. "Officials Worry Trump May Back Erik Prince Plan to Privatize War in Afghanistan." *NBC News*, August 17. Retrieved December 16, 2018 (www.nbcnews.com/news/military/officials-worry-trump-may-back-erik-prince-plan-privatize-war-n901401?cid=sm_npd_ms_tw_ma).

Lee, Michelle Ye Hee. 2015. "Does the United States Really Have 5 Percent of the World's Population and One Quarter of the World's Prisoners?" *The Washington Post*, April 30.

Leonhardt, David. 2008. "A Free-Market-Loving, Big-Spending, Fiscally Conservative Wealth Redistributionist." *The New York Times*, August 24.

Levin, Sam. 2018a. "Facebook Documents Published by UK—The Key Takeaways." *The Guardian*, December 5.

———. 2018b. "Is Facebook a Publisher? In Public It Says No, But in Court It Says Yes." *The Guardian*, July 3.

Lewis, Michael. 2018. *The Fifth Risk*. New York: W.W. Norton & Company.

Lichtenstein, Nelson. 2006. "Wal-Mart: A Template for Twenty-First Century Capitalism." Pp. 3–30 in *Wal-Mart: The Face of Twenty-First Century Capitalism*, edited by Nelson Lichtenstein. New York: The New Press.

Lieber, Chavie. 2019. "Suicide Attempts and Mental Breakdowns: 911 Calls From Amazon Warehouses Reveal That Some Workers Are Struggling." *Vox*, March 11.

Liptak, Adam, and Jack Nicas. 2019. "Supreme Court Allows Antitrust Lawsuit Against Apple to Proceed." *The New York Times*, May 13.

Lohr, Steve. 2019a. "State Attorneys General Said to Be Near Formal Investigation of Tech Companies." *The New York Times*, August 19.

———. 2019b. "Chris Hughes Worked to Create Facebook. Now, He Is Working to Break It Up." *The New York Times*, July 25.

Lohr, Steve, Mike Isaac, and Nathaniel Popper. 2019. "Tech Hearings: Congress Unites to Take Aim at Amazon, Apple, Facebook and Google." *The New York Times*, July 16.

Longman, Phillip, and Paul S. Hewitt. 2014. "After Obamacare." *Washington Monthly*, January/February.

Lopez, German. 2017. "The Opioid Epidemic, Explained." *Vox*, December 21.

Lynn, Barry. 2006. "Breaking the Chain: The Antitrust Case Against Wal-Mart." *Harpers*, July.

———. 2010. *Cornered: The New Monopoly Capitalism and the Economics of Destruction.* Hoboken, NJ: John Wiley & Sons, Inc.

———. 2015. "The New China Syndrome." *Harper's*, November.

Mac, Ryan, Charlie Warzel, and Alex Kantrowitz. 2018. "Growth at Any Cost: Top Facebook Executive Defended Data Collection in 2016 Memo—And Warned That Facebook Could Get People Killed." *BuzzFeed News*, March 29.

MacFarquhar, Neil. 2018. "Inside the Russian Troll Factory: Zombies and a Breakneck Pace." *The New York Times*, February 18.

MacLean, Nancy. 2017. *Democracy in Chains: The Deep History of the Radical Right's Stealth Plan for America.* New York: Viking.

Madrick, Jeff. 2014. "Innovation: The Government Was Crucial After All." *The New York Review of Books*, April 24.

Madrigal, Alexis C. 2017. "Silicon Valley's Big Three vs. Detroit's Golden-Age Big Three." *The Atlantic*, May.

Manjoo, Farhad. 2017a. "Apple's Silence in China Sets a Dangerous Precedent." *The New York Times*, July 31.

———. 2017b. "What the Tax Bill Fails to Address: Technology's Tsunami." *The New York Times*, December 20.

———. 2018a. "How to Combat China's Rise in Tech: Federal Spending, Not Tariffs." *The New York Times*, July 18.

———. 2018b. "It's Time for Apple to Build a Less Addictive iPhone." *The New York Times*, January 17.

———. 2018c. "How Tech Companies Conquered America's Cities." *The New York Times*, June 20.

Manyika, James, Susan Lund, Jacques Bughin, Kelsey Robinson, Jan Mischke, and Deepa Mahajan. 2016. "Independent Work: Choice, Necessity, and the Gig Economy." *McKinsey & Company*. Retrieved May 22, 2019 (www.mckinsey.com/featured-insights/employment-and-growth/independent-work-choice-necessity-and-the-gig-economy).

Martin, Timothy W. 2017. "401(k) Pioneers Lament What They Started—Retirement-Saving Vehicles Fall Short of Early Backers Rosy Expectations." *Wall Street Journal*, January 3.

Martineau, Paris. 2018. "How the Pentagon's Move to the Cloud Landed in the Mud." *Wired*, October 10.

Masters, Kiri. 2018. "A Simple Guide to Amazon's Complicated Advertising Business." *Forbes*, June 8.

Matsa, Katerina E., and Elisa Shearer. 2018. "News Use Across Social Media Platforms 2018." *Pew Research Center*. Retrieved May 10, 2019 (www.journalism.org/2018/09/10/news-use-across-social-media-platforms-2018/).

Mayer, Jane. 2016 *Dark Money: The Hidden History of the Billionaires Behind the Rise of the Radical Right*. New York: Doubleday.

Mazzucato, Marianna. 2011. *The Entrepreneurial State*. London: Demos.

———. 2013. "Taxpayers Helped Apple, But Apple Won't Help Them." *Harvard Business Review*, March 8.

McCracken, Harry. 2019. "Meet the Woman Behind Amazon's Explosive Growth." *Fast Company*, April 11.

McGoey, Linsey. 2015. *No Such Thing as a Free Gift: The Gates Foundation and the Price of Philanthropy*. London: Verso.

McGreal, Chris. 2009. "Revealed: Millions Spent by Lobby Firms Fighting Obama Health Reforms." *The Guardian*, October 1.

McKeever, Brice. 2015. "The NonProfit Sector in Brief 2015: Public Charities, Giving, and Volunteering." *Urban Institute*, Washington, DC. Retrieved August 25, 2016 (www.urban.org/research/publication/nonprofit-sector-brief-2015-public-charities-giving-and-volunteering).

McKibben, Bill. 2018. "How Extreme Weather Is Shrinking the Planet." *The New Yorker*, November 26.

Medin, Milo, and Louie Gillman. 2019. *The 5G Ecosystem: Risks and Opportunities for DoD*. Defense Innovation Board, Washington D.C., United States.

Meek, James. 2014. *Private Island: Why Britain Now Belongs to Someone Else*. London: Verso.

Meier, Barry. 2018. "Origins of an Epidemic: Purdue Pharma Knew Its Opioids Were Widely Abused." *The New York Times*, May 29.

Metz, Cade. 2015. "Why WhatsApp Only Needs 50 Engineers for Its 900M Users." *Wired*, September 15.

———. 2017. "How Facebook's Ad System Works." *The New York Times*, October 12.

Michaels, Samantha. 2018. "Leaked Memo Reveals Trump's Gift to Private Prison Companies." *Mother Jones*, January 30.

Miller, Claire Cain. 2016. "The Long-Term Jobs Killer Is Not China. It's Automation." *The New York Times*, December 21.

Mills, C. Wright. 1956. *The Power Elite*. New York: Oxford University Press.

Mitchell, Stacy, and Olivia Lavecchia. 2018. "Report: Amazon's Next Frontier: Your City's Purchasing." *Institute for Local Self-Reliance*. Retrieved September 20, 2018 (https://ilsr.org/amazon-and-local-government-purchasing/).

Mizruchi, Mark S. 2013. *The Fracturing of the American Corporate Elite*. Cambridge, MA: Harvard University Press.

———. 2017. "The Power Elite in Historical Context: A Reevaluation of Mills's Thesis, Then and Now." *Theory and Society* 46: 95–116.

Mokyr, Joel. 2002. *The Gifts of Athena: Historical Origins of the Knowledge Economy*. Princeton: Princeton University Press.

———. 2003. "The Knowledge Society: Theoretical and Historical Underpinnings." *AdHoc Expert Group on Knowledge Systems*, United Nations, NY.

———. 2011. "The Commons of Knowledge: A Historical Perspective." *The Annual Proceedings of the Wealth and Well-Being of Nations*, Volume IV (https://papers.ssrn.com/sol3/papers.cfm?abstract_id=2176273).

Mokyr, Joel, Chris Vickers, and Nicolas L. Ziebarth. 2015. "The History of Technological Anxiety and the Future of Economic Growth: Is This Time Different?" *Journal of Economic Perspectives* 29(3): 31–50.

Moses III, Hamilton, David H. M. Matheson, E. Ray Dorsey, Benjamin P. George, David Sadoff, and Satoshi Yoshimura. 2013. "The Anatomy of Health Care in the United States." *JAMA* 310(18): 1947–1964.

Mossialos, Elias, Martin Wenzl, Robin Osborn, and Dana Sarnak, eds. 2016. *International Profiles of Health Care Systems*. New York, NY: The Commonwealth Fund. Retrieved March 24, 2016 (www.commonwealthfund.org/~/media/files/publications/fund-report/2016/jan/1857_mossialos_intl_profiles_2015_v7.pdf).

Mozur, Paul. 2017a. "The World's Biggest Tech Companies Are No Longer Just American." *The New York Times*, August 17.

———. 2017b. "China Spreads Propaganda to U.S. on Facebook, a Platform It Bans at Home." *The New York Times*, November 8.

Mozur, Paul, Mark Scott, and Mike Isaac. 2017. "Facebook Faces a New World as Officials Rein in a Wild Web." *The New York Times*, September 17.

Mozur, Paul, Daisuke Wakabayashi, and Nick Wingfield. 2017. "Apple Opening Data Center in China to Comply With Cybersecurity Law." *The New York Times*, July 12.

Mueller III, Robert S. 2019. "Report on the Investigation Into Russian Interference in the 2016 Presidential Election." Volumes I & II. (Redacted version of 4/18/2019).

Mulrooney, John J. 2017. "Current Navigation Points in Drug Diversion Law: Hidden Rocks in Shallow, Murky, Drug-Infested Waters. *Marquette Law Review* 101: 333.

Mundy, Liz. 2017. "Why Is Silicon Valley So Awful to Women?" *The Atlantic*, April.

Murgia, Madhumita. 2019. "Google Accused of Secretly Feeding Personal Data to Advertisers." *The Financial Times*, September 4.

National Center for Education Statistics. 2019. "Public Charter Enrollment." *National Center for Education Statistics*. Retrieved July 11, 2019 (https://nces.ed.gov/programs/coe/indicator_cgb.asp).

Nicas, Jack. 2018a. "Google Shrugs Off $5.1 Billion Fine With Another Big Quarter." *The New York Times*, July 23.

———. 2018b. "Apple Says It Will Buy Back $100 Billion in Stock." *The New York Times*, May 1.

Nicas, Jack, and Matthew Rosenberg. 2018. "A Look Inside the Tactics of Definers, Facebook's Attack Dog." *The New York Times*, November 15.

Nickel, Patricia Mooney. 2012. *Public Sociology and Civil Society: Governance, Politics, and Power*. Boulder, CO: Paradigm.

Nocera, Joe. 2015. "Jeff Bezos and the Amazon Way." *The New York Times*, August 21.

Once Considered. 2017. "Once Considered a Boon to Democracy, Social Media Have Started to Look Like Its Nemesis." *The Economist*, November 4.

Open Secrets. 2015. "Influencing and Lobbying." *Open Secrets*. Retrieved March 23, 2016 (www.opensecrets.org/lobby/list_indus.php).

Oprysko, Caitllin, and Zach Montellaro. 2019. "Pennsylvania GOP Rep. Tom Marino to Retire This Month." *Politico*, January 17.

Orrange, Robert M. 2017. "Complex Organization and Work." Pp. 226–235 in *The Cambridge Handbook of Sociology*, Vol. 1, edited by Kathleen Odell Korgen. New York: Cambridge.

Ortutay, Barbara. 2018. "Facebook Isn't Backing Off Messenger Kids, Despite Critics." *USA Today*, February 16.

Paradise Papers Reporting Team. 2017. "Paradise Papers: Apple's Secret Tax Bolthole Revealed." *BBC News*, November 6. Retrieved August 20, 2018 (www.bbc.com/news/world-us-canada-41889787).

Parker, Richard. 2005. *John Kenneth Galbraith: His Life, His Politics, His Economics*. Chicago: The University of Chicago Press.

Pauly, Madison. 2018. "Trump's Immigration Crackdown Is a Boom Time for Private Prisons." *Mother Jones*, May/June.

PBS Newshour. 2019. "How Federal Case Against Drug Distributor Could Change Opioid Fight." *PBS Newshour*, April 24. Retrieved May 29, 2019 (www.pbs.org/newshour/show/how-federal-case-against-drug-distributor-could-change-opioid-fight).

Perlroth, Nicole, Sheera Frenkel, and Scott Shane. 2018. "Facebook Exit Hints at Dissent on Handling Russian Trolls." *The New York Times*, March 19.

Petrovic, Misha, and Gary C. Hamilton. 2006. "Making Global Markets: Wal-Mart and Its Suppliers." Pp. 107–141 in *Wal-Mart: The Face of Twenty-First Century Capitalism*, edited by Nelson Lichtenstein. New York: The New Press.

Pew Research Center. 2015. "U.S. Public Becoming Less Religious." Retrieved May 7, 2018 (http://assets.pewresearch.org/wp-content/uploads/sites/11/2015/11/201.11.03_RLS_II_full_report.pdf).

Phillips, Matt. 2018. "Apple's $1 Trillion Milestone Reflects Rise of Powerful Megacompanies." *The New York Times*, August 2.

Pilkington, Ed. 2017a. "Why the UN Is Investigating Extreme Poverty . . . in America, the World's Richest Nation." *The Guardian*, December 1.

———. 2017b. "A Journey Through the Land of Extreme Poverty: Welcome to America." *The Guardian*, December 15.

Pollitz, Karen, Jennifer Tolbert, and Rosa Ma. 2014. "Survey of Health Insurance Marketplace Assister Programs." Washington, D.C.: Kaiser Family Foundation. (http://kff.org/health-reform/report/survey-of-healthinsurance-marketplace-assister-programs).

Porter, Michael E., and Mark R. Kramer. 2002. "The Comparative Advantage of Corporate Philanthropy." *Harvard Business Review*, December.

Porzecanski, Katia, Gillian Tan, and Sonali Basak. 2019. "Billionaires Under Fire Confront Wealth Gap at Milken Conference." *Bloomberg Businessweek*, May 1.

Private Security Contracting in Iraq and Afghanistan. 2007. "Hearing Before U.S. House of Representatives Committee on Oversight and Government Reform." October 2. (https://oversight.house.gov/legislation/hearings/hearing-on-private-security-contracting-in-iraq-and-afghanistan-0).

Przybylski, Andrew K., and Netta Weinstein. 2017. "A Large-Scale Test of the Goldilocks Hypothesis: Quantifying the Relations Between Digital-Screen Use and the Mental Well-Being of Adolescents." *Psychological Science* 28(2): 204–215.

Rajagopalan, Megha, Lam Thuy Vo, and Aung Naing Soe. 2018. "How Facebook Failed the Rohingya in Myanmar." *BuzzFeed News*, August 27.

Ramm, Benjamin. 2017. What the Myth of Faust Can Teach Us." *BBC Culture*, September 26. Retrieved September 7, 2018 (www.bbc.com/culture/story/20170907-what-the-myth-of-faust-can-teach-us).

Ravitch, Dianne. 2014. *Reign of Error: The Hoax of the Privatization Movement and the Danger to America's Public Schools*. New York: Vintage Books.

Reagan, Gillian. 2009. "The Evolution of Facebook's Mission Statement." *Observer*, July 13.

Reich, Robert. 2015. *Saving Capitalism: For the Many, Not the Few*. New York: Vintage Books.

The Rise. 2019. "The Rise of Millennial Socialism." *The Economist*, February 14.

Risen, James, and Matthew Rosenberg. 2015. "Blackwater's Legacy Goes Beyond Public View." *The New Times*, April 14.

Ritzer, George. 2015. "Prosumer Capitalism." *Sociological Quarterly* 56(3): 413–445.

Ritzer, George, and Steven Miles. 2019. "The Changing Nature of Consumption and the Intensification of McDonaldization in the Digital Age." *Journal of Consumer Culture* 19(1): 3–20.

Rohr, John A. 1986. *To Run a Constitution: The Legitimacy of the Administrative State*. Lawrence: The University of Kansas Press.

Romm, Tony. 2018. "Apple, Amazon, Facebook and Google Spent Nearly $50 Million—A Record—to Influence the U.S. Government in 2017." *Recode*, January 23.

Roose, Kevin. 2018a. "On Russia, Facebook Sends a Message It Wishes It Hadn't." *The New York Times*, February 19.

———. 2018b. "How Facebook's Data Sharing Went From Feature to Bug." *The New York Times*, March 19.

Rosenberg, Matthew, Nicholas Confessore, and Carole Cadwalladr. 2018. "How Trump Consultants Exploited the Facebook Data of Millions." *The New York Times*, March 17.

Rosenthal, Elisabeth. 2017. *An American Sickness: How Healthcare Became Big Business and How You Can Take It Back*. New York: Penguin Books.

Ruggie, John G. 2013. *Just Business: Multinational Corporations and Human Rights*. New York: W.W. Norton & Company.

Rushe, Dominic. 2019 "The Kings of Capitalism are Finally Worried About the Growing Gap Between Rich and Poor." *The Guardian*, April 24.

Saba, Jennifer. 2017. "The Retailers That Can Resist the Amazon Onslaught." *The New York Times*, August 28.

Sainato, Michael. 2019. "'We Are Not Robots': Amazon Warehouse Employees Push to Unionize." *The Guardian*, January 1.

Salamon, Lester M. 2012. *The State of Nonprofit America*. Washington, DC: Brookings Institution Press.

———. 2015. *The Resilient Sector Revisited*. Washington, DC: Brookings Institution Press.

Sanger, David E., Julian E. Barnes, Raymond Zhong, and Marc Santora. 2019. "In 5G Race With China, U.S. Pushes Allies to Fight Huawei." *The New York Times*, January 26.

Sanger-Katz, Margot. 2018. "After Years of Quiet, Democratic Candidates Can't Stop Talking About Health Care." *The New York Times*, August 1.

Sanger-Katz, Margot, and Haeyoun Park. 2017. "Obamacare More Popular Than Ever, Now That It May Be Repealed." *The New York Times*, February 1.

Santhanam, Laura. 2018. "How Voters Viewed Trump, Health Care and Immigration, According to Exit Polls." *PBS Newshour*, November 8. Retrieved November 16, 2018 (www.pbs.org/newshour/politics/how-voters-viewed-trump-health-care-and-immigration-according-to-exit-polls).

———. 2019. "What Purdue Pharma's Settlement With Oklahoma Means for the Opioid Crisis." *PBS Newshour*, March 26. Retrieved May 29, 2019 (www.pbs.org/newshour/health/what-purdue-pharmas-settlement-with-oklahoma-means-for-the-opioid-crisis).

Satariano, Adam. 2018a. "Uber Claims to Have Changed. A London Judge Will Decide." *The New York Times*, June 24.

———. 2018b. "Uber Regains Its License to Operate in London, a Win for Its New CEO." *The New York Times*, June 26.

Satariano, Adam, and Jack Nicas. 2018. "E.U. Fines Google in Android Antitrust Case." *The New York Times*, July 18.

Scahill, Jeremy. 2007. "Pull the Plug on the Mercenary War." *The Nation*, April 30.

———. 2010. Blackwater's New Sugar Daddy: The Obama Administration." *The Nation*, June 28.

Schechner, Sam, and Natalia Drozdiak. 2018. "The Woman Who Is Reigning in America's Technology Giant: European Union Antitrust Chief Margrethe Vestager Has Become the De Facto Global Regulator for U.S. Companies Such as Google and Apple." *Wall Street Journal*, April 4.

Schlosser, Eric. 1998. "The Prison-Industrial Complex." *The Atlantic*, December.

Schneider, Mercedes K. 2015. *Common Core Dilemma: Who Owns Our Schools*. New York: Teachers College, Columbia University.

———. 2016. *School Choice: The End of Public Education?* New York: Teachers College Press, Columbia University.

Schumpeter, Joseph A. 1942. *Capitalism, Socialism, and Democracy*. New York: Harper & Brothers.

Schwartz, Peter, and Peter Leyden. 1997. "The Long Boom: A History of the Future, 1980–2020." *Wired*, July 1.

Segal, David. 2015. "Prison Vendors See Continued Signs of Captive Market." *The New York Times*, August 29.

Selby, Alan. 2017. "Timed Toilet Breaks, Impossible Targets and Workers Falling Asleep on Feet: Brutal Life Working in Amazon Warehouse." *Mirror*, November 25.

Selman, Donna, and Paul Leighton. 2010. *Punishment for Sale: Private Prisons, Big Business, and the Incarceration Binge*. Lanham, MD: Rowman & Littlefield.

Selyukh, Alina. 2018. "Long Kept Secret, Amazon Says Number of Prime Customers Topped 100 Million." *NPR The Two Way*, April 18. Retrieved September 13, 2018 (www.npr.org/sections/thetwo-way/2018/04/18/603750056/long-kept-secret-amazon-says-number-of-prime-customers-topped-100-million).

Sennott, Charles M. 2004. "Security Firm's $293m Deal Under Scrutiny." *The Boston Globe*, June 22.

Shah, Reema. 2014. "Beating Blackwater: Using Domestic Legislation to Enforce the International Code of Conduct for Private Military Companies." *Yale LJ Online* 123: 2559.

Shane, Scott, and Daisuke Wakabayashi. 2018. "'The Business of War': Google's Employees Protest Work for the Pentagon." *The New York Times*, April 4.

Shapiro, Ari. 2019. "Disney Heiress Calls for Wealth Tax: 'We Have to Draw a Line'." *NPR All Things Considered*, June 28. Retrieved July 10, 2019 (www.npr.org/2019/06/28/736993245/disney-heiress-calls-for-wealth-tax-we-have-to-draw-a-line).

Shaw, Tamsin. 2018. "Beware the Big Five." *The New York Review of Books*, April 5.

Shearer, Elisa, and Jeffrey Gottfried. 2017. "News Use Across Social Media Platforms." *Pew Research Center*. Retrieved May 10, 2019 (www.journalism.org/2017/09/07/news-use-across-social-media-platforms-2017/).

Shephard, Alex. 2018. "Is Amazon Too Big to Tax?" *The New Republic*, March 1.

Singer, Natasha. 2012. "Mapping, and Sharing, the Consumer Genome." *The New York Times*, June 16.

———. 2018. "Timeline: Facebook and Google Under Regulators' Glare." *The New York Times*, March 24.

Singer, Peter W. 2003. *Corporate Warriors: The Rise of the Privatized Military Industry*. Ithaca, NY: Cornell University Press.

———. 2004. "Nation Builders and Low Bidders in Iraq." *The New York Times*, June 15.

Sjoberg, Gideon. 1960. *The Preindustrial City: Past and Present*. New York: Free Press.

———. 1983. "Afterword." Pp. 271–279 in *Bureaucracy as a Social Problem*, edited by W. Boyd Littrell, Gideon Sjoberg, and Louis A. Zurcher. Greenwich, CT: JAI Press.

———. 1999. "Some Observations of Bureaucratic Capitalism: Knowledge About What and Why?" Pp. 43–64 in *Sociology for the Twenty-First Century: Continuities and Cutting Edges*, edited by Janet L. Abu-Lughod. Chicago: The University of Chicago Press.

———. 2005. "The Corporate Control Industry and Human Rights: The Case of Iraq." *Journal of Human Rights* 4(1): 95–101.

———. 2009. "Corporations and Human Rights." Pp. 169–188 in *Interpreting Human Rights: Social Science Perspectives*, edited by Rhiannon Morgan and Bryan S. Turner. New York: Routledge.

Sjoberg, Gideon, Richard A. Brymer, and Buford Farris. 1966. "Bureaucracy and the Lower Class." *Sociology and Social Research* 50(3): 325–337.

Sjoberg, Gideon, and Leonard D. Cain. 1971. "Negative Values, Countersystem Models, and the Analysis of Social Systems." Pp. 212–229 in *Institutions and Social Exchange: The Sociologies of Talcott Parsons and George C. Homans*, edited by Herman Turk and Richard L. Simpson. Indianapolis, IN: Bobbs-Merrill Company.

Sjoberg, Gideon, Elizabeth A. Gill, and Leonard D. Cain. 2003. "Countersystem Analysis and the Construction of Alternative Futures." *Sociological Theory* 21(3): 210–235.

Sjoberg, Gideon, Elizabeth A. Gill, and Joo Ean Tan. 2003. "Social Organization." Pp. 411–432 in *The Handbook of Symbolic Interactionism*, edited by Larry T. Reynolds and Nancy Herman-Kinney. Walnut Creek, CA: Alta Mira.

Sjoberg, Gideon, Elizabeth A. Gill, and Norma Williams. 2001. "A Sociology of Human Rights." *Social Problems* 48(1): 11–47.

Sjoberg, Gideon, Ted R. Vaughan, and Norma Williams. 1984. "Bureaucracy as a Moral Issue." *Journal of Applied Behavioral Science* 20(4): 441–453.

Smith, Jason Scott. 2006. *Building New Deal Liberalism: The Political Economy of Public Works, 1933–1956*. New York: Cambridge University Press.

Smith, Sandy. 2018. "Richard Florida Calls for Truce in Amazon HQ2 Bidding War." *Philadelphia Magazine*, January 31.

Sommer, Jeff. 2017. "The Mind Boggling Ascent of Amazon and Jeff Bezos." *The New York Times*, July 28.

Sorkin, Andrew Ross. 2017. "20 Years On, Amazon and Jeff Bezos Prove Naysayers Wrong." *The New York Times*, May 15.

———. 2019a. "What Trump's Huawei Reversal Means for the Future of 5G." *The New York Times*, July 1.

———. 2019b. "How Shareholder Democracy Failed the People." *The New York Times*, August 20.

Sorkin, Andrew Ross, Stephen Grocer, Tiffany Hsu, and Gregory Schmidt. 2019. "5G Is the New Arms Race With China." *The New York Times*, January 28.

Stewart, James S. 2016. "Facebook Has 50 Minutes of Your Time Each Day. It Wants More." *The New York Times*, May 5.

Stolberg, Sheryl G., and Astead W. Herndon. 2019. "'Lock the S.O.B.s Up': Joe Biden and the Era of Mass Incarceration." *The New York Times*, June 25.

Stone, Brad. 2013. *The Everything Store: Jeff Bezos and the Age of Amazon*. New York: Random House.

Strauss, Karsten. 2016. "America's Most Reputable Companies, 2016: Amazon Tops the List." *Forbes*, March 29.

Streitfeld, David. 2013. "A New Book Portrays Amazon as Bully." *The New York Times*, October 22.

———. 2014. "Writers Feel an Amazon-Hachette Spat." *The New York Times*, May 9.

———. 2018. "Amazon Hits $1,000,000,000,000 in Value, Following Apple." *The New York Times*, September 4.

Sumagaysay, Levi. 2019. "Lack of Diversity in Tech: House Hearing Explores Harms, Solutions." *San Jose Mercury News*, March 6.

Surowiecki, James. 2016. "Why Don't We Have a Universal Basic Income?" *The New Yorker*, June 20.

Swisher, Kara. 2018. "The Expensive Education of Mark Zuckerberg." *The New York Times*, August 2.

Tankersley, Jim. 2019. "Warren's Plan Is Latest Push by Democrats to Raise Taxes on the Rich." *The New York Times*, January 24.

Taylor, Timothy. 2017. "Adam Smith on the Benefits of Public Education." *Conversable Economist*, September 1. Retrieved January 10, 2018 (https://populardemocracy.org/sites/default/files/FraudandMismgmt5-3-14%28FINALx3.0%29REV.pdf).

Tejada, Carlos. 2017. "Google, Looking to Tiptoe Back Into China, Announces A.I. Center." *The New York Times*, December 13.

Teles, Steven. 2013. "Kludgeocracy in America." *National Affairs* 17: 97–114.

Thompson, Derek. 2018. "Amazon's HQ2 Spectacle Isn't Just Shameful—It Should Be Illegal." *The Atlantic*, November 12.

Thompson, Nicholas, and Fred Vogelstein. 2018. "Inside the Two Years That Shook Facebook—and the World." *Wired*, February 12.

Tiku, Nitasha. 2018. "Facebook Funded Most of the Experts Who Vetted Messenger Kids." *Wired*, February 14.

Tollefson, Jeff. 2018. "China Declared World's Largest Producer of Scientific Articles." *Nature*, January 18.

Too Much. 2016. "Too Much of a Good Thing." *The Economist*, March 26. Retrieved August 6, 2018 (www.economist.com/briefing/2016/03/26/too-much-of-a-good-thing).

Turner, Adair. 2016. *Between Debt and the Devil: Money, Credit, and Fixing Global Finance*. Princeton, NJ: Princeton University Press.

Turner, Fred. 2006. *From Counterculture to Cyberculture: Stewart Brand, the Whole Earth Network, and the Rise of Digital Utopianism*. Chicago: The University of Chicago Press.

Turner, Jonathan M. 2019. "Hit the Road, Jack: Uber Drivers are Independent Contractors According to NLRB." *The National Law Review*. Retrieved September 26, 2019 (www.natlawreview.com/article/hit-road-jack-uber-drivers-are-independent-contractors-according-to-nlrb).

Twenge, Jean M. 2017. "Have Smartphones Destroyed a Generation?" *The Atlantic*, September.

Twenge, Jean M., Gabrielle N. Martin, and W. Keith Campbell. 2018. "Decreases in Psychological Well-Being Among American Adolescents After 2012 and Links to Screen Time During the Rise of Smartphone Technology." *Emotion* 18(6): 765–780.

Urban Justice Center. 2018. "The Prison Industrial Complex: Mapping the Private Sector Players." *Urban Justice Center*. Retrieved June 28, 2019 (https://static1.squarespace.com/static/58e127cb1b10e31ed45b20f4/t/5ade0281f950b7ab293c86a6/1524499083424/The+Prison+Industrial+Complex+-+Mapping+Private+Sector+Players+%28April+2018%29.pdf).

Valet, Vicky. 2018. "America's Most Reputable Companies 2018." *Forbes*, April 17.

Vaughan, Ted R., and Gideon Sjoberg. 1984. "The Individual and Bureaucracy: An Alternative Meadian Interpretation." *Journal of Applied Behavioral Science* 20(1): 57–69.

Vogel, Kenneth P., and Cecilia Kang. 2017. "Senators Demand Online Ad Disclosures as Tech Lobby Mobilizes." *The New York Times*, October 19.

Wagner, Kurt. 2018. "Facebook's Acquisition of Instagram Was the Greatest Regulatory Failure of the Past Decade, Says Stratechery's Ben Thompson." *Recode*, June 2.

Wakabayashi, Daisuke. 2019. "Google Ends Forced Arbitration for All Employee Disputes." *The New York Times*, February 21.

Wakabayashi, Daisuke, and Katie Benner. 2018. "How Google Protected Andy Rubin, the 'Father of Android'." *The New York Times*, October 25.

Wakabayashi, Daisuke, Erin Griffith, Amie Tsang, and Kate Conger. 2018. "Google Walkout: Employees Stage Protest Over Handling of Sexual Harassment." *The New York Times*, November 1.

Wakabayashi, Daisuke, and Scott Shane. 2018. "Google Will Not Renew Pentagon Contract That Upset Employees." *The New York Times*, June 1.

Warren, Elizabeth, and Amelia Warren Tyagi. 2003. *The Two-Income Trap: Why Middle-Class Mothers and Fathers Are Going Broke*. New York: Basic Books.

Warzel, Charlie, and Ash Ngu. 2019. "Google's 4,000-Word Privacy Policy Is a Secret History of the Internet." *The New York Times*, July 10.

Waters, Richard. 2017. "Silicon Valley Aims to Engineer a Universal Basic Income." *Financial Times*, May 3.

Weber, Max. [1904/1905] 1958. *The Protestant Ethic and the Spirit of Capitalism*. New York: Scribner.

———. [1921] 1968. *Economy and Society*. Vols. 1–3. Berkeley: University of California Press.

Wedel, Janine. 2009. *Shadow Elite: How the World's New Power Brokers Undermine Democracy, Government, and the Free Market*. Philadelphia, PA: Basic Books.

———. 2014. *Unaccountable: How Elite Power Brokers Corrupt Our Finances, Freedom, and Security*. New York: Pegasus Books.

———. 2015. "Forget the McDonnells. We're Ignoring Bigger, More Pernicious Corruption Right Under Our Noses." *The Washington Post*, January 12.

———. 2017. "From Power Elites to Influence Elites: Resetting Elite Studies for the 21st Century." *Theory, Culture & Society* 34(5–6): 153–178.

Weiss, Linda. 2014. *America Inc.? Innovation and Enterprise in the National Security State*. Ithaca, NY: Cornell University Press.

Weller, Chris. 2017. "8 Basic Income Experiments to Watch Out for in 2017." *Business Insider*, January 24.

Wessler, Seth F. 2016. "The Obama Administration Continues Pulling Away From Private Prison Companies." *The Nation*, September 2.

Wingfield, Nick. 2017. "Amazon's Ambitions Unboxed: Stores for Furniture, Appliances and More." *The New York Times*, March 25.

———. 2018. "Amazon Pushes Facial Recognition to Police. Critics See Surveillance Risk." *The New York Times*, May 22.

Wingfield, Nick, and Patricia Cohen. 2017. "Amazon Plans Second Headquarters, Opening a Bidding War Among States." *The New York Times*, September 7.

Wingfield, Nick, Paul Mozur, and Michael Corkery. 2018. "Retailers Race Against Amazon to Automate Stores." *The New York Times*, April 1.

Winkler, Adam. 2018. *We the Corporations: How American Businesses Won Their Civil Rights*. New York: Liveright Publishing.

Wong, Julia. 2018. "'Good for the World'? Facebook Emails Reveal What Really Drives the Site." *The Guardian*, December 5.

———. 2019. "The Cambridge Analytica Scandal Changed the World—But It Didn't Change Facebook." *The Guardian*, March 18.

Wood, Robert W. 2019. "Despite Sweeping California Gig Worker Law, Uber Says It Won't Treat Drivers as Employees." *Forbes*, September 11.

World Economic Forum. 2017. "Shaping the Future of Retail for Consumer Industries." *Report to Annual Meeting*. (www3.weforum.org/docs/IP/2016/CO/WEF_AM17_Future of RetailInsightReport.pdf).

Wu, Tim. 2016. *The Attention Merchants: The Epic Scramble to Get Inside Our Heads*. New York: Vintage Books.

Wu, Tim, and Stuart A. Thompson. 2019. "The Roots of Big Tech Run Disturbingly Deep." *The New York Times*, June 7.

Yahoo! Finance. 2018a. "Apple Inc." Retrieved August 27, 2018 (https://finance.yahoo.com/quote/AAPL?p=AAPL).

———. 2018b. "Facebook Inc." Retrieved August 27, 2018 (https://finance.yahoo.com/quote/FB/profile?p=FB).

———. 2019. "Alphabet Inc. (GOOGL)." Retrieved August 22, 2019 (https://finance.yahoo.com/quote/GOOG/).

Yergin, Daniel, and Joseph Stanislaw. 2002. *The Commanding Heights: The Battle for the World Economy.* New York: Free Press.

Zahn, Max, and Sharif Paget. 2019. "'Colony of Hell': 911 Calls From Inside Amazon Warehouses." *Daily Beast*, March 11.

Zernike, Kate. 2015. "Massachusetts's Rejection of Common Core Test Signals Shift in U.S." *The New York Times*, November 21.

———. 2016a. "How Trump's Education Nominee Bent Detroit to Her Will on Charter Schools." *The New York Times*, December 12.

———. 2016b. "Betsy DeVos, Trump's Education Pick, Has Steered Money From Public Schools." *The New York Times*, November 3.

Zhong, Raymond, and Paul Mozur. 2018. "Tech Giants Feel the Squeeze as Xi Jinping Tightens His Grip." *The New York Times*, May 2.

Index

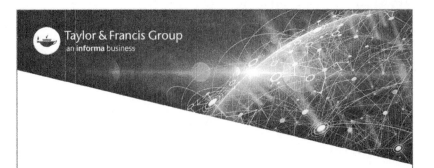